The Language Teacher Education Casebook

Storytelling is a powerful tool for understanding. This casebook includes seventy dilemma-based narrative cases, providing language teachers with a thorough overview of key topics in language education. The cases cover a broad range of language teaching and learning concerns relevant to the development of pre- and in-service language teachers. They include narratives of language teachers, learners, teacher educators, researchers, administrators, and other professionals working in a variety of educational settings, such as schools, universities, private language institutions, and informal contexts, and in multilingual contexts around the world. Cases illustrate theoretical principles and concepts current in the field, in the form of moral or practical dilemmas that require resolving by readers. Case components include discussion questions, related research topics with suggested methods for carrying out research, and reading resources. A facilitator guide provides suggestions for conducting classroom and online discussions, creating case-based assignments for assessment, and mentoring teacher research.

GARY BARKHUIZEN is Professor of Applied Linguistics at the University of Auckland, New Zealand. His recent books include *Language Teacher Educator Identity* (2021), *Language Teachers Studying Abroad* (Ed., 2022), and *Narrative Inquiry in Language Teaching and Learning Research*, second edition (with Benson and Chik, 2025).

The Language Teacher Education Casebook

Gary Barkhuizen
University of Auckland

Shaftesbury Road, Cambridge CB2 8EA, United Kingdom

One Liberty Plaza, 20th Floor, New York, NY 10006, USA

477 Williamstown Road, Port Melbourne, VIC 3207, Australia

314–321, 3rd Floor, Plot 3, Splendor Forum, Jasola District Centre, New Delhi – 110025, India

103 Penang Road, #05–06/07, Visioncrest Commercial, Singapore 238467

Cambridge University Press is part of Cambridge University Press & Assessment, a department of the University of Cambridge.

We share the University's mission to contribute to society through the pursuit of education, learning and research at the highest international levels of excellence.

www.cambridge.org
Information on this title: www.cambridge.org/9781009444163

DOI: 10.1017/9781009444132

© Gary Barkhuizen 2026

This publication is in copyright. Subject to statutory exception and to the provisions of relevant collective licensing agreements, no reproduction of any part may take place without the written permission of Cambridge University Press & Assessment.

When citing this work, please include a reference to the DOI 10.1017/9781009444132

First published 2026

Cover image: Richard Drury/Getty Images

A catalogue record for this publication is available from the British Library

Library of Congress Cataloging-in-Publication Data
Names: Barkhuizen, Gary Patrick author
Title: The language teacher education casebook / Gary Barkhuizen, University of Auckland.
Description: Cambridge, United Kingdom ; New York, NY : Cambridge University Press, 2025. | Includes bibliographical references and index.
Identifiers: LCCN 2025018057 | ISBN 9781009444163 hardback | ISBN 9781009444149 paperback | ISBN 9781009444132 ebook
Subjects: LCSH: Language teachers – Training of | Language and languages – Study and teaching
Classification: LCC P53.85 .B37 2024 | DDC 418.0071–dc23/eng/20250626
LC record available at https://lccn.loc.gov/2025018057

ISBN 978-1-009-44416-3 Hardback
ISBN 978-1-009-44414-9 Paperback

Cambridge University Press & Assessment has no responsibility for the persistence or accuracy of URLs for external or third-party internet websites referred to in this publication and does not guarantee that any content on such websites is, or will remain, accurate or appropriate.

For EU product safety concerns, contact us at Calle de José Abascal, 56, 1°, 28003 Madrid, Spain, or email eugpsr@cambridge.org

Contents

List of Figures	*page* vi
Acknowledgments	vii
Introduction	1
The Cases	22
Facilitator Guide	28
1 Classroom Language Teaching	38
2 Language Learners	63
3 Teacher–Student Relationships	88
4 Language Assessment	112
5 Classroom Management	137
6 Professional Development	162
7 Teacher Research	187
8 Professional Service	213
9 Leadership	240
10 Teacher Wellbeing	267
Bibliography	293
Index	300

Figures

0.1	A strong case method pedagogical approach	*page* 12
0.2	Cases used strategically within a course	13
0.3	Cases used as one-off instructional activities	13
0.4	Research as an extension of classroom case method instruction	16

Acknowledgments

Producing this casebook has involved several special people. Many thanks to graduate students and research assistants who worked on case construction and helped with research, including Kethakie Nagahawatte, Jovan Cavor, and Yanqiu Yang, and especially Rosa Pezoa Tudela, who, in addition, contributed to the design and analysis of a student teacher feedback questionnaire.

Graduate MTESOL and MA Applied Linguistics students as well as undergraduate TESOL and Education students at the University of Auckland in the following courses engaged with the case method in their classes and provided extensive feedback: LANGTCHG 757, LANGTCHG 734, and LANGTCHG 207.

Minh Nguyen, University of Otago, recruited students to comment on the case method approach and on some specific cases in the early stages of conceptualizing the book. Nur Arifah Drajati, Universitas Sebelas Maret, Indonesia, made available large numbers of her teacher education students to work on cases and complete a questionnaire to record their experiences in the later stages.

Research and conference funding was provided by the School of Cultures, Languages and Linguistics, University of Auckland (2023, 2024), and from the SOTL (Scholarship of Teaching and Learning) fund, University of Auckland (2024).

Thank you also to the many colleagues who attended my conference and workshop presentations on the case method and this casebook and asked questions and provided feedback, which all prompted revisions and additions to the text.

Thanks, finally, to the editorial and production teams at Cambridge University Press for their expert advice, and patience.

Introduction

A case is a narrative that describes some action unfolding over time. It includes characters doing things together in particular places and reveals their thoughts, beliefs, feelings, and decision-making processes. But a case is more than just a description of interesting events. Cases illustrate theoretical principles and concepts worth reflecting on and knowing about, and they typically expose those principles in the form of moral or practical dilemmas that require resolving by readers.

This casebook presents cases in the field of language teacher education and continuing professional development (PD), and so the cases are narratives about the professional lives of language teachers, teacher educators, and researchers as they go about their work with learners and with their colleagues in the places where they work. The cases are always complex – they raise issues, they present dilemmas, and they uncover the struggles and joys of teaching and learning to teach.

Cases have been incorporated into case method pedagogies in professional preparation programs in fields such as law, business, and medicine for over a hundred years (Merseth, 1996), with the Harvard University Law School introducing the method as early as 1870. Banks (2017) describes the method as used in the field of law as "a reasoning process that facilitates the discovery of general principles of law from specific cases" (p. 51). He goes on to add that studying case law in this way facilitates logical reasoning, or "thinking like a lawyer" (p. 51).

In the case of this language teacher education casebook, the aim is for language teachers who work through the cases to begin "thinking like a teacher." In conjunction with reading and reflecting on the cases, working on cases also means engaging in discussion in the form of collaborative question and answer sessions facilitated by teacher educators or PD facilitators. Regarding legal training, Banks (2017) explains that this case dialogue method "strengthens not only a student's substantial knowledge ... it also creates the type of analytical problem-solving skills that lawyers [language teachers] need to know in making judgments about what the law [teaching] means or how to apply it in everyday practice" (p. 52). Casebooks and the case method have now been used in fields as diverse as international health research (Capron, et al.

2009), hedge fund fraud (Johnson, 2010), neuropsychology (Orsini, 1988), and financial management (Kumar, 2016).

Author Statement

Several years ago, I was teaching a graduate course in TESOL (Teaching English to Speakers of Other Languages) management and leadership. The course content included theories and strategies relevant for language teachers in their professional work in schools and for those planning to take up leadership roles in the future. Course materials and the lectures were sufficiently interesting and informative, but when I decided to introduce short written cases into class discussions, I noticed a discernible increase in student engagement. The hypothetical cases were only about 200 words long, but each involved a central character (e.g., a teacher, head of department, school principal) who was struggling with a management issue in their working contexts.

The cases were in the form of short narratives. They were, even in their brevity, rich in contextual detail and interesting enough to grab the attention of the students. They really did increase the students' involvement in class discussion, but more importantly, got them reflecting on and critiquing the course content. I didn't take the use of cases much further in my teacher education courses at the time, although over the years I have always included narratives in one way or another in my teaching, for example students writing their own narratives for later self-analysis or me and my students reviewing narrative research studies rich with descriptions of personal struggles and successes.

Narrative Inquiry

At about the same time that I was introducing cases into my management course, I was beginning to learn about and employ narrative inquiry methods in my research work. Central to narrative inquiry are stories – stories of life and professional experience. The researcher's aim is to understand the narrator's perspective of their experiences, how they make sense of their world, whether it be language learning or language teaching. I have come to be a strong advocate for narrative research methods, firmly believing that we understand our lives through telling, listening to, and reflecting on stories. Stories include characters, not only the main narrator, who interact and have relationships with each other and also position themselves vis-à-vis each other. These relationships unfold in particular physical places and social spaces, which can be at a micro level, such as in classrooms, or at broader institutional or community levels. The relationships are also influenced by much broader, macro contexts, such as global ideas and discourses about, for example, language learning, teacher education, multilingualism, globalization, and developments in Artificial Intelligence (AI) and technology. Stories, of course, also embody action – something happens with and to these characters. These experiences, how they unfold, and how they are narrated by the characters, is what makes narrative research so interesting. Like with all good stories, we want to know what happened, when, with whom, where, and why?

Research and Pedagogy

And this is where my interests in research and pedagogy begin to align. Both narrative inquiry and the case method:

- include stories of life experiences, unfolding in spatiotemporal contexts rich in detail;
- examine stories that are multilayered, complex, and often of a dilemmic nature;
- critically analyze these life experiences and propose resolutions to perceived dilemmas.

As a researcher, my interest in stories and always wanting to know "what happened?" eventually crossed back into the teacher education classroom in the form of cases. I have been using the case method now for the past few years in both undergraduate and postgraduate teacher education classes. I have written the cases myself, many of which are in this book. They are hypothetical but based on my experiences as a language teacher, researcher and reader of research, teacher educator, and educational manager at high school and in higher education. I am convinced that the case method has a lot to offer language teacher educators and professional development facilitators, and recent research in general education and language teacher education would appear to support this view. I am excited to present the cases in this book and hope that those who engage with them find them useful, instructive, and interesting.

Cases in Teacher Education

Case method pedagogy emerged and gained popularity in the field of general teacher education in the late twentieth century (Merseth, 1991; Shulman, 1992), and then made an appearance in L2 (second language) teacher education a few years later (Jackson, 1997; Kelch & Malupa-Kim, 2014; Reichelt, 2000). Case-based methodologies have appeared on and off in small-scale research projects; for example, the critical analysis of one case study in a foreign/second language methodology course (Haley, 2004) and the writing and use of cases in a teacher education program in Hong Kong (Tinker Sachs & Ho, 2011).

Cases have also been incorporated into language teacher education textbooks; for example, Bailey's (2006) case-based approach to language teacher supervision, and an earlier casebook for use in teacher education courses published by TESOL International (Richards, 1998). A more recent series of three casebooks features genuine US-based cases that promote a sociocultural approach to second language teacher education (Zlateva & Gooden, 2018), inclusive pedagogical practices in language education (Gooden, 2021), as well as decolonizing pedagogical practices (Gooden, 2024).

This Casebook

Also drawing on a sociocultural theoretical perspective, the design and content of this casebook is underpinned by several language teacher education (LTE) conceptual positions.

1. The first of these comes from Kubanyiova (2020): a "language teacher education knowledge base must be enriched by critical perspectives on the roles and tasks of language teachers in the face of [the] existing socio-political climate of language education in their specific contexts" (p. 53). Keywords here are "critical perspectives," which the cases and discussions foster, "socio-political climate," which raises awareness in teachers of both micro- and macro-ideologies infiltrating their language classroom practices, and "specific contexts," which locate their developing knowledge-base within their physical and social spaces of practice.
2. Wright (2010), supported by others such as Richards and Farrell (2005), recommends that language teacher education should place "an emphasis on the student teacher's learning to teach, and becoming a thinking teacher" which means "a great deal of reflective activity programmed into learning experiences" (p. 271). Reading the cases and answering and discussing the accompanying questions collaboratively with others offers such reflective opportunities.
3. Working on the cases together in class or online or in a workshop – with fellow teachers and a teacher educator – generates a dialogic space (Bakhtin, 1981) that facilitates critical reflection and "opportunities for the participants to construct professional knowledge through conversations with one another" (Doecke, 2004, p. 207), or to put it another way, "to engage in dialogic discussions with others about their work" (Owen, 2020, p. 165).
4. Contemplating the research topics suggested with each of the cases, and potentially taking them up as actual projects, progresses the reflective process even further. Johnson and Golombek (2020) propose that "LTE pedagogy must have a self-inquiry dimension, involving teacher educators and teachers working together or by themselves" (p. 124). The research

topics include suggestions for carrying out an actual inquiry and recommend appropriate types of research and research methods.

The casebook, therefore, aims to prepare teachers who think, critically, like teachers through reflection, collaborative dialogue, and research in relation to the content and dilemmas of the cases, and by connecting that content and the outcome of their reflections to their own work contexts and development.

The Cases

This casebook presents seventy cases in ten chapters arranged according to the teacher education or PD topics they address. While each chapter may focus broadly on one topic, in working through the cases it will become evident that the chapter topics interrelate, together contributing to developing an understanding of issues, current ideas, and debates in language teacher education and professional development. At the same time, although each of the cases in their respective chapters may target only one or two particular issues or dilemmas, close analysis will often reveal more than such a narrow dilemmic focus. This, of course, is to be expected, considering the complex nature of teachers' professional work.

As mentioned above, the cases in this book are invented – they are hypothetical, yet realistic, written for the purposes of this casebook. They cover a broad range of topics in language teaching and learning relevant to the development of pre- and in-service language teachers in current times. The cases include the stories of language teachers, learners, teacher educators, researchers, administrators, and other professionals working in a variety of educational settings, such as schools, universities, private language institutions, and informal contexts, and in multilingual geographical contexts around the world (up to forty countries). The personal, situational, and institutional descriptions in each case are usually generic enough so that readers can transfer the cases' themes and dilemmas to their own locales and then imagine what they would do to make sense of and resolve similar dilemmas in their work.

Terms and Conditions

Language teaching and language teacher education are global practices, but the way in which these practices and their theoretical underpinnings are understood, critiqued, and implemented in local geopolitical contexts varies considerably. This diversity is captured in the cases, especially in the following ways:

1. Terminology varies according to local usage; for example, elementary versus primary school, or student teacher versus teacher learner. Another example is language student versus learner.

2. Some terminology may suggest political connotations, such as the use of English as a Second Language (ESL) learner, versus, say, English Language Learner (ELL) or English as an Additional Language (EAL) learner, or multilingual learner.
3. Reference to teachers, too, can vary or be political, such as ESL and ESOL (English for Speakers of Other Languages) teacher, and NNEST (non-native English-speaking teacher) and NEST (native English-speaking teacher).
4. Languages are referred to in the cases as first (L1), second (L2), native, non-native, mother-tongue, dominant, and majority languages in different contexts.

Readers may be unfamiliar with some of these terms, or they may perceive them to be inappropriate or discriminatory. If so, this offers an opportunity to either learn what they mean or to reflect on and critique their use when analyzing the cases from the perspective of their own work experience and teaching contexts.

Likewise, readers may react negatively to some of the content of the cases, including context-specific teaching and learning practices, the nature of the dilemmas raised, what the characters do and feel, and how they interact with each other. They might also be offended by positions taken on educational policy, or by cultural practices and beliefs they are unfamiliar with or that they oppose. Stereotypes may emerge in the cases – cultural, ethnic, national, socio-economic – but these are included in the hope that they can be reflected upon, discussed, questioned, related to one's own conditions, and learned from. The role of case method facilitators is obviously important in this process. They will know best what is appropriate for their particular context; from case selection, to managing class discussion, to guiding the selection and implementation of research topics. The Facilitator Guide gives further advice in this regard.

Character, Action, and Context Disclaimer

As mentioned above, the cases in this book are invented by the author – they are hypothetical, imagined, written for the purposes of this casebook. Any resemblance in the cases to actual events, incidents, locations, institutions, names, or people is entirely coincidental.

What Is the Case Method?

Broadly speaking, the *case method* is a type of case-based pedagogy, which Zlateva and Gooden (2018) describe as "a means of developing teacher thinking, attitudes, and beliefs about issues in the field. Language teachers practicing it are not passive recipients of theories, principles, and strategies. ... Case studies give teachers the opportunity to reflect on their reasoning" (p. 10). Two further excerpts from the literature reinforce these ideas:

1. The first is from Haley (2004): Case-method instruction can be employed for the "illustration of theoretical principles, providing precedents for practices, posing moral or ethical dilemmas, modeling 'thinking like a teacher,' and providing alternative images of practice" (p. 291).
2. Harrington, Quinn-Leering, and Hodson (1996) also make reference to reflection and subsequent practice, this time focusing on the dilemmic nature of the case method: "dilemma-based pedagogy [is] intended to provide students of teaching with opportunities to recognize specific events as problematic, gain an understanding of them, reflect on them and on the consequences of action, and devise sensible, moral and educative ways of acting in doing so" (p. 26).

The case method in language teacher education involves using cases for teaching about language teaching. Teacher educators and PD facilitators embed cases in their teaching to stimulate critical reflection and encourage teachers to resolve dilemmas and imagine (future) teaching practice. The cases, whether authentic or hypothetical, are analyzed and discussed in class (or online) in various possible arrangements (see Facilitator Guide) and the outcomes of the deliberations are applied by the teachers to their own (future) working contexts.

Reflecting this common goal and pedagogical approach, notwithstanding a wide variety of actual classroom practices, the case method has been referred to in several different ways, including case-based teaching (Prince & Felder, 2007), case-based instruction (Mostert, 2007), case-based learning (Jackson, 1997), the case-study method (Kelch & Malupa-Kim, 2014; Reichelt, 2000), and most famously the casebook method (Banks, 2017). Emphasizing the contribution to learning of discussion, question and answer exchanges, and collaborative decision-making, the approach has also been referred to as the Socratic method, inductive learning, and discussion-based learning.

The Case Method in Language Teacher Education

Recent, and even early, discussions of the case method in language teacher education (Gooden, 2024; Reichelt, 2000; Tinker Sachs & Ho, 2011) have drawn on sociocultural theoretical perspectives to justify the use of cases in teacher learning and professional development. It is not difficult to see why.

In a 2020 journal article, Johnson and Golombek put forward eight interrelated propositions which they believe constitute language teacher education pedagogy as a central domain for the knowledge-base of language teacher education. These propositions have their foundation in a Vygotskian sociocultural theoretical perspective, and thus Johnson and Golombek envision that:

> the dialogic interactions that unfold in our LTE programs as the very external forms of social interaction and activities ... will become internalized psychological tools for teacher thinking, enabling our teachers to construct and enact theoretically and pedagogically sound instructional practices for their students. (p. 118)

In the case method, the "dialogic interactions" are the collaborative discussions about the cases mediated by the teacher educators and PD facilitators, as they enact case-based pedagogies that support the professional development of the teachers. It is the teacher educators (or PD facilitators) who select cases and set up and engage in case discussions with the teachers. The following four propositions are particularly relevant to the case method and exemplify further how this process works.

1. *LTE Pedagogy Must Be Located*

Language teacher education takes place in particular contexts: the contexts where teachers do their learning but also the contexts described and explored within the cases. Johnson and Golombek (2020) remind us that "context is not limited to specific geopolitical boundaries but includes socio-political, socio-historical, and/or socioeconomic contexts that shape and are shaped by local and global events" (p. 120).

What happens locally in language teacher education, therefore – in classrooms, in the cases, in teacher research projects – is interconnected with much broader scales of context, larger ideological discourses with which teacher educators and student teachers engage. Through the use of cases, teacher educators provide opportunities for teacher learners to reflect on and make sense of their development in the contexts of both their teacher education and (future) teaching.

2. *LTE Pedagogy Must Create Opportunities to Externalize Everyday Concepts While Internalizing Relevant Academic Concepts Through Authentic, Goal-Directed Activities of Teaching*

What this proposition means is that teacher educators need to support teacher learners to unite their everyday concepts – gained from experience and often implicit and unanalyzed – with the new academic concepts they come across in teacher education programs or professional development activities. The academic concepts are those generated by research and other scholarship (theorizing) in the field of language teaching and learning; they are the "theory" in the complex theory–practice relationship.

One of the claims repeatedly made about the benefits of the case method is that it helps teachers to bridge the gap between theory and practice (Darling-Hammond & Hammerness, 2002; Gooden, 2024; Haley, 2004). Studying cases means teachers explore and internalize principles or theories of teaching within the rich context of the narratives and make connections to their own experience and practice.

3. *LTE Pedagogy Must Contain Structured Mediational Spaces Where Teachers Are Encouraged to Play/Step into Being and Becoming a Teacher*

The case method provides structured mediational spaces. In the process of creating these spaces for teachers, in which they take part in goal-directed case discussions and research activities, teacher educators and PD facilitators become mediators, providers of emotional support, and instructors of academic concepts (Johnson & Golombek, 2020).

Their goal, through the cases, is ultimately to enable teacher learners to think like a teacher and "try out emerging teacher identities, alternative instructional practices, and new modes of engagement in teaching" (Johnson & Golombek, 2020, p. 123). Mediational spaces should be safe for teachers – safe "to be creative, express their ideas freely, risk responses that might differ from the majority opinion, and challenge others' views and assumptions of a case" (Jackson, 1997, p. 8).

4. *LTE Pedagogy Must Have a Self-Inquiry Dimension, Involving Teacher Educators and Teachers Working Together or by Themselves, in Which They Seek to Trace Teacher Professional Development as It Unfolds Over Time and Place*

As teachers engage in their teacher education or professional development work, they must, according to this proposition, engage in self-inquiry; that is, to reflect deeply on and ask questions about their ongoing development over time in order to understand it and position it within their sociocultural, institutional contexts of practice.

Accompanying each of the seventy cases in this casebook are two research topics and recommendations for how to carry out the inquiry. Johnson and Golombek (2020) suggest that teacher educators mediate this process of self-inquiry or teacher research by, for example, working with the teachers to provide feedback, commentary, and support during the inquiry activities. If this is not feasible, teachers can work independently or in collaboration with other teachers after reading and reflecting on the cases.

What Is a Case?

Definitions of what a case is vary considerably according to the professional discipline in which they are used, how they are used, and what their purpose is. A simple definition is as follows: "A case is a description of an actual or hypothetical yet realistic/real-world situation in which a person or persons face a problem or challenge" (Kelch & Malupa-Kim, 2014, p. 10). Merseth (1996) adds some details, saying that a case is:

> often presented in narrative form that is based on a real-life situation or event. It attempts to convey a balanced, multidimensional representation of the context, participants, and reality of the situation. Cases are created explicitly for discussion and seek to include sufficient detail and information to elicit active analysis and interpretation by users with differing perspectives. (p. 722)

- Cases are narratives, situations, selections of research data, or other authentic documents and policies shaped into case form.
- They present interesting and provocative issues, problems, or questions for discussion, reflection, and action.
- Cases can be short (a few hundred words) to many pages long.
- They can be written by an instructor (a teacher educator or PD facilitator), by teacher learners (Reichelt, 2000), or both (Tinker Sachs & Ho, 2011), or be made available in a casebook, like this one.
- Cases can be complete, providing a record of something that happened with a resolution or a story ending.
- Cases can also be open-ended (Jackson, 1997) or unresolved, ending in a dilemma, an unsolved problem, or a story without a conclusion. This casebook uses unresolved, dilemma-based narrative cases.

Dilemma-Based Narrative Cases

Dilemma-based or decision-making cases (Jackson, 1997) focus on dilemmas or critical incidents in language teaching and teacher professional development that are presented from the perspective of teachers, teacher educators, researchers, or institutions. The cases in this casebook have the following features, grouped into three main categories.

1.   Narrative

- There is always a story, a plot that runs through the case, usually with some dramatic tension.
- The stories include characters – teachers, teacher educators, researchers, administrators and leaders, and language learners. There are usually one or

two central characters who interact with each other or with other people in the story, typically in unequal relationships of power.
- The cases always exhibit a temporal or time dimension; the events or action of the narrative cases unfold over time. Historical life-events and imagined futures are also part of the storylines.
- The characters in the cases interact with each other and perform their actions in physical places and social spaces. The places are usually physical language classrooms, institutions, and communities, but also committees, professional networks, and digital online spaces.
- The cases, like good stories, have high tellability, that is, the extent to which they convey their content and action in an effective manner (novel, unusual, unique) (Ochs & Capps, 2001). They aim to create strong interest and draw the students into the events, content, and dilemmas discussed.
- The cases in this casebook are hypothetical yet realistic. They have been written – invented – specifically for the casebook but draw on the author's vast experience of language teaching, teacher education, doing and reading research, and managing language teaching programs, departments, and schools.

2. *Dilemma-Based*

- Harrington (1995) provides a useful definition of what case dilemmas are and do:

  Dilemmas present situations for which there are competing, often equally valid solutions. Using dilemma-based cases in preservice programs helps students begin to understand and accept the tentativeness in knowing, with certainty, what action to take; provides opportunities to marshal and evaluate evidence for judging alternative interpretations and actions; and can illuminate the moral dimensions of teaching. (p. 2)

- Characters in the cases, usually toward the end of the narrative, are confronted with situations (dilemmas, decisions, story conclusions) that need resolving. Teachers working on the cases need to do the same, as they make their own decisions while providing analyses and justifications to support those decisions.
- The cases aim to be interesting and sometimes challenging and to express some urgency and tension in order to engage readers.
- The cases can also be somewhat ambiguous, with no quick or easy solutions, reflecting the complexities of real-life teaching situations (Jackson, 1997).
- The narratives are complex and multidimensional to encourage alternative interpretations.

12 Introduction

3. *Context Rich*

- The narrative cases are locally located and situated. They reflect the local social, cultural, educational, and political contexts within which the action takes place and in which the characters live their professional lives.
- The cases aim as far as possible to be globally situated, reflecting global ideas, debates, and issues in language teacher education and continuing professional development.
- Characters, places, and actions are richly contextualized, like in the real world of language teaching and professional practice, so that readers are able to "probe the issues at stake and are compelled to exercise evidence-based judgment in the dynamic process of exchanging perspectives and opinions" (Gooden, 2024, p. 15).
- The characters, what they do, and the dilemmas they face in the cases are credible so that teachers can identify with them, care about them, and imagine being or working with them.

How Are Cases Used?

A great deal of variation exists in the ways in which teacher educators and PD facilitators use cases in their programs, courses, and workshops. The Facilitator Guide section that follows offers specific suggestions for their use in classrooms and online. Here three broad approaches are outlined.

1. *Cases Used Within a "Strong" Case Method Pedagogical Approach*

In this approach, the curriculum is driven by case method pedagogy. Here, the case-oriented curriculum is reminiscent of the practices of the Harvard Law School from many years ago and continuing today. In other words (see Figure 0.1), the curriculum is designed around the cases.

The design of a particular course, its content, and the cases to be used in the course are decided on at the same time, with the cases determining what the course will look like and what will be in it.

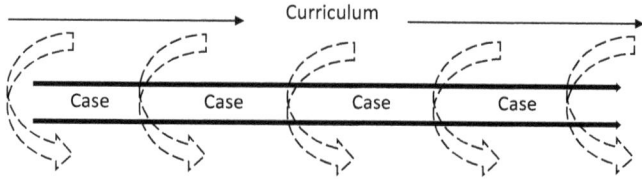

Figure 0.1 A strong case method pedagogical approach

2. *Individual Cases Used Strategically (and Regularly) Within a Course, Class, or a Series of Workshops*

In this approach, the curriculum is not designed around the cases – they do not drive the shape of a course, or its content, or how it is delivered. The course, and its content, is primary and cases are introduced at strategic and regular times for specific purposes to supplement the course content (see Figure 0.2).

A teacher educator could, for example, insert a case into a course to transition into a new topic, or at the end of a unit within a course to consolidate what has previously been covered.

3. *Individual Cases Used as One-Off Instructional Activities*

In this instructional approach, cases are used here and there within a course without any pre-planning and certainly not to orient the content of the course or to direct its structure (see Figure 0.3).

Cases may, for example, be used as an icebreaker, to develop group cohesion, or even as a time filler. A clear relationship must still exist, nevertheless, between the cases and the course objectives and content.

What Are the Benefits of the Case Method for Teachers?

Many claims have been made about the benefits or advantages for teachers engaging with case method pedagogy, and also when engaging with each other

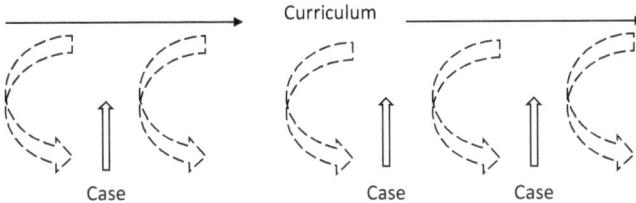

Figure 0.2 Cases used strategically within a course

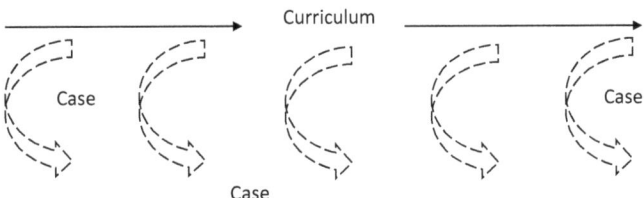

Figure 0.3 Cases used as one-off instructional activities

when working on cases. The (language) teacher education literature has generated countless lists of these benefits (see e.g., Jackson, 1997; Mostert, 2007; Lundeberg, 1999; Tinker Sachs & Ho, 2011). A further collated list can be found below, after a few representative quotes from this literature.

Quotes from the Literature

- Jackson (1997): "The case method can sharpen the critical thinking, analytical, and communication skills of both novice and experienced teachers and help ready them for the complex challenges they could face in the world of professional practice" (p. 1).
  - Critical thinking
  - Analytical skills
  - Communication skills
  - Ready for challenges of professional practice
- Tinker Sachs and Ho (2011): "The use of cases enhances reflective thinking about teaching in a social setting. Reflective thinking about teaching can lead teachers to analyze and theorize their practice and bridge the theory/practice divide" (p. 276).
  - Reflective thinking
  - Analyzing and theorizing practice
  - Bridging the theory/practice divide
- Mostert (2007): "Case-based instruction argues for an increased emphasis on the study of teachers' perspectives and knowledge rather than theory, thereby allowing for the emergence of the voice of the teacher as central to what happens in classrooms, rather than the views imposed by researchers because teachers are inextricably linked to the actions and decisions of teaching" (pp. 435–436).
  - Teachers' perspectives and knowledge
- Schröter & Röber (2022). "Rather than being restricted to a passive or receptive role description, course participants are encouraged to contribute actively to the course content by discussing and evaluating the case material. In doing so, students stand a much better chance, if compared to formal settings of frontal classroom teaching, to relate their prior (work) experience to the subject matter, feel emotionally involved in the learning process and build teams with their classmates. In this way, the case method blends cognitive with affective learning modes . . ., which also helps making knowledge more memorable and retrievable" (p. 263).
  - Contributing actively to course content
  - Relating prior experience to the subject matter
  - Feeling emotionally involved
  - Making knowledge more memorable and retrievable

List of Primary Benefits

1. Since the cases relate closely to – or may even drive – the curriculum and course content, they serve an instructional purpose in relation to the topic being taught. The teachers learn about the topic by engaging with the cases (Kunselman & Johnson, 2004).
2. As discussed above regarding a sociocultural theoretical perspective on language teacher education, the case method prompts the externalizing of *everyday concepts* (what teachers know from their experiences) while internalizing relevant *academic concepts* (Johnson & Golombek, 2020); similar in meaning to bridging the theory/practice divide. Teachers make sense of theory through the cases by relating it to their own knowledge.
3. Case discussions and reflection/research on the content and dilemmas of cases encourage teachers to make connections to (a) their personal life experiences, (b) their (imagined future) teaching practice, and (c) workplace and educational contexts with which they are familiar.
4. Consequently, applying what has been learned to real-world problems ("thinking like teachers") is another major outcome for teachers who have worked on cases.
5. The case method, through in-classroom or online discussions, promotes reflective practice. Teachers also refine their reflective practice skills and learn how to become reflective practitioners.
6. Through the many ways the case method requires classroom and online discussions, group work, and completion of research tasks, teachers learn to collaborate in groups, to argue a position, and to listen to, understand, tolerate, and learn from alternative views.
7. And they do so vicariously through the actions, beliefs, attitudes, and decisions of the characters in the cases. This offers readers a relatively safe space in which to put forward and debate their ideas.
8. Case reading, collaborative discussions, and reflection lead to ideas for self-inquiry and research. So, moving beyond cases and drawing on knowledge gained by participating in the case method, teachers are informed and inspired to do research.
9. The development of the following related skills is also supported by the literature:
   - Processing and analyzing skills (Haley, 2004)
   - Reasoning and decision-making skills (Heitzmann, 2008)
   - Coping with ambiguities (Bailey, 2006)
   - Critical thinking (Gooden, 2024)
   - Problem solving (Darling-Hammond & Hammerness, 2002)

Cased-Based Teacher Research

Case method pedagogy is typically classroom based. Although teacher learners may read a case prior to a class to prepare for later case-based class work or engage in some post-class work on a case (e.g., written reflection or an assignment), the main case-based instruction takes place in the classroom. This is where facilitator-led discussions occur, or teachers collaborate in groups to work on tasks related to the case. Figure 0.4 shows connections between reading, discussing, and reflecting on the case, activities that typically take place in the classroom. The arrows depict the association of these case-based activities with teachers' practice, both current and in the future.

On the right side of Figure 0.4, teacher research is introduced as an extension to classroom-based case method instruction. Research extends the case method beyond the classroom, although it is still connected to and inspired by cases. Teacher research can be collaborative, involving pairs or groups of teachers working on a common research project, for example, but normally involves independent work in the form of course assignments, graduate-level dissertations or theses, or teacher research conducted as part of one's continuing professional practice. Each case in this casebook includes two related research topics and suggests practical methods for carrying out the research. These are described further in the Facilitator Guide section.

Who Is the Casebook For?

Language Teacher Education

Language teacher education is a process that serves like a bridge "to link what is known in the field with what is done in the classroom, and it does so through the individuals whom we educate as teachers" (Freeman, 1989, p. 30). "Individuals" here are pre-service or in-service teachers who learn to teach and learn about teaching. Freeman (2016) expands his conceptualization of

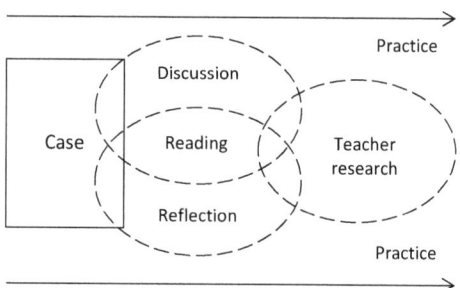

Figure 0.4 Research as an extension of classroom case method instruction

language teacher education "to describe the connecting, building, and refining of knowledge and know-how through formal processes of professional preparation and further development" (p. 9).

- This casebook is intended for use with pre-service and in-service teachers who engage in formal processes of preparation and further development. These are normally undergraduate and graduate teacher preparation programs in institutions such as university or colleges of education.

Continuing Professional Development

Mercer, Farrell, and Freeman (2022) state that continuing professional development "recognizes that professionals often actively maintain and expand their professional knowledge, skills, and attitudes in response to changes in circumstances and professional understandings over time. As such, professional development is an ongoing, long-term endeavour that professionals engage in throughout their careers" (p. 8).

- This casebook is intended for use with professionals who engage in ongoing, long-term development endeavors throughout their careers. These normally include workshops, seminars, webinars, and short courses, offered by institutions, online, or at conferences, for example, and are not associated with a formal program or qualification.

Programs and Courses

- Graduate programs in TESOL and Applied Linguistics.
- Graduate programs in Education, Multilingual Education, Bilingual Education, and International Education.
- Formal, accredited teacher training courses such as CELTA (Certificate in English Language Teaching to Adults) and DELTA (Diploma in English Language Teaching to Adults).
- In-service professional development workshops.
- Undergraduate programs in TESOL and Applied Linguistics.

People

- Pre-service language teachers in undergraduate programs.
- Pre-service and in-service teachers in formal, accredited teacher training courses.

- Pre-service and in-service language teachers in graduate-level programs, including coursework doctoral students.
- In-service teachers participating in continuing professional development workshops and short courses.
- Teacher educators in the process of formal instruction with pre-service and in-service teachers.
- Teacher educators undertaking self-study.
- Professional development facilitators undertaking self-study or in the process of instruction with in-service teachers.
- Teacher educators and language teachers participating in in-house institutional professional development.
- Curriculum designers and policy makers involved in language teacher education.
- Teacher researchers undertaking independent or collaborative research.
- Teacher researcher mentors.

Organization of the Casebook

Following this Introduction, a description of the components of The Cases is presented. There are seven cases in each of the ten chapters. The components of a case consist of the case itself, a set of keywords and pre-reading reflections that come before the presentation of the case, and then discussion questions, research topics, and reading resources after the case.

A Facilitator Guide follows the description of the case components. The Guide suggests ways in which teacher educators and professional development workshop facilitators can use cases in their instruction. It focuses particularly on classroom, online, and workshop activities for the purposes of discussions, reflection, assignments, and research.

The casebook covers ten main topic areas, each in a separate chapter. Although these topics and cases are presented in separate chapters, they are obviously very much interrelated. Some cases, therefore, contain content that could easily appear in other chapters as well. Many traditional themes as well as those more recently covered in discourse on language teacher education are spread across all ten topic areas, but typically one or more will appear as the main theme in any one particular case.

Chapter 1: Classroom Language Teaching

This opening chapter goes straight to the heart of what language teachers do – classroom teaching. It includes cases set in seven different countries and in primary, high, and private language schools, as well as college and university. It covers topics as diverse as teaching in large classes, translanguaging, and using AI in an academic writing class.

Chapter 2: Language Learners

Each case in this chapter examines the experiences of a language learner from a different country, usually from the perspective of their teacher. Learners are the people who teachers interact with the most in their professional lives and are often the cause of dilemmas they encounter. The chapter covers topics such as gender identity in the classroom, teaching dedicated older learners, and teaching a learner with suspected ADHD (Attention Deficit Hyperactivity Disorder).

Chapter 3: Teacher–Student Relationships

Teachers' relationships with their students are the focus of this chapter. These relationships can determine the outcomes of learning, but also affect the professional and emotional lives of teachers. The cases in this chapter examine how teacher–student relationships unfold in diverse multicultural contexts and cover topics such as being a Black teacher in Japan, compromising the privacy of a gay primary school teacher in Canada, and knowing students' names.

Chapter 4: Language Assessment

All teachers are in some way involved in the assessment of their learners, whether it be informal classroom-based assessments or preparing them for external examinations. This chapter offers cases that raise dilemmas teachers face when their work relates to language learner assessment. It covers topics such as too much internal assessment, the pressure of external public examinations, post-entry university language assessment, and students copying off each other.

Chapter 5: Classroom Management

Effective language teaching and learning means managing instructional activities in the classroom, managing students and any issues they present, and managing one's own professional conduct and learning. Cases in this chapter examine management issues, from New York City in the USA, to Thailand, to Poland, and include topics such as the field trip (that never happened), planning too much lesson content, and managing a new student in class.

Chapter 6: Professional Development

Besides teaching, managing their classrooms, and assessing learners, teachers also take care of their own development, sometimes with the support of their workplace institutions or professional associations. This chapter presents cases that offer opportunities to examine a variety of types of teacher professional development including doing a PhD part-time, conducting workshops for teacher colleagues, and going on a short-term study-abroad exchange.

Chapter 7: Teacher Research

Doing useful research, or wanting to do research, or not having sufficient skills to do research are ongoing concerns for teachers, despite an increasing expectation that teacher research should be part of a teacher's professional life. Cases in this chapter look at high school teacher-researchers in Vietnam, an MA student choosing a dissertation topic in the UK, and an ethical dilemma experienced by a student teacher while on a teaching practicum in the US.

Chapter 8: Professional Service

There are multiple dimensions to the work that language teachers and teacher educators do in their institutions, and beyond, besides teaching in classrooms and doing research. They all perform some sort of professional service, be it administrative or committee work or taking on management and leadership roles. Professional service is the focus of this chapter, and cases include meeting with dissatisfied parents, serving on a Department of Education working group, and giving a talk to pre-service teachers.

Chapter 9: Leadership

Some teachers and teacher educators take on quite significant leadership roles, such as serving as a new president of a teacher association in Thailand, but all teachers exhibit leadership in some way. It may be relatively small-scale, such as attempting to decolonize the curriculum in one program in Colombia or establishing a collaborative teacher research group in a school in Botswana. Diverse teacher leadership possibilities such as these are represented in the cases in this chapter.

Chapter 10: Teacher Wellbeing

As teachers go about their work of teaching in classrooms, doing research, and performing leadership duties, their psychological and emotional wellbeing is constantly under pressure in the workplace. This final chapter presents cases where wellbeing dilemmas are exposed. It includes a teacher educator who is under pressure from management to retire, a teacher coping with a heavy post–study-abroad workload, and a teacher having to deal with students' complaints.

In the Bibliography, references relating to the two Research Topics connected to each of the seventy cases are listed. These are divided into two sections: The first includes general research methodology texts in applied linguistics or language teaching and learning, and the second section includes references to specific methods of data collection and analysis. The casebook ends with References cited in the Introduction.

The Cases

Each of the ten chapters contains seven cases, and each case is structured the same way. A case has several related components which serve a particular purpose in case method instruction. To describe and illustrate these components a sample case from Chapter 5: Classroom Management will be used. The Facilitator Guide suggests ways in which these case components can be used in classrooms and professional development workshops.

Title

The title briefly describes what the case is about.

Purpose

Titles are brief and aim to identify the main topic of the case and signal its contents. They pique the reader's interest and help them decide whether the case is suitable for a particular course, lesson, or workshop. The title of the sample case is:

The Field Trip (That Never Happened)

Keywords

A list of five keywords or phrases follows the title.

Purpose

The keywords provide further information about the case, beyond what the title offers, to help readers anticipate what the case is about. Specifically, the keywords indicate:

- The country or countries in which the narrative of the case is located.
- The type of institution or educational sector in which the character(s) in the case work; for example, primary school, university, private language school.
- The main character(s) in the case and the type of work they do.
- What the main action or topic of the case is.
- What the dilemma in the case is or what causes the dilemma.

Here are the keywords from the sample case, The Field Trip (That Never Happened):

Keywords
- Canada
- Private school
- Part-time ESL teacher
- Planning a field trip
- Parents' queries and concerns

Pre-reading Reflection

Before the presentation of the case, there are three pre-reading reflection questions. As the name suggests, these are to be done before reading the case.

Purpose

The pre-reading reflection orients readers to the case. It gets them thinking about the topic of the case, usually by drawing on their personal experiences of the same or similar circumstances as those presented in the case. The questions are not always obviously related to the case topic, but their relevance will become clearer after analyzing the case. In other words, the pre-reading reflections "warm up" readers before tackling the case. The sample case pre-reading reflection questions are as follows:

Pre-reading Reflection

1. Do you have memories of going on a school field trip when at elementary or secondary school? How was it?
2. What health and safety risks might apply to day trips off school grounds?
3. What are some of the language learning benefits of going on short field trips? Imagine one specific type of trip.

24   The Cases

The Case

The dilemma-based narrative is the main component in the series of related case components.

Purpose

As described in the Introduction, a case in this casebook is a narrative in which one or two central characters – teachers, teacher educators, language learners, researchers – engage in professional action in particular spatiotemporal contexts and experience dilemmas that need resolving.

In the sample case used here, a part-time ESL teacher at a private school in Canada decides to take her small class on a field trip to a neighboring park to "observe nature," such as the sky, grass, any breeze, birds, and the weather, in preparation for a climate change project. When the teacher, Xiaoming Chen, starts putting together the paperwork for the field trip, she encounters some pressure and resistance from the students' parents. They have plenty of difficult questions and alternative suggestions for how the work could be done, which eventually leads to Xiaoming abandoning the field trip.

Discussion Questions

A series of five discussion questions follows the case. These questions relate directly to the content of the case and can be the start or form the basis of classroom discussion.

Purpose

The discussion questions are of varying types:
- Recalling case content and clarifying its meaning.
- Evaluating actions and decision-making.
- Giving personal opinions of the content, actions, or decision-making.
- Taking the perspective of the character(s) and performing alternative actions.
- Providing a rationale or motivation for actions or decisions.
- Considering personal emotional responses to the content and understanding what they mean.
- Suggesting alternative actions or decisions.
- Suggesting resolutions to dilemmas.
- Imagining future actions and experiences of the characters.

Research Topics

The sample case from Chapter 5 about Xiaoming and her abandoned field trip has the following five questions:

Questions

1. One query raised by the parents has to do with Xiaoming's experience. Do you think she is experienced enough to lead her planned field trip? Why or why not?
2. Can you think of an alternative way of handling the parental consent form process?
3. How do you feel about some parents' attitude regarding students remaining on the school grounds and in their classroom instead of going on the field trip? Was a field trip justified to successfully complete the climate change project?
4. Did Xiaoming make the right decision to abandon the field trip? What would you have done?
5. How could the school have supported Xiaoming both before she sent out the forms to parents and when they were returned?

Research Topics

Immediately following the case are two research topics, which are related to the topic of the case. Methods for carrying out the research are suggested – both data collection and analysis, and sometimes reporting the findings. The research is designed to be as feasible as possible for graduate students or busy practicing teachers and teacher educators.

Purpose

As explained above (see Figure 0.4), research extends the case method beyond the classroom. The aim of doing research is to draw on knowledge gained from engaging with the case to (a) learn more about the topic, (b) further the teacher's professional development, (c) produce findings that might be useful to their own classroom, or more broadly, their workplace, (d) produce findings to report in a publication or a conference presentation, (e) complete a class assignment, (f) contribute to a qualification, and (g) continue with ongoing teacher research as part of the teacher's professional practice. Research based on the research topics could take the form of:

- Self-study
- Class assignments
- Dissertations and theses
- Independent or collaborative teacher research
- Teacher educator research

The sample case of Xiaoming and the abandoned field trip includes the following research topic. (Note: M9 cross-references to relevant research methodology literature provided in the Bibliography.)

Research Topic

Investigating the Roles and Responsibilities of Part-Time Language Instructors
What roles and responsibilities are appropriate for part-time language instructors? How is their workload monitored and protected? What support do they get in their schools?

1. In one school or institutional language department, meet with the administrator (e.g., human resources manager, principal) who is responsible for appointing part-time language instructors.
2. *Interview* (M9) the administrator to inquire about the process of appointing part-time language instructors, and ask about: how they are appointed, their teaching workload allocations, their teaching and administration responsibilities, what support they get for classroom management issues, and how their work is evaluated and their wellbeing monitored.
3. Now conduct *semi-structured interviews* (M9) with the part-time instructors in the school or department. Ask them the same set of questions.
4. Compare the instructors' and the administrator's answers to the questions.
5. Do part-time language instructors feel that they are exploited? Are they over-worked? Are they assigned responsibilities for which they do not feel qualified? Do they feel supported and protected?

Resources

The case ends with a list of three relevant resources (and their URLs) – mostly open-access publications such as journal articles and topic-related webpages.

Purpose

The resources can be used by both the teacher educator/PD facilitator and teacher learners who work on the cases.
  For the instructors:

- The resources provide background information about the topic.
- They can be utilized when preparing a lesson in which the associated case will be used.
- Resources can be incorporated into classroom case-based activity.
- One or more of the resources may be assigned as pre-reading before class, or as further reading after class.

For the teacher learners:

- The resources could be consulted before or after class to gain a deeper understanding of the topic of the case.
- Readings could be consulted for research purposes.

The following is one of the resources from the sample case:

Resources

DeWitt, J. & Storksdieck, M. (2008). A short review of school field trips: Key findings from the past and implications for the future. *Visitor Studies*, *11*(2), 181–197. https://doi.org/10.1080/10645570802355562

Facilitator Guide

This Facilitator Guide suggests ways in which the case components can be used. Merseth (1996) states that in the case method, the facilitator "plays a very important role – guiding, probing, directing, giving feedback or sometimes simply observing the exchanges and contributions among the class members" (p. 727). The Guide first addresses general facilitator guidelines that apply to the use of this casebook in all types of teacher education and professional development situations where the casebook is used. "Facilitator" in this section means a teacher educator working in an institution, a teacher trainer, or a facilitator of continuing PD workshops. These broad guidelines are followed by more specific suggestions for using the case components (a) in classroom or workshop discussions, (b) in online discussions, (c) for assignments, and (d) for the purposes of research.

General Guidelines

1.   Being Flexible

Facilitators should aim to be flexible with all aspects of case method pedagogy. This means keeping an eye on teacher participant engagement, monitoring their interest and comprehension of the content of the cases, checking on their understanding of the language of the case components, monitoring their levels of motivation, and then making necessary changes to instruction when issues are detected. Consequently, facilitators also need to be constantly reflective about their own practice, evaluating and understanding their planning and the effective application of case work. Changes could be, for example:

- slowing down, or speeding up;
- omitting some planned activity or a case component;
- assigning individual work instead of group work;
- or even abandoning a case altogether.

2. Adapting, Adding To, and Translating Case Components

Facilitators know their teacher learners best – their educational and cultural backgrounds, their level of language proficiency, their teaching experience and working contexts. Facilitators, therefore, should be willing to adapt, translate, and add to the case components to suit their teacher participants by, for example:

- paraphrasing or translating parts of the case components (i.e., *Discussion Questions*, *Research Topics*, one or more case paragraphs) if the language is too difficult for the teacher learners.
- shortening a case, but not losing relevant contextual details.
- re-writing questions to suit the teaching and learning contexts of the teachers.
- developing course assessments or creating reflection tasks from the *Research Topics*.
- adding supplementary materials relevant to the topic of the case, such as policy and syllabus documents, internet links, social media, and teaching materials.
- inserting examples from a local context or explanatory notes within a case to make the cases more relevant and meaningful to a particular group of teachers.
- adding to the five discussion *Questions* to suit the teachers.
- allowing teachers to use AI or translation apps to help with language comprehension.

3. Encouraging Active Engagement

At all times, at all stages, facilitators should encourage teacher participants to engage actively with the case components. As Capron et al. (2009) say, "The goal is for participants to *learn through actively engaging with the case studies*. Participants are encouraged to apply knowledge, reasoning, and their experiences and contexts to a real-life situation (the case study) and to learn from each others' responses" [emphasis in original] (p. 17). This could involve:

- creating a safe environment in which to reflect on, discuss, and research the cases;
- listening carefully to participant contributions and re-phrasing where necessary for those who might not understand them (either because of the content or because of language problems);
- trying to get many different teachers to contribute during discussions and other case-related activities;
- offering affirming and encouraging feedback;
- demonstrating self-enthusiasm for case method instruction.

4. Being Comfortable with Debate and Disagreement

Discussions of the dilemma-based narrative cases in this casebook inevitably result in different opinions about how the cases should be resolved. Disagreements may also arise about the meaning of the content of cases, the interpretation of underlying theories, and the relevance of a topic for the participants' teaching contexts. Answers to the discussion questions will also vary, as they should. Facilitators, therefore, could manage difference by:

- welcoming different points of view;
- encouraging all participants to be supportive rather than competitive;
- avoiding and deflecting personal or culturally insensitive arguments;
- helping participants to look at issues and dilemmas from multiple perspectives.

5. Developing Tolerance for Ambiguity and Uncertainty

Facilitators who believe that their role is to deliver information would probably not be comfortable using the case method (Wasserman, 1994). Effort, therefore, needs to be made by facilitators to develop tolerance for ambiguity and uncertainty and for not always needing to know the correct or best answer. And the same applies to teacher learners who would prefer to passively absorb information delivered by their instructors. Facilitators should strive to enable tolerance for ambiguity and uncertainty in their teacher learners. This could be achieved by:

- combining case methods with more traditional (and possibly preferable) teacher-fronted instruction, thereby teaching inductive learning when using the case method;
- summarizing discussions, decisions, and dilemma resolutions at regular intervals – perhaps in writing – so that teachers feel that concrete progress is being made;
- regularly checking on the emotional wellbeing of both the teacher participants and the facilitator.

Class and Workshop Discussions

Preparing for Class or Workshop Discussions

- Carefully select an appropriate case and know it well. The case should align with the lesson content and represent any theoretical principles or concepts being taught.

- Consult the *Resources*, if necessary, to learn more about the topic of the case.
- If the teacher participants will be doing preparation before class, ask them to read the *Keywords* and to do the *Pre-reading Reflection* at home before coming to class. They could also read the case.
- Assign them a task such as writing a short narrative of their own experience related to the topic of the case.
- Ask them to read one or more of the case *Resources* before class. Alternatively, they could read the abstracts or selected sections from the *Resources*.

Reading the Case in Class

- Start by setting aside a short period of time for teacher participants to refresh their memories about the *Keywords* and *Pre-reading Reflection* (or to consider them for the first time if they didn't do so at home before the class or workshop). They could do this silently and independently, or perhaps in pairs.
- Read the case aloud, paragraph by paragraph, from beginning to end. Stop along the way to check on teacher comprehension, although stopping too often might distract from the flow of the narrative and should perhaps only be done after a full reading of the case.
- Alternatively, assign a reader or readers to read the case aloud (readers could be assigned before class to give them an opportunity to practice).
- After the first reading, give teachers a few minutes to read the case again silently by themselves to ensure full comprehension of the narrative, and to identify and begin considering any dilemmas.

Facilitating Classroom Discussions

- Many options are possible for how case discussions can take place, and facilitators will know which are most appropriate for their particular teacher learners.
- One obvious possibility is for the facilitator to engage teachers in a facilitator-led discussion, whereby the facilitator leads the discussion with the whole class or workshop group. This might be more feasible in small classes. In this arrangement:
  a. Seek to maintain equal and fair distribution of turns and not favor specific vocal participants or groups of participants; address the entire class when speaking.
  b. Work through the five *Questions* (including revised or additional questions) one by one until saturation has been reached.
  c. Encourage teacher participants to speak clearly and directly, and support them by paraphrasing, repeating, and translating, if necessary.

d. Make reference, if applicable, to the three *Resources* or any supplementary materials if these have been consulted.

- Another option, after reading the case, is to divide the class or workshop participants into small groups. In this arrangement:
  a. assign each group a *Question* or two to discuss;
  b. in a facilitator-led discussion, allow each group a turn to report on their discussion;
  c. encourage contributions from all class members.

- A third option also involves post-reading group work. This time each group writes down their discussion responses to the assigned *Question(s)* on poster-sized paper and then in turn presents their answers in front of the class. While they present:
  a. lead the whole-class discussion based on the groups' reports;
  b. support the presenting group members, encouraging equal participation and clarity of argument.

- For all three options, and any others that might be organized, discourage participants or groups from raising private issues, and while pursuing valid and relevant lines of argument, gently direct discussion away from potentially irrelevant or harmful ideas.

After Class Case Work

- Ask teacher participants to summarize classroom case discussions in writing, in a teacher casebook journal.
- Also in their journal, participants could reflect on the case's applicability to professional practice, with examples.
- Suggest or require teacher learners to read one or more (or sections) of the three *Resources* to consolidate their understanding of the case, the resolutions of the dilemma in the case, and the case topic more generally.
- Assign work on any supplementary materials, which could be discussed or presented at the next class meeting.
- Ask teachers to summarize answers to the five discussion *Questions* and then post them online on a learning management system (LMS) (see next section).

Online Discussions

Learning management systems, such as Moodle, Blackboard Learn, and Canvas, offer plenty of opportunities for individuals to engage with each other in online digital spaces, and this includes language teacher learners discussing cases. Again, there are many ways of doing so, and facilitators will know what is appropriate and feasible in their contexts, taking into account available technology, facilitator and teacher technological skills, course or workshop syllabus requirements, time, and other practical constraints. Three broad options include the following.

Discussing the Case Completely Online

- Post the *Keywords*, *Pre-reading Reflection*, the *Case*, and *Questions* components of one case online in a specifically designated discussion forum.
- Provide clear instructions on how to go about the discussion.
- Preferably, only do an online case discussion after having completed a discussion in class so that participants are familiar with both the components and discussion procedures.
- Ask teacher participants to read the *Keywords*, *Pre-reading Reflection*, and the *Case*, and then to post answers to one or two of the five *Questions* in the discussion forum.
- Pairs or groups of teachers may wish to consult with each other about the case prior to posting their individual comments.
- Encourage them to read the posts of all other teachers, and to reply to two or three (or more) of them.
- Monitor the activity in the discussion forum.
- Other possibilities include:
  a. discussing or doing tasks related to the *Resources* or sections of them online;
  b. working on any supplementary materials created by the facilitator;
  c. discussing one or both *Research Topics* or planning possible projects based on the topics;
  d. planning and posting teaching materials, lesson plans, policy statements, or short video commentaries created by the teachers after discussing the case online.

Discussing the Case Online with Facilitator Intervention

This option is similar to the one above, but this time it involves participation by the facilitator beyond merely monitoring the online activity from a distance.

- Reply to the teacher participants' posts, encouraging further comment by the poster.
- Also comment on teachers' replies to other posts. The purpose of these comments is to extend the conversation, suggest alternative interpretations, and to get teachers to dig deeper into topics and viewpoints.

- If synchronous online videochat is possible via the LMS, such as with Zoom, hold a short meeting to summarize discussions, highlight controversies, settle arguments, or conduct a question and answer (Q&A) session.
- Engage with teachers in their reading of any *Resources*.
- Work with teachers on supplementary materials and their posts containing materials, policy statements, or videos that they may have produced.
- Consult with individual teachers or groups of teachers who are considering or planning to do research based on the *Research Topics*. Work through the topics to ensure understanding and check the purpose and feasibility of a potential project. Plan follow-up, face-to-face meetings.

Combining In-Class and Online Discussion

Two main options, among others, are possible when combining in-class and online case work. One is to start work on the case in class and then move online.

- Do most of the case discussion in class, working through the components and answering the *Questions*.
- In the online discussion forum, request teachers to ask questions about any of the five *Questions* they had issues with or concerns about in class. They could also write down their in-class answers and seek clarification or responses from other class members.
- Assign work on supplementary materials or *Resources* that relate to the case that was discussed in class.
- After discussing the case in class, ask teachers to read the *Research Topics* at home and then bring suggestions to the online discussion forum for taking the research projects further. They might suggest steps for planning a project or considering its feasibility within their places of work, for example.

A second option is to begin case work online and then continue later in class.

- Introduce the topic of the case online in a short, written description and ask teachers to reflect on that topic from the perspective of their own professional experience.
- Provide a very brief note of related theoretical principles and concepts.
- Present the teachers with the *Keywords* and *Pre-reading reflection* to prepare them for reading the case later in class.
- Post short quotes from the *Resources* and ask teachers to comment on those, or answer questions posted in the discussion forum.

Cases for Assignments

Many of the case activities presented so far can be converted into course or workshop assignments for assessment purposes, if desired or required. Below are just five examples that illustrate the possibilities.

- Teacher participants are given a case to analyze independently. They answer the five *Questions* or complete any other case-related task created by the facilitator.
- Teachers answer the five *Questions* independently, then meet with another class or workshop member and compare answers. In their written assignment, they first report their own answers, and then in a separate section compare their answers with their partner's. A final section could be a reflection on the case analysis process, including the collaboration with their partner.
- Teachers work together on a case in a group assignment, answering the *Questions* or performing another task and then submitting a jointly written report. The assignment could also take the form of a PowerPoint (or similar) presentation to the rest of the class, which could include a Q&A session.
- In a simple online assessment, teacher participants post answers to the case *Questions* on the available LMS discussion forum, and then the quality of these is assessed by the facilitator. This could be a one-off exercise, or several postings could be made during the course for different cases.
- Individual teachers construct a multimodal PowerPoint (or similar) presentation including voice, sound, and images to convey their understanding of case dilemmas, to suggest research ideas, and to integrate supporting information from the *Resources*. The presentations are posted online for comments (and grading) from the facilitator and other class members.

Cases for Research

Research is now considered to be an integral part of language teachers' professional work (Curtin & Uştuk, 2024), and their teacher education programs or continuing PD initiatives are recognized places for developing research knowledge and skills. As Figure 0.4 in the Introduction shows, engaging in research is an extension of classroom-based case method pedagogy. Two *Research Topics* are attached to each of the seventy cases in this casebook. Case-embedded research can be collaborative, involving whole-class discussion and reflection or pairs or groups of teachers working on a common research project, for example. However, it normally involves independent work in the form of course assignments, graduate-level dissertations or theses, or teacher research conducted as part of one's continuing professional practice.

If, after having read and discussed the *Research Topics*, a study is conducted that requires the collection of real data from human participants, ensure that ethics approval is obtained from a relevant institutional review board or ethics committee and that informed consent is obtained from any research participants.

Research Topics for Reflection and Discussion

- Integrate one or both *Research Topics* into case method work in a class or workshop.
- Confirm the teacher participants' understanding of the topics, aims, and methods of the proposed research.
- Discuss the relevance, feasibility, and potential implications of the project in the context of the teachers' workplace.
- Debate which of the two *Research Topics* the teachers prefer, and why, and consider alternatives and extensions to the two topics and their proposed methods.
- Transfer some of the above reflection and discussion activities to an online LMS platform.

Research for Assignments

- Teachers draft a full research proposal based on one of the *Research Topics*, and with reference to the related case.
- Reduce the scope of a selected *Research Topic*. Participants then independently carry out a small-scale study for the purposes of an assessed course assignment.
- Adapt a *Research Topic* so that class members can use each other as research participants. This will probably eliminate the need for ethics approval.
- Combine a *Research Topic* (and its associated case) with other course or workshop materials to create an assignment.

Research for Dissertations or Theses

Teachers doing graduate qualifications (e.g., MA and PhD level) will encounter the case-related *Research Topics* in their coursework or the PD workshops in which they participate. These graduate students may go on to do independent research in the form of dissertations and theses, and thus move out of the hands of case method facilitators. Nevertheless, they may still be inspired both by the *Research Topics* they come across when examining the associated cases and by the case work done with facilitators and other class members during their classes and workshops.

- As a class, suggest ways in which *Research Topics* could be developed into a dissertation or thesis topic for an MA or PhD project.
- Focusing on the methods of data collection and analysis, consider their scope and whether they would be appropriate for a project the size of a dissertation or thesis. Suggest what adaptations and extensions might have to be made to the methods.
- Together, suggest different research topics based on the reading and discussion of the case.

Teacher Research

Teacher research is the ongoing research language teachers engage in as part of their professional practice. It could be classroom-based action research, exploratory action research, or any other type of qualitative and quantitative research. Teachers might be primary or secondary school teachers or university-based academics, and they might do their research independently or in collaboration with each other. Facilitators of the case method in teacher education courses and PD workshops will encounter teachers who are doing research.

- Discuss the case *Research Topics* in relation to the teacher participants' experiences and work contexts.
  a. Are the topics relevant to the teachers' work experience?
  b. Would the proposed topics and methods be feasible?
  c. What constraints might the teachers experience?
  d. How would the topics and methods have to be adapted to suit their needs and preferences?
  e. Are the topics motivating for this particular group of teachers?
- Teachers draft a research proposal based on one of the *Research Topics*.
- Teachers discuss one or two *Research Topics* with their colleagues at work to gauge their interest in collaborating on a research project, and then report back to the class.
- If time allows, teacher participants conduct a study based on one of the *Research Topics* and write a brief report on the findings. This can be shared with the class, in class or online.

1 Classroom Language Teaching

Cases in this chapter

1.1	Working as a Teacher Assistant	*page* 38
1.2	Using AI in an Academic Writing Class	41
1.3	Translanguaging During Independent Group Play	44
1.4	Engaging English Language Learners	48
1.5	Global Englishes in a Rural Classroom	51
1.6	Criticism of an Intensive TEFL Course	55
1.7	Teaching in Large Classes	58

1.1   Working as a Teacher Assistant

Keywords
- United States and Uganda
- High school
- English as a New Language (ENL) teacher assistant
- Working with an experienced teacher
- Observing language errors being taught

1.1.1   Pre-reading Reflection

1. What would you do if you were observing a language class as a peer teacher and noticed your teacher colleague teaching obvious language errors to the learners?
2. Do you have any experience of working as or working with a teacher assistant? What is the role of an assistant in a language classroom?
3. What issues could arise in the relationship between classroom teachers and their assistants?

Harry is from Uganda in Africa and has lived in the US for two years. He obtained his BA degree in teaching from a university in Uganda and then taught in a high school in Kampala, the capital city, for three years before being awarded a scholarship to study toward an MA degree in TESOL (Teaching English to Speakers of Other Languages) at a university in New York City. He graduated after two years but could not immediately find a fixed-term teaching position in the US,

1.1 Working as a Teacher Assistant

which he was allowed to do as a condition of both his scholarship and passport visa. However, a job as a language teacher assistant opened up at a public school in the neighborhood where Harry was living in New York. Short-term funding had been allocated by the city for special assistance to support schools that were struggling with larger than normal intakes of students across all grades. For years, teachers had been complaining about increased class sizes, heavy workloads, under-prepared students, and disruptive classroom behavior. The school decided to spend the funds on hiring a teacher assistant to work with the English as a New Language (ENL) teachers in the school, which catered for immigrants and recent refugees in the area. The assistant would move from class to class throughout the day to assist teachers with various tasks such as facilitating group work, monitoring discipline, and helping to prepare materials and lesson plans.

Harry believed he was easily qualified enough to manage these tasks. He applied for the job and was hired as a teacher assistant soon after graduation at the start of his third year living in the US. Harry soon discovered that the work was both manageable and enjoyable, although he didn't really find it very challenging. He got on well with the students, engaging productively with them during group work and one-on-one discussions, for example. He produced useful lesson plans collaboratively with the teachers and loved seeing them come to life in the classroom. With some mentoring, he began grading assignments and tests and became quite efficient at it, earning the praise of colleagues. By all accounts, Harry was doing a fine job.

One of the teachers Harry assisted, Matt, was a native English speaker with about ten years' teaching experience. Harry noticed that the students loved him; he was funny, he was approachable, and the students could follow what he was covering in lessons, which he moved along at a good pace. However, Harry also noticed that Matt often made obvious language errors when he was teaching; not so much in his own language use, but in the content of what he was actually teaching the students. For example, one day Harry was observing a teacher-fronted lesson. The Grade 11 class was having a discussion and one of the students used the sentence, "I should have gone yesterday." Matt interrupted the student, saying that what she should have said was, "I should have went yesterday" because "went is in the past." Harry knew this was not right, and could even identify the grammatical rule to explain why. However, being the assistant, he didn't feel he should say anything in class.

Harry had heard many similar "corrections" in this Grade 11 class, but this particular one played on his mind. He decided he would talk to the teacher about the example. When they next consulted, Harry politely spoke about the grammatical point, raising it more as a topic of interest than as a criticism of Matt's teaching. Matt did engage in the conversation, but not for long, and indicated to Harry that perhaps he hadn't been living in the US long enough to fully understand the nuances of American English grammar. Harry didn't push the issue, and the topic of conversation changed to the upcoming lesson.

1.1.2 Questions

1. Do you think the school made an appropriate decision by appointing Harry?
2. How does Harry benefit from the appointment and what does he lose out on?
3. Is "I should have went yesterday" wrong? Harry believed that the teacher made both a *language* and an *instructional* mistake in class. What do you think?
4. Did Matt have a point about Harry not having lived in the US long enough to be familiar with American English usage? How might Matt have approached their conversation from an alternative perspective?
5. Besides talking to the teacher about his language errors, as he did, what else might Harry have done?

1.1.3 Research Topics

Examining the Teacher–Teacher Assistant Relationship

How do language teachers and teacher assistants decide who does what in the classroom? Why do they make these decisions? Are issues of power, or time, or expertise involved, for example? Do they work well together? Do they appear to get along?

1. Locate a teaching context where a language teacher works with a teacher assistant (or a student teacher, or co-teacher).
2. *Observe* (M3) their classroom during a language lesson. Draw a map of the classroom and note the position of the teacher and assistant and how they move around the room. What do they do in these positions? Write down their words and actions.
3. After class, meet with the teacher and the assistant together and show them the map. First describe what you observed, and then ask them to explain (a) why they moved the way they did and (b) their actions in the places they moved to.
4. Ask them, individually, to write you a follow-up email in which they reflect on their working relationship, specifically how effective they think it is and if their collaborative work benefits their learners.
5. Would moving in a different pattern change their working relationship? Do they work well together?

Questioning the Purpose of a Teacher Assistant

What is it that a teacher assistant does in a language classroom? What is their purpose? Do language teachers always need or desire a teacher assistant? Which language teachers need them more?

1. Do an *archive or document search* (M6) on the role of teacher assistants in language classrooms (or classrooms of other subjects). The webpages of

Ministries or Departments of Education, or teacher education textbooks, may have useful information.
2. Review these documents and list five benefits and five challenges for teachers who work in classrooms with teacher assistants.
3. Design a short *questionnaire* (M17) based on this list. Ask respondents to rank the significance of the benefits and challenges from their perspective.
4. Distribute the questionnaire to teachers (both those who work with assistants and those who don't) in your professional networks.
5. Is it beneficial having a teacher assistant in the classroom?

1.1.4   Resources

Gibbs, K. & Beamish, W. (2024). Teacher aides' voices: Perspectives on teaching pedagogy. *Educational Research, 66*(2), 155–170. https://doi.org/10.1080/00131881.2024.2309910

Miquel, E., Monguillot, M., Soler, M., & Duran, D. (2024). Reciprocal peer observation: A mechanism to identify professional learning goals. *Education Inquiry,* https://doi.org/10.1080/20004508.2024.2370116

Stacey, K., Harvey, S., & Richards, R. (2013). Teachers working with ESOL paraprofessionals in a secondary context: Examining supervision. *Teaching and Teacher Education, 36,* 55–67, https://doi.org/10.1016/j.tate.2013.07.002

1.2   Using AI in an Academic Writing Class

Keywords
- Singapore
- Academic writing support courses
- University students
- Using AI (Artificial Intelligence) for completing coursework
- Extending AI to assessments

1.2.1   Pre-reading Reflection

1. Using AI for assessment purposes is proving challenging for educational institutions. Should it be?
2. What's the difference between using AI for assignment writing and plagiarism?
3. Would you be tempted to use AI for a writing task if it saves time and gets a good result?

Peter and Chen, both from Malaysia, are two international graduate students at the same university in Singapore. They are in the first semester of their one-year master's degrees in education and social studies, respectively. Both want to become teachers in the future. They are doing well in their studies but are struggling with academic writing – their lecturers have recommended they attend a course at the university's English language center. This is where they met. The course they are doing is designed especially for graduate students whose first language is not English, and it aims mainly to help them with their university studies but also their future working lives. The course is credit bearing and the students pay extra for it. Toward the end of the course, they meet for coffee one morning in the university cafeteria and have the following conversation about their upcoming assignment, which involves writing a conference proposal of 500 words. They will subsequently have to present their proposal to the class.

CHEN: How far have you got with your proposal? I'm still thinking about my topic. I don't think the instructions were very clear about the theme of the conference.

PETER: I think we can choose our own conference theme. It would be boring in the presentations if everyone does the same. Anyway, we are doing different subjects, so our conferences should be different.

CHEN: So, how far are you with the assignment?

PETER: I haven't really started. It's only 500 words, and I'm planning to use AI to write the draft for me.

CHEN: Really?

PETER: Why not? We've been using AI all through the course anyway, so we might as well use it for the assignment.

CHEN: I see what you mean. But when Prof used it with us, it was for brainstorming – remember that task we did on essay planning? Oh, and also for summarizing. We had to summarize that passage from one of the ministry's policy documents and then revise it to make it look like we had written it ourselves.

PETER: Yes, I remember. That was quite fun, and my summary was really good. I can't see why my proposal can't be just as good if I use that AI tool. Why do you think Prof spent so much time showing us how to use AI if we can't continue to use it?

CHEN: But it's for an assessment, not class work. I guess that's the difference. I think she was clear about us not using AI for assessments. I'll have to go back and check the instructions. Perhaps we could ask her in class this afternoon? Or maybe we could talk to some of the others in class and see what they think.

PETER: Not sure about that. Perhaps wait a bit.

CHEN: I remember also Prof saying she uses AI a lot and can easily recognize language produced by ChatGPT. She said something about certain words keep coming up and the structure of sentences. So, I guess it's best not to use AI for the assessment. What if she gives you zero!

PETER: But how can she prove it? She will need evidence to fail someone, surely.

CHEN: I guess. But I'm not going to take the chance. Anyway, I want to see how I do by myself. This course isn't necessary for my degree. It's for my own learning. I want to see how I can do. Maybe I have learned something.

PETER: Up to you. I'm really busy and don't think I have time to work too much on the 500 words. I'll first try AI and see how it goes. Perhaps I can disguise it well. I still think I've learned quite a bit on this course, anyway.

1.2.2 Questions

1. What was the writing course teacher trying to achieve by introducing and using AI in her writing course? What were her pedagogical goals?
2. Why did Peter suggest that Chen "wait a bit" before asking the teacher or their classmates about whether they could use AI for the assignment?
3. Do you think Peter should take a chance and use AI for his proposal writing assignment? Give reasons for your answer.
4. If you were doing this course assignment, would you be more like Chen or more like Peter? Give a reason for your choice.
5. As the course teacher, would you give a student zero if they used AI for the assignment?

1.2.3 Research Topics

Exploring Writing Teachers' Attitudes to AI Use
What are writing teachers' attitudes to the use of AI by students in their classes? Is their attitude different when students write for assessment and when they write for coursework? How do they control the use of AI in their classes?

1. Design a *survey* (M17) with both *closed-item questions* (i.e., agreeing with statements, selecting answers to a given question) and *open-ended questions* (i.e., comment on closed-item answers, write a sentence or short paragraph about a given topic or question) that asks teachers to consider their attitudes to AI use in the classes.
2. On a smaller scale, distribute the survey to writing teachers within one institution (e.g., a school or a university); on a larger scale, distribute to teachers across institutions.
3. If feasible, conduct short *interviews* (M9) with some of the respondents to discuss their answers, and to probe their attitudes further.
4. Are teachers generally for or against the use of AI? What are their reasons?

Analyzing Students' Reasons for Using AI Without Permission
Why would writing students use AI for writing assessments when they have been instructed not to? Is this considered cheating? Is doing so the same as or worse than plagiarism? Does it make a difference if students are taking a writing class or if they are taking a content subject class, for example, second language acquisition or sociolinguistics?

1. Design a set of questions on an anonymous platform such as *Google Forms* or *Qualtrics* (M17). Because of the nature of the topic, students might not want to respond if the *survey* is not anonymous.
2. Focus the questions on possible reasons why students would use AI without permission. List five possible reasons for a writing class and five reasons for a content subject class. Ask respondents if these reasons apply to them; they could comment on each answer. Leave space for the respondents to add further reasons.
3. Are students deliberately devious, or are there strategic reasons for using AI?

1.2.4 Resources

Marzuki, Widiati, U., Rusdin, D., Darwin, & Indrawati, I. (2023). The impact of AI writing tools on the content and organization of students' writing: EFL teachers' perspective. *Cogent Education*, *10*(2), 2236469. https://doi.org/10.1080/2331186X.2023.2236469

Merkel, W. (2020). A case study of undergraduate L2 writers' concerns with source-based writing and plagiarism. *TESOL Journal*, 11:e503. https://doi.org/10.1002/tesj.503

Koltovskaia, S., Rahmati, P., & Saeli, H. (2024). Graduate students' use of ChatGPT for academic text revision: Behavioral, cognitive, and affective engagement. *Journal of Second Language Writing*, *65*, 101130. https://doi.org/10.1016/j.jslw.2024.101130

1.3 Translanguaging During Independent Group Play[1]

Keywords
- Türkiye
- Primary school
- Independent play in German lessons
- Students translanguaging
- Teachers and parents complaining

1.3.1 Pre-reading Reflection

1. How familiar are you with the term "translanguaging"? How is it different from code-switching?

---

[1] This case draws on the research of Moses and Capurro (2024). See the full reference in the Resources below the case.

2. Some teachers (and schools) argue that only the target language should be used in target language lessons. This debate is an old one. What is your position?
3. To what extent should parents' interference in classroom teaching and learning practices be tolerated?

Ms. Aydem teaches at a private primary school located in a city in central Türkiye. The students' parents can afford to pay fees, and they expect the teachers to be good and the learning to be evident. They expect to see results. Ms. Aydem teaches German as a foreign language to primary grades (about ages six to eight). The school has elected German as its compulsory foreign language because the immediate community traditionally has close ties with family in Germany and potential exists for students to take up employment or further study in Germany when they finish high school. Besides learning German, students at the school usually also know some English; their parents send them to private institutes for lessons or they hire tutors. They believe that knowledge of English is also important for their futures.

Ms. Aydem is known as an innovative teacher. She does what is required of the German language syllabus and is always in step with the other German teachers in the same grades. She acknowledges that this is important for assessment and reporting purposes. However, she likes to introduce activities into her classes that are popular with students and are effective in getting students to use German for communicative purposes. She believes this is important for her own professional development, which ultimately benefits the learners. These activities can take up quite a bit of class time, and so she must remain aware that they can't be so demanding or time-consuming that they squeeze out the scheduled classwork. Ms. Aydem tries to use German as much as possible in class, and she encourages her students to do the same, although, as she says, "all languages are welcome."

One activity that has proven to be effective for keeping students engaged and which seems to get them to use more German is independent play in groups. What this entails is dividing the class into small groups of four or five students. Each group is then left on its own to play for a specified period of time, usually about twenty minutes. The play is not haphazard; typically, a topic, or task, or some materials are assigned, and some related German vocabulary is provided to be incorporated into the play. Once this is set up, the group members are left alone to play independently without or with very limited teacher intervention. Ms. Aydem has noticed over the two or three years that she has organized play sessions in her lessons that the students tend to speak more German than when participating in other class activities, particularly focus-on-form communicative tasks.

The students in Ms. Aydem's play groups don't use only German. They also use Turkish, and some English can also be heard. What they are doing when interacting with each other is called *translanguaging*; that is, making use of all the semiotic resources they have available to them to achieve the goals of the play activity. These include linguistic and material resources, as well as others such as movement and facial expressions. Ms. Aydem is immensely satisfied with the way the play unfolds in her class. However, she has received criticism from two directions. The first is from one of her colleagues, Mr. Demir, who happened to be in her classroom one day while he was waiting for her to finish a lesson. He was surprised to hear so much Turkish spoken during her German lesson. He commented to her that the play probably promoted this, and later mentioned to other language teachers in the school what he had observed. The second criticism came from the students' parents. Ms. Aydem's students obviously talk to their parents about what they do in class. The parents do not see a place for play activities in the curriculum. They do not perceive play to be a serious school activity, especially if Turkish is used in German lessons. Surely, they argue, only German should be used in German lessons.

1.3.2   Questions

1. What are some of the benefits of *play* in language classes, especially with young learners?
2. Ms. Aydem appears to be a responsible teacher. What makes her responsible, and what risks does she appear to take in her teaching?
3. What do you think are some of the learning benefits of translanguaging during play?
4. Why might Mr. Demir, his colleagues, and the students' parents resist translanguaging practices in Ms. Aydem's class?
5. Would you support Ms. Aydem continuing to incorporate play into her German classroom lessons? What advice would you offer her to prevent further criticism from others?

1.3.3   Research Topics

Investigating Translanguaging and Language Learner Identity
How does translanguaging in the classroom affect the construction of language learners' identities? Is the process of identity construction different from when learners are forced to use only the target language? Do language learners have translingual identities?

1. Identify a group of language learners, adults or young learners who practice translanguaging during their language lessons in the classroom.
2. Provide each of them with a blank *body outline silhouette* (M2) and ask them to color it in using different colors to represent the different languages they use in the classroom. In other words, they use different colors for different languages on different parts of the body outline.
3. Invite them to write words or sentences to explain the colors and to give reasons for why they are located where they are on the body silhouette.
4. Below the silhouette, ask students to write a short paragraph (100 words), with reference to their silhouette, describing how they see themselves as language learners in the language classroom.
5. What are the students' language learner identities during language lessons? Does using multiple languages change who they are?

Describing Language Teachers' Perspectives on Translanguaging in the Classroom

Do language teachers promote translanguaging in their language classrooms? Or do they try to prohibit or control translanguaging? What are their reasons for their choices? Do teachers know the difference between translanguaging and code-switching?

1. A simple interview study would be an appropriate way to discover language teachers' knowledge and opinions about translanguaging.
2. Design a *semi-structured interview* (M9) schedule that asks questions about teachers' knowledge of translanguaging: what it is; how it differs from code-switching; whether they allow, promote, or prohibit translanguaging in their classrooms; and the reasons for their answers to these questions.
3. Interview teachers of different languages in one school. Record the interviews and transcribe them. Compare their interview data.
4. Is translanguaging a common practice? Do teachers know more about code-switching than translanguaging? Is this important for teachers to know?

1.3.4   Resources

Brevik, L. M. & Holm, T. (2023). Affinity and the classroom: Informal and formal L2 learning. *ELT Journal, 77*(1), 83–93. https://doi.org/10.1093/elt/ccac012

Cenoz, J. & Santos, A. (2020). Implementing pedagogical translanguaging in trilingual schools. *System, 92,* 102273. https://doi.org/10.1016/j.system.2020.102273

Moses, L. & Capurro, C. T. (2024). Literacy-based play with young emergent bilinguals: Explorations in vocabulary, translanguaging, and identity work. *TESOL Quarterly, 58*(1), 423–450. https://doi.org/10.1002/tesq.3236

1.4 Engaging English Language Learners

Keywords
- China
- College English teachers
- Exam-oriented teaching
- Teachers plan new strategy
- Learners rejecting classroom activities

1.4.1 Pre-reading Reflection

1. Should studying and passing a course in English or any other language be compulsory at university?
2. Testing and examinations can be very powerful, determining the way language courses are taught. This can be both good and bad. Can you think of examples?
3. How can teachers get students to interact with each other briefly and easily in large classes? Think of some examples.

At Normal University located in a large urban center in Northeast China all students are required to take at least one English language course as part of their undergraduate degree. Non-English majors take a compulsory course that covers the four basic skills – listening, speaking, reading, and writing. However, in practice, the exam-oriented teaching focuses on grammar-translation and other content typically tested in the final assessment. And the students know this. They therefore do not attempt to engage with the small amount of classroom material that does not appear to be applicable to the exam. They are not interested in it, and more broadly, are not particularly interested in learning English in the first place. They don't see the language as being relevant to their current or future lives in China – very few plan to study, work, or live in another country – and would rather dedicate their study time to their major subjects. The English teachers, of course, know all this too.

However, from experience the teachers also know that some of the students will indeed encounter English in their future lives. In addition, they feel that they have a professional responsibility, and a personal commitment, to implement the communicative-oriented curriculum that the department has decided they should follow, even though in practice they do not fully implement it. The outcome is that most students learn to pass the exam but do not learn to use much English. This unsatisfactory situation really upsets the English teachers at Normal University and has been continuing for years.

Recently, two new teachers joined the faculty, Ms. Chen and Ms. Zhang, both with MA degrees and both with about five years' English teaching experience at universities in other cities. Soon after arriving at Normal University, they detected the conditions that led to the other teachers in the department being unhappy and the students, although passing the course, being unmotivated. Being young and energetic, they decided to do something about it. They recognized that the department was huge, consisting of many English teachers and hundreds of students doing the compulsory course, but they thought they could start small, working with a group of teachers interested in making a change. They recruited three other English teachers who had informally expressed similar concerns during a faculty meeting. The five teachers knew that they could not change the assessment regime, so decided that a useful strategy would be to gradually and subtly insert into the usual grammar-translation, exam-focused instruction simple activities that required very brief interactional encounters in class. For example:

1. Turn to your neighbor and read this sentence aloud. Then listen to them reading it aloud.
2. Show two students a photo on your phone. Describe the photo using three different English words. Each take a turn. Write down all nine words.
3. Think about the lesson we have just completed. Write down one question you have about the lesson. Read this question to your neighbor and listen carefully to the answer.

The teachers planned to trial a limited number of these sorts of brief communicative encounters at strategic times per lesson over a few weeks, and then report back to each other. The outcome was that the students would have none of it. Perhaps one or two attempted some engagement with their classmates, but most sat silently ignoring the instruction or looking at their phones without engaging. Knowing that the organizational structures of the department and the students' attitudes were too powerful to change, Ms. Chen and Ms. Zhang were not too disappointed. The other three teachers, however, decided not to continue with the initiative. Ms. Chen and Ms. Zhang were determined to continue reflecting on their classroom practice and the possibilities for change; and they firmly believed that in small ways they could be successful in getting their students to become more engaged in using English both during lessons and after class as well.

1.4.2 Questions

1. Do you think the teachers at Normal University are right when they say their students will encounter English in their future lives?
2. Why do the English teachers at the university persist in teaching to the exam, even though their department promotes a communicative-oriented language teaching curriculum?
3. Why was Ms. Chen's and Ms. Zhang's strategy of introducing brief communicative encounters into lessons not successful? Was it because of the teachers, the students, or something broader? What would you have done differently?
4. What reason do you think the other three English teachers gave Ms. Chen and Ms. Zhang for discontinuing their involvement with the change strategy?
5. Ms. Chen and Ms. Zhang are determined to make changes to their teaching and their students' English learning. Do you think they are fighting a losing battle?

1.4.3 Research Topics

Analyzing Learner Engagement in Group Work
What types of small group tasks or activities lead to better student engagement – with the language, the task itself, and with each other? Do their levels of engagement change when the task changes? How does students' group work engagement relate to their motivation?

1. Collaborate with a language teacher to plan an *action research* (M1) project that focuses on learner engagement during small group work.
2. Think of an activity or task that you and the teacher believe will engage the learners in the task and get them to interact with each other.
3. Groups should be about four to five members. When the teacher facilitates the lesson and the group work, observe the group action, noting what you see – who is talking, to whom, what language they are using, and whether they are on task. Can you see their levels of motivation or engagement?
4. Discuss the lesson with the teacher after class to learn their perspective on the group work engagement. Consider how the task or activity could be changed for further use in a later lesson. Then observe that group work and discuss the outcome again with the teacher.
5. Did the planned group activity or task promote group engagement? Did any change to the activity result in better engagement? What was the level of motivation of the students in the groups?

Asking Why Learners Don't Engage in Classroom Activities
Why don't learners want to engage with what happens in the classroom? What are their perceptions of classroom activities and their teacher practices? What reasons do they give for not wanting to engage? Are they motivated to learn or to participate in class activities?

1. Randomly select a group of learners (up to ten) from a classroom which has been described by its teacher as consisting of learners who lack enthusiasm for class work.
2. After gaining their permission, extract them from the class and meet together as a *focus group* (M8) for an hour.
3. Before you meet, prepare a schedule of five to ten questions that ask them about: their reasons for learning the target language, what they enjoy about language lessons, how much they believe they learn during language lessons, what they don't like about language lessons, and how they plan to use the language in the future.
4. After asking a question, try to facilitate a discussion. Give all learners an opportunity to talk. Record the discussion.
5. Transcribe the focus group discussion to discover the main themes that relate to the five to ten focus questions. You could then take these themes to a second focus group, perhaps from another language class.
6. What are the main themes? Does a second focus group confirm them, or raise different themes? How do the students see themselves using the language in the future? Does the answer to this question have anything to do with their classroom engagement?

1.4.4 Resources

Li, J., Wang, C., Zhao, Y., & Li, Y. (2023). Boosting learners' confidence in learning English: Can self-efficacy-based intervention make a difference? *TESOL Quarterly, 58*(4), 1518–1547. https://doi.org/10.1002/tesq.3292

Wang, Y., Xin, Y., & Chen, L. (2024). Navigating the emotional landscape: Insights into resilience, engagement, and burnout among Chinese High School English as a Foreign Language Learners. *Learning and Motivation, 86*, 101978. https://doi.org/10.1016/j.lmot.2024.101978

Yung, K. W-H. (2021). Engaging exam-oriented students in communicative language teaching by "packaging" learning English through songs as exam practice. *RELC Journal, 54*(1), 280–290. https://doi.org/10.1177/0033688220978542

1.5 Global Englishes in a Rural Classroom

Keywords
- South Africa

- Rural high school
- Teachers of English as an Additional Language
- Introducing Global Englishes
- Not relevant to context

1.5.1   Pre-reading Reflection

1. When you think of a rural school, what image comes to mind?
2. What are some differences between Standard English and Global Englishes? Can you think of any examples? Do you know what *Global Englishes* means?
3. How would you define a *multilingual* language learning classroom? In what ways are the language learning classrooms you're familiar with multilingual?

Indawo High School is located in a rural area in the Eastern Cape, South Africa. It is, on paper, a large school, though numbers fluctuate term by term, as students come and go or drop out altogether without notice. The size of the teaching staff is also not stable, with new appointments not taking up positions when the term begins and others remaining absent for extended periods. However, at its core, Indawo High School has a group of committed teachers who turn up to school and endeavor to work steadily through the curriculum. Very few students pass the final-year external examination and finish school, probably less than 20 percent. The majority quit school two or three years early to take up employment on local farms or move to cities in the province to look for other work. They find it impossible to pass their subjects at school and certainly don't see a future in higher education.

Indawo High School has few facilities. The single school building is reached via a dirt road and electricity is available intermittently throughout the day. The one school computer is in the principal's office. Multiple grades are taught in the same classrooms, often by the same teacher. All students at the school follow the English as an Additional Language (EAL) syllabus, with isiXhosa being their (and the teachers') first or home language. English is introduced as a subject early in the local school system – in the early primary school grades – and then used as a medium of instruction, also during the primary school years. In rural areas, however, students have very limited exposure to English outside the classroom, and inside the classroom the teaching is generally regarded as poor quality, mainly due to lack of adequate teacher training and the low level of English proficiency of the teachers. The learners, notwithstanding a communicative-oriented English curriculum, speak very limited English, and their literacy skills are well below what they should be for their grades.

A directive has recently come through from the regional Department of Education stating that schools should begin looking into including Global

1.5 Global Englishes in a Rural Classroom

Englishes in their high school classrooms. The statement says that examples of Global Englishes can be integrated into lessons by adapting existing classroom materials. The rationale for their decision is that "we are now living in a multilingual world" and that "so-called standard English is a minority variety." The directive from the department has not provided a timeline for the introduction of Global Englishes or indicated where any additional materials will come from, or indeed, what Global Englishes are. Further information is promised.

In the meantime, the English teachers have heard rumors that one of the ministers in the local government has recently attended an international TESOL conference in the US at which she listened to a presentation on Global Englishes in the multilingual classroom. The presentation was very convincing; it stressed, with examples from many countries, that learners should not necessarily learn the language spoken only by "native" speakers, since most speakers of English are in fact "non-native." The presenter also said something (the rumor was not clear on this) about it not being as important to pass English exams with accurate answers as it was to be able to "get your message across." This final point really worried the English teachers. Of course, they were also concerned about getting access to examples of Global Englishes, not knowing themselves what the concept actually meant, and they wondered how relevant this whole idea was to their rural context where English was almost never heard or used. They also wondered how their classrooms were multilingual. The teachers were prepared to give it a go, though, when the time came.

1.5.2 Questions

1. Pick out keywords from the case that indicate the rural nature of Indawo High School. How do these keywords compare with your image of what rural schools are?
2. How would you judge the decision to introduce Global Englishes into English language teaching in this region's rural schools? Specify why you think it is a good or bad decision.
3. Consider the English teachers' reaction to the top-down policy decision to introduce Global Englishes into the English syllabus. In what ways do you agree or disagree with them?
4. Considering the facilities and expertise available in the school, what support might the school offer the English teachers to implement the Global Englishes initiative?
5. The teachers are prepared to "give it a go." If you were a teacher in the same context, would you feel the same?

1.5.3 Research Topics

Exploring Language Teaching with a Rural School English Teacher
What stories do rural school English teachers have to share about their teaching experiences? What do their stories say about the constraints they endure? How much English do they hear and use in their classrooms?

1. Use your networks to contact an English teacher working in a rural primary or high school. Request permission to have a conversation with them on a smartphone, using an app such as WhatsApp or Zoom.
2. Invite the teacher to *share stories* (M16) of their teaching experiences in the school where they work.
3. Instead of asking questions, say to the teacher, "Tell me about … " – for example, "Tell me about your students, what a typical English lesson looks like, the amount of English that is used in the classroom, the materials you use, your aspirations as an English teacher." Engage in the conversation with the teacher so that you tell the stories together. Record the conversation.
4. Write a story or stories of the teacher's experiences.
5. Do rural school teachers have sufficient resources? What are their goals, and are they different from those of teachers in well-resourced urban schools?

Understanding Global Englishes
What does Global Englishes mean? How can the concept be made useful and relevant for English teachers? Is Global Englishes something that English teachers should be interested in? If so, which teachers?

1. Do a *digital literature search* (M6) on the internet to explore the meaning of Global Englishes. Write down definitions of the concept that you come across until you feel satisfied that you have a good understanding of what it means.
2. From these definitions, compose a short *PowerPoint* (or similar) *presentation* (M12) with brief accompanying notes suitable for English teachers.
3. Distribute the PowerPoint presentation to teachers in your institution or program. Request feedback.
4. Make changes to the presentation and prepare to present it at a workshop at a local teachers' conference.
5. What will your message to your audience be? How do you think they will respond to your presentation?

1.5.4 Resources

Cameron, A. & Galloway, N. (2019). Local thoughts on global ideas: Pre- and in-service TESOL practitioners' attitudes to the pedagogical implications of the globalization of English. *RELC Journal, 50*(1), 149–163. https://doi.org/10.1177/0033688218822853

da Costa, N. & Rose, H. (2024). The impact of Global Englishes classroom-based innovation on school-aged language learners' perceptions of English: An exercise in practitioner and researcher partnership. *System, 121*, 103263. https://doi.org/10.1016/j.system.2024.103263

Shan, L. W. & Aziz, A. A. (2022). A systematic review of teaching English in rural settings: Challenges and solutions. *International Journal of Academic Research in Business and Social Sciences, 12*(6), 1956–1977. http://dx.doi.org/10.6007/IJARBSS/v12-i6/14233

1.6 Criticism of an Intensive TEFL Course

Keywords
- Egypt
- Private language school
- Under-qualified, experienced English teacher
- Intensive TEFL certificate
- Being critical of the course

1.6.1 Pre-reading Reflection

1. Do you think that being a proficient speaker of English, or a native speaker, is enough to work as an English teacher?
2. How effective are short (e.g., four weeks), intensive courses for training language teachers?
3. How long do you think a language teacher should teach before they can be called an *experienced* teacher?

Denver has lived and worked in a large city in Egypt for just over ten years. Soon after graduating from a US university with a four-year liberal arts degree, he decided to travel through Europe for a few months. His degree was not a teaching qualification, and he didn't particularly see himself working as a teacher in the future. While traveling through Italy, he met a group of young Egyptian backpackers who told him about life and work in Egypt. He decided to follow them home, since he still had a month or so left of his scheduled time abroad. Soon after arriving, and running out of funds, he managed to get some part-time work teaching English for a few hours a week at a private language school. One of his travel companions had a contact at the school. Apparently, being a native speaker of English and having a degree was enough for him to get the job.

Denver really enjoyed the work, even though he had absolutely no teaching experience or any relevant qualifications. He was determined to learn about English teaching and studied the language in his own time. He also searched the internet for appropriate resources and sites that helped him with lesson planning and designing materials and assessments. After a few weeks it was clear to the school (and himself) that he was doing well, and so they asked him to stay on for a while with more hours added onto his workload per week. To jump ten years ahead, Denver has never left Egypt, except for holidays back home to the US about once a year. He's moved schools a few times, and over the years developed into an expert and confident teacher. He's had success with his students, and his managers have always given him good evaluations.

However, in later years Denver became aware of developments in the employment requirements of schools, including private schools that needed accreditation approval from higher authorities. Although no formal statement had yet been made by his school, Denver believed that it would soon be announced that an English teaching qualification would be required to procure full-time employment. To preempt any difficulties – he loved his job and really did want to stay at the school – he decided to enrol in a four-week intensive TEFL (Teaching English as a Foreign Language) course offered in the city. It is an internationally recognized certificate, and he knew his school and its governing body would be satisfied with the qualification to ensure his continued employment.

Denver sailed through the TEFL course, which was offered during his summer break. He drew on his considerable teaching experience to contribute to his learning and to class discussions, as well as to complete assignments and participate in the teaching practice. At times, he found himself mentoring some of the inexperienced student teachers on the course, and even offered advice to the trainer here and there when he appeared stuck with providing answers or suggesting pedagogical solutions. Even though the course was "easy" for Denver, he found it a worthwhile experience for his professional development. At the end of the course all student teachers were asked to complete a course evaluation. Denver was positive overall on the anonymous form, though he made quite a few critical comments, especially about the apparent inexperience of the trainer, the lack of challenging assessments, and the slow pace of some of the lessons. Denver, of course, passed the course and was awarded his certificate, thus holding on to his job at this school. Some time later, he thought back to the course evaluation he had submitted after

1.6 Criticism of an Intensive TEFL Course

the course had ended. He felt some shame about his comments, guilt even, and wondered if his comments had come across as arrogant and gratuitous. He felt sorry for the trainer, who overall did a good job. He wished he had been more positive.

1.6.2 Questions

1. How typical today are Denver's early experiences of English teaching, i.e., traveling abroad and getting a job with limited qualifications?
2. Do you think it was necessary for Denver to obtain the TEFL certificate? What else might he have done?
3. Why are the schools in Egypt beginning to require formal language teaching qualifications? What has changed from when Denver first started to teach?
4. Denver felt he benefitted from the TEFL course. Considering his experience, how do you think he benefitted?
5. Was Denver right to be so critical in his course evaluation? Why do you think he regretted what he wrote?

1.6.3 Research Topics

Analyzing a Short-Course Teacher Training Webpage
How do intensive teacher training (TEFL or TESOL) courses advertise themselves on their public webpages? What promises do they make? Do their courses look inviting? Do they look convincing? Are the courses accredited?

1. Search the internet for the webpage of an intensive teacher training (TEFL or TESOL) course. Find one in a location near where you live and work.
2. Do a critical *discourse analysis* (M5) of the webpage. Examine the words used – what is their meaning, where are they placed, how large or small are they? How persuasive is the message of the words? What pictures, graphics, or colors are included on the landing page of the website and in the hyperlinks – and what do they add to the message? If there are videos, what are they about? How are they produced?
3. Summarize the analysis by writing a list of bullet points, each one making a statement about what was found. Organize this list into a few paragraphs describing the findings. Is the webpage trustworthy? Does the teacher training appear to be thorough and effective? Is the program internationally accredited?
4. On a personal level, does the course look interesting and inviting to you? Would you want to do the course?

Examining Motivations for Teaching Abroad
Why do teachers, especially young, recently qualified teachers, go abroad to teach? What motivates them to explore teaching contexts in other countries? What challenges do they face and what successes do they achieve?

1. Many TESOL and TEFL teachers work abroad before settling down into a job in their home countries. Some stay abroad to work.
2. Identify about ten teachers who have worked abroad and have now returned to teach in their home country. Ask them to write a short *reflective piece* (M14) in the form of a journal entry which includes the following: where they taught abroad, why they decided to go overseas to teach, one critical incident that occurred while abroad, one major challenge they faced, how they developed as a language teacher while working overseas. They can end the reflection with why they decided to return home, and how they felt when they did.
3. Do a thematic analysis of the ten written journal entries by searching for the main themes in each journal (e.g., challenges, motivations, emotions on return). Try to group similar themes into broader categories.
4. Which themes or categories are common across the entries? Which are unique to a particular teacher? Does the country where the teachers worked make a difference? Does their age or gender?

1.6.4 Resources

Edgar, J. A. & Lautenbach, G. (2022). Online TEFL certificates: Are they enough? *IDEAS: Journal on English Language Teaching and Learning, Linguistics and Literature, 10*(2), 1101–1116. https://doi.org/10.24256/ideas.v10i2.2795

Stroebe, W. (2020). Student evaluations of teaching encourages poor teaching and contributes to grade inflation: A theoretical and empirical analysis. *Basic and Applied Social Psychology, 42*(4), 276–294. https://doi.org/10.1080/01973533.2020.1756817

Yaccob, N. S., Yunus, M. M., & Hashim, H. (2022). Globally competent teachers: English as a second language teachers' perceptions on global competence in English lessons. *Frontiers in Psychology, 13*, 925160. https://doi.org/10.3389/fpsyg.2022.925160

1.7 Teaching in Large Classes

Keywords
- United Kingdom
- High school EAL teaching
- Art in the English language classroom

1.7 Teaching in Large Classes

- Lack of teaching space
- Curriculum constraints

1.7.1   Pre-reading Reflection

1. Imagine being a language teacher in a class of sixty-five high school students.
2. What are the biggest challenges you think you would experience?
3. What would your top two strategies be for managing the class?

Anne, a first-year teacher, joined an urban school in the UK in 2017. This was her first teaching job after completing a postgraduate certificate that prepares teachers to teach in UK secondary schools. Anne, White and British, obtained her undergraduate degree in the UK focusing on fine arts and English literature. When she started teaching, she was twenty-three years old.

Many of the students in Anne's school were recent immigrants and the school also attracted many study-abroad students from around the world, particularly countries in the Middle East. The school's very active International Office had secured a number of contracts with institutions in these countries, meaning that study-abroad student numbers remained healthy. The majority of the immigrant and study-abroad students was described by the school as EAL students: English as an Additional Language students. Separate classes were set up for them, whereby they were withdrawn from the mainstream for up to an hour each day to focus on English learning. The school had its own EAL Department, and Anne was one of five EAL teachers.

In her first term, Anne was assigned a Year 11 EAL class (fifteen- to sixteen-year-old students). On the first day of school, there were fifteen students in the class. By the end of that first week, there were just over twenty. Anne was anticipating a maximum of eighteen students – at least, that is what the head of the EAL Department had told her. She was a little upset about this increase, for several reasons. Firstly, workload; having over twenty students would mean extra preparation and coursework marking. There were also discipline issues to consider with larger classes. But more important for her than workload at this stage was a class activity she had planned for the first two to three weeks of the term.

For this activity, she wanted to draw on her fine arts background. The aim of the activity was for students to produce self-portraits over a period of time. Students would each be assigned a space on a board attached to a classroom wall where they could place photos, drawings, notes, written paragraphs, and other artefacts that reflected their multicultural identities.

Each day they could add something new. Anne had planned various writing and speaking activities based on the developing self-portraits.

As the class size grew – it was finally twenty-seven by the end of the second week of term – the self-portraits project slowly began to disintegrate. The disruption came from three directions: (1) It became difficult for students to move easily around the classroom. To get to their portraits, they needed easy access to the board on the wall. But with so many students in the room they had to squeeze past each other and move chairs and desks and step over carry-bags, and in doing so often knocked students' artefacts off the board. The self-portraits started to look shabby. (2) Because there were now so many students, the planned writing and speaking activities (and even contributing to the construction of the self-portraits) were taking too long and could almost never be completed satisfactorily. (3) There was pressure from the head of department to make faster progress with the prescribed activities that other Year 11 EAL classes were doing at the same time. By the end of the third week, the self-portraits project was abandoned.

1.7.2 Questions

1. What discipline issues might Anne have faced as the class size increased? Consider the number of students, the physical size of the room, and Anne's inexperience as a teacher.
2. Did you think Anne's self-portraits project was a good idea for a language class? What were its strengths and limitations?
3. The official curriculum has considerable power to stifle teachers' creativity in the classroom. How did this unfold in Anne's classroom? What could she have done about it?
4. What could Anne have done to rescue the self-portraits project?
5. What is an ideal class size for language teaching? What is the reason for your answer? What factors does a school manager have to consider when determining class size?

1.7.3 Research Topics

Exploring Teacher Emotions in Large Language Classes
How does teaching in large classes make teachers feel? How do their emotions affect their teaching methods, their relationships with their students, and their conversations with institutional administrators?

1. *Observe a language lesson* (M3) in a large class. Note down as much of the classroom action as you can, particularly aspects of the lesson that you believe relate to the size of the class. After class, record

a conversation with the teacher about some of your observations. Point to the size-related aspects of the lesson and ask the teacher: "How does this make you feel?"
2. Repeat this exercise with two or three other teachers in the same institution.
3. Hold a face-to-face or online *focus group discussion* (M8), with all the teachers involved, about your findings from the observations and the conversations. Record the discussion.
4. Search the data (observation notes, conversations, focus group discussion) for any *keywords or phrases* (M10) that refer to or express an emotion.
5. Are there similarities and differences among the teachers in relation to the research topic? What is the biggest problem they identify? How strongly do they feel about this problem?

Investigating Learner Perceptions of Learning in Large Classes
Are language learners aware of any pedagogical constraints caused by classroom size or student numbers? How do they feel about being in large classes? Do they believe it affects their learning?

1. Work with a teacher who teaches large language classes or select one of your own.
2. Incorporate into a language lesson a writing task that focuses on learning in large classes.
3. For example, design a *narrative frame* (M16, a story template with sentence starters that forms a coherent narrative when the sentences have been completed) that requires students to reflect on and write a story about the questions above.
4. The frame should have about seven to eight starters only and could be completed in hard copy or digitally.
5. Analyze the frames for themes, essentially by grouping all responses to the same starters together and examining them for what they mean in relation to the research questions.
6. Do learners enjoy being in large classes? Do they experience any benefits or challenges?

1.7.4 Resources

Anderson, J. (2016). *What to consider when teaching English in large classes.* British Council. https://www.britishcouncil.org/voices-magazine/what-con sider-when-teaching-english-large-classes (Accessed August 20, 2024).

Panhwar, A. H. & Bell, M. J. (2022). Enhancing student engagement in large ESL classes at a Pakistani university. *Educational Action Research, 31*(5), 964–980. https://doi.org/10.1080/09650792.2022.2089191

Tin, T. B. (2013). Towards creativity in ELT: The need to say something new. *ELT Journal, 67*(4), 385–397. https://doi.org/10.1093/elt/cct022

2 Language Learners

Cases in this chapter

2.1	Demotivated Language Learners	*page* 63
2.2	Dedicated Older Language Learners	67
2.3	Teaching a Student with Suspected ADHD	70
2.4	Disruption in a Multigrade Language Classroom	74
2.5	Young Learners with Limited Class Time for Learning	77
2.6	Gender Identity in the Classroom	81
2.7	An Immigrant Learner's Problems and Successes	84

2.1 Demotivated Language Learners

Keywords
- Sri Lanka
- Rural schools
- Poor communities
- Unmotivated students
- Engaging language learners

2.1.1 Pre-reading Reflection

1. Being a teacher of unmotivated language learners is one of the major difficulties language teachers experience. Why is it such a challenge for teachers?
2. Give two examples of what teachers can do to motivate their learners. Think of a specific context for your answer.
3. How might learners' motivation affect the motivation levels of their teachers?

During the final stages of her career, Mrs. Perera taught English language to Grade 9 and 10 students (aged about thirteen to fourteen) at a government school located in a semi-urban, coastal area in the southern part of Sri Lanka. She had worked as an English language teacher for almost thirty years in the secondary public school system. During her service, she had taught in five different schools. Three of these were located in rural settings, while the one before her last school was situated in an urban center. She received a transfer to her final school as part of a periodic shuffling of teachers carried out by the Ministry of Education.

A couple of months after starting to teach at this school, Mrs. Perera realized that most students were not keen to learn English and lacked discipline. They talked constantly in the classroom, walked in and out of the room when they wanted to, and engaged in other activities during lessons. Some students would even disappear from the classroom before she arrived in class. Mrs. Perera slowed her teaching pace, allowed more time for activities, and followed the students more closely during these activities, hoping that they would show more interest. She also made it a point to include fun activities during class, such as singing songs and playing games. She noticed that only a few students showed an increase in interest. These were always the students seated in the front rows.

Mrs. Perera was not happy about the situation in her classes. One day in the staffroom, she spoke to her fellow teachers about the students' lack of interest and discipline. It wasn't a surprise for her to hear similar stories from them. But what did surprise her was the attitude of some of the teachers. One teacher who was not an English teacher stated, "There is no use trying. They are not interested. It is a waste of our time. They are simply waiting to finish or drop out of school to join the army or go fishing." Mrs. Perera realized that members of the community where the school was located mainly worked in the fishing industry, and young people who didn't become part of the family's fishing business joined the army's lower ranks to fight in the war. Joining the military was considered noble and a way of earning a decent salary. Both these occupations did not require a solid education, and English was not a requirement at all.

Mrs. Perera felt her heart sink. She understood that her students did not recognize any value in learning English for the futures they aspired to. She remembered a similar community at one of the rural schools she had worked at previously. It was in a rural agricultural community. Students stopped attending school during harvesting because they had to lend a hand to support their families. And they didn't show much interest in education. In that school, too, some teachers perceived their work to be futile and did not show much enthusiasm in their work. As a young teacher in the early stages of her career, Mrs. Perera was not discouraged by the situation. She was energetic and determined to do her best.

However, Mrs. Perera became disheartened when she realized that the situation of poor communities and their aspirations had not changed much since she became a teacher decades ago. She decided to focus on the few students in the front rows during lessons and to let go of the rest of the class. She felt it was beyond her control, and she did not have that youthful enthusiasm anymore to try to keep everyone engaged. Five years after that, Mrs. Perera retired.

2.1.2 Questions

1. Do you think it is the responsibility of language teachers to influence their learners' aspirations for the future?
2. In what ways could teachers maintain their drive and desire to teach in the face of larger structural constraints that impact learners' motivation? Think of the schools and communities where Mrs. Perera taught, for example.
3. In the end, why did Mrs. Perera stop seeking ways to engage the whole class during her lessons?
4. What strategies could Mrs. Perera have used to increase her students' engagement and interest in learning if she had continued to try?
5. What advice regarding student motivation might Mrs. Perera have offered a new English teacher joining the school?

2.1.3 Research Topics

Exploring English Language Learners' Imagined Life After Secondary School
What plans do English language learners have for life after school? Do these plans involve using English? What jobs do they desire to do? Will they study further? Do their plans affect their levels of motivation to learn English while at school?

1. Design a *questionnaire* (M17) for secondary school students learning English as an additional or foreign language in a context that you have access to. Focus on one institution or even one class and ask questions about their life and career aspirations and the role of English in their plans. Ask about their motivation to learn English and if their motivation is related to their life goals.
2. Include about fifteen to twenty questions so that a broad range of topics can be covered. Open-ended questions requiring short written answers would be appropriate for the *questionnaire design* (M17).
3. Analyze the questionnaire data and then select five respondents that have provided interesting or relevant answers. Invite these students for *one-on-one, semi-structured interviews* (M9) to probe their questionnaire responses further. Point to their answers and ask them to explain or elaborate. Record the interviews.
4. What do the students want to do after school? Do their plans influence their in-class engagement with the lesson materials and activities and

with the teacher? Is their motivation affected by their after-school aspirations?

Discovering If Language Learner Motivation Affects Teacher Motivation
How does language learner motivation affect teacher motivation? Do unmotivated learners influence the level of enjoyment and the enthusiasm that teachers feel about their work in the classroom? What other emotions do teachers experience when working with unmotivated language learners?

1. Engage two language teachers with two different levels of learners – for example, a primary school teacher and a university language teacher.
2. In a small-scale *ethnographic study design* (M7), spend time with the two teachers over a period of time, which could be brief depending on feasibility. Observe one or two of their classes (or more if time and practicality allow); speak to them after these lessons about their teaching and about their students; ask them about the fluctuations in their motivation levels, and what causes them; try to gain an understanding of the context of the teaching and learning – the facilities, the kinds of learners, the program and courses, the materials used, the institution.
3. Audio-record conversations and write fieldnotes about your observations.
4. Ask: what is going on with these two teachers and their learners? Aim to understand the big picture of their work together.
5. How well do they work together? Do the learners affect the teachers' emotions? Are the teachers always motivated, or unmotivated?

2.1.4 Resources

Getie, A. S. (2020). Factors affecting the attitudes of students towards learning English as a foreign language. *Cogent Education*, *7*(1), 1738184. https://doi.org/10.1080/2331186X.2020.1738184

Jahedizadeh, S., Ghanizadeh, A., & Ghonsooly, B. (2016). The role of EFL learners' demotivation, perceptions of classroom activities, and mastery goal in predicting their language achievement and burnout. *Asian-Pacific Journal of Second and Foreign Language Education*, *1*, 16. https://doi.org/10.1186/s40862-016-0021-8

Sakui, K., & Cowie, N. (2012). The dark side of motivation: Teachers' perspectives on 'unmotivation'. *ELT Journal*, *66*(2), 205–213. https://doi.org/10.1093/elt/ccr045

2.2 Dedicated Older Language Learners[1]

Keywords
- Mexico
- Language institute
- Spanish speakers learning Turkish
- Turkish TV dramas
- Learners not taken seriously

2.2.1 Pre-reading Reflection

1. What is it about TV soap operas that makes them addictive? Who might they appeal to?
2. It becomes harder to learn an additional language when one is over sixty years of age. Say why you agree or disagree with this statement.
3. Do you think there are methods more appropriate for teaching older language learners?

Turkish TV dramas or *novelas* are very popular in Mexico. Powerful storylines take viewers on a rollercoaster ride of romance, drama, and suspense. The actors are attractive and the settings in which the action unfolds are typically exotic and beautiful. Nora is hooked on *novelas*. She is an eighty-two-year-old woman who lives alone in a suburb of a large Mexican city. Her house is big and is usually filled with extended family over weekends. On weekday afternoons, when the *novelas* are on TV, five of her neighbors pop over to view them. All female, her friends range in age from their mid-seventies to early eighties. They have their favorite shows, know the names of all the characters, follow the plot closely, and dissect each episode at the end of the afternoon. Nora has a strong desire to visit Türkiye one day, and one by one she has convinced her friends to join her. They believe it is quite feasible in a couple of years' time when they will have saved enough money and planned the trip with a travel company that caters for older travelers. In the meantime, they have decided that it would be a good idea to learn some Turkish.

The women felt that knowing some basic Turkish vocabulary and phrases would be a good start – words to do with greetings and types of food, making simple requests, and asking for help and directions. They also thought it would be useful to be able to read some of the writing they see on buildings or in shops and tourist attractions. Their English isn't very good, and they didn't expect to see any Spanish in Türkiye. Fortunately for Nora and her friends, there is an

---

[1] This case was inspired by stories told during a personal visit to a family in Mexico.

institute that teaches Turkish not far away from where they live. A twenty-minute bus ride would take them to the front door. The aim of the Turkish classes at the institute is to promote Turkish language and culture overseas and to prepare those who might want to work or study abroad in Türkiye.

The group hoped that there would be a class specifically for older learners, but this was not the case. So, when they enrolled and started their class, a conversation class for beginners, they found themselves in a general class of about fifteen adult learners from their early twenties upward. They were noticeably the oldest in the class. After the first lesson, they felt optimistic. They learned a few vocabulary items, which they immediately recognized from the *novelas*, and wrote these down in their notebooks. They were pleased that the conversation classes would incorporate some writing. The young female teacher was energetic and took time to introduce herself on day one, and then on following days she slowly covered the content of each lesson. Her Spanish was excellent. The six-week course consisted of three one-hour lessons per week.

By the end of week two, Nora started to feel that she was falling behind – she found herself forgetting the material she learned in the first week. On the bus on the way home, she mentioned this to her friends. To her surprise, they felt the same. One of the friends said that she had noticed the teacher spending more time with the younger learners. She thought she might have been imagining things, so didn't want to say anything about it. The five friends decided that during the next lesson they would observe the teacher more closely. And when they did, they noticed that she hardly ever asked them any questions or looked toward them when she was teaching from the front of the room. Nora and her friends wondered if they weren't being taken seriously, perhaps because they were older learners. Nevertheless, they still looked forward to their lessons and were motivated to learn. They could already identify newly learned words in the episodes of the *novelas* they were watching. This encouraged them even more.

2.2.2   Questions

1. Are Nora and her friends right when they say that learning some basic Turkish vocabulary would be useful on their trip to Türkiye? In what ways?
2. Nora and co-learners found themselves in the wrong class. What kind of class might have been more appropriate for them?
3. Assuming their observations of the teacher were accurate, why you do think the older learners might have been neglected by the teacher during class activities?
4. What could the teacher have done to engage the older learners more productively in classroom work?

5. Do you think someone from the group of older learners should say something to the teacher? If so, what should they say and how? If they don't, what do you think the consequences might be?

2.2.3 Research Topics

Reviewing Empirical Studies on Older Learners
What do we mean by older language learners? Or third-age learners? What special learner characteristics do they have? How are they defined in the literature?

1. Open the links to the two journal articles in the *Resources* section below – the articles are Open Access.
2. Read the *literature review* (M6) sections of the articles to see if you can find descriptions or definitions of *older learner* or *third-age learner*.
3. Then scan the other sections of the articles for use of the terms *older learner* or *third-age learner*. How are these terms used? How do they enhance your understanding of what an older language learner is?
4. Now, in a few sentences, write your own extended definition of who an older language learner is.
5. Is there an age range or age limit? What is their learning goal? How well do they learn? How do they prefer to learn? Which teaching and learning methods appeal to them?
6. Think about what you can do with your written extended definition. Who can you share it with? Can it be used to start a research project, or to write a policy for your institution?

Conducting a Life History Interview
What are the life experiences of an older language learner? What is their language and cultural background? What language(s) do they speak and use in their daily lives? What is their imagined L2 identity?

1. Find an older language learner who would be willing to share their sociolinguistic life experiences with you. If you don't already know a potential participant, make contact through your professional and institutional networks and request to be introduced ethically and caringly.
2. Conduct a *life history interview* (M9) with the older learner. Start slowly by developing a rapport with the learner and sharing some of your own life experience. Say, "Tell me about . . . ", and gently start to invite the learner to share aspects of their sociolinguistic life, including their linguistic, cultural, educational, and working background. Invite the sharing of stories.

3. Be well prepared with an interview schedule before starting the interview. Let the interviewee talk freely about these topics, but don't wander too far off the scheduled topics.
4. The interview should be fairly lengthy, roughly an hour or two. Record the interview.
5. After transcribing the interview, analyze it by *re-storying* the learner's experiences; in other words, construct a story of their sociolinguistic experiences in chronological order. This method of analysis is called *writing as analysis* (M16).
6. What major events in the learner's life relate to their current language learning? How does the learner describe their imagined future language identity?

2.2.4 Resources

Bosisio, N. (2019). Language learning in the Third Age. *Geopolitical, Social Security and Freedom Journal*, *2*(1), 21–36. https://doi.org/10.2478/gssfj-2019-0003

Kacetl, J., & Klímová, B. (2021). Third-Age learners and approaches to language teaching. *Education Sciences*, *11*(7), 310. https://doi.org/10.3390/educsci11070310

Vivarelli, N. (2021). Why Turkish dramas are conquering Hispanic audiences in the U.S. on Univision (EXCLUSIVE). *Variety*, May 21, 2021. https://variety.com/2021/tv/news/turkish-dramas-u-s-hispanic-audiences-univision-1234978398/ (Accessed October 28, 2024).

2.3   Teaching a Student with Suspected ADHD

Keywords
- Florida, USA
- Junior high school
- English as a Second Language (ESL) teacher
- Teaching a language learner with special educational needs
- Consulting the school counselor

2.3.1   Pre-reading Reflection

1. Are you familiar with the symptoms of ADHD (Attention Deficit Hyperactivity Disorder)?

2.3 Teaching a Student with Suspected ADHD

2. Sometimes just one or two students can repeatedly disrupt an entire class. How do you think that makes teachers feel?
3. Is it always good practice to seek advice when issues arise with one's teaching?

Jenny Ferreira teaches English as a Second Language in a middle school on the southeast coast of Florida, USA. She has an MA in TESOL from the local university and has been at the school for nearly ten years. Jenny is happy at the school and has no plans to move. Her small family is well settled in the city, where her two children attend a good elementary school in the suburb where they live. All her students are Spanish speaking and come from a range of Caribbean and Central American countries. She loves them dearly and wishes the very best for them. She sees many students come and go, mostly to enter high school, but some move back to their home countries. She is never sure why this is the case, but Jenny always tries to give them the best opportunity to learn while they are in her class.

The ESL classes at the school are small, about fifteen to twenty students. One of Jenny's classes consists entirely of students who have come through from the elementary feeder school close by. They know each other and, besides the occasional argument and fight, they get along well. Their English is also quite good, but they need another semester or two in the ESL program. Pedro is a twelve-year-old in the class. He is a delightful boy who is quick to answer questions and to volunteer to help Jenny organize groups and hand out worksheets. Pedro has a great sense of humor and is popular with the other students. Jenny finds him charming and easy to get along with. At times, however, he seems a little distracted. For example, one minute he'll be working on a task in his group and then the next he'll be talking to a neighbor in another group. Jenny then has to move him back to his own group. At other times, he sits quietly and appears to be drifting off into dreamland, not paying attention to anything happening around him. Then suddenly he is full of energy again, chatting to other students and shouting out answers to questions.

Jenny has noticed that he is not learning at the same pace as the other students in the class. On a recent round of assessments, Pedro performed well below the class average. His spoken English is good, but he is struggling with writing and some of the communicative tasks the students do in pairs or groups. He also can't seem to focus for long on the short reading passages they work on in class. His comprehension of these does not seem to be improving. Of course, Pedro isn't the only middle school student Jenny has come across in her career who is boisterous in class and doesn't always concentrate on the task at hand. But there is just something about Pedro's behavior that seems different.

Then one day Jenny is scrolling her social media and comes across an interview with a woman who describes how her life has changed since she was diagnosed with ADHD. In the interview she explains in detail what her symptoms are and how these affect her work, her interactions with others, and her family life. As a teacher, Jenny feels she needs to know more. Some of those symptoms look very familiar to her, and she particularly thinks of Pedro. Does he exhibit similar symptoms? Does he have ADHD? Jenny is not a psychologist or a medical doctor and she knows she has to be very careful about making any such evaluations. She is not sure if she should report her thoughts to the school counselor. It could be devastating for Pedro if she gets things wrong or speaks to the wrong people. But Jenny is worried about Pedro's English learning, and she feels she needs to say something.

2.3.2 Questions

1. Jenny appears to be settled in her ESL teaching job at the school. Do you think it's time she moved on, or gained another qualification? Give a reason for your answer.
2. Pedro probably isn't the first student to exhibit ADHD symptoms in Jenny's classes over the years. Why do you think she has only begun to notice them now?
3. Might Pedro not have ADHD? What else could be the cause of his behavior in class?
4. How could Jenny educate herself about ADHD and its relationship to language learning and teaching? What could her school do to support teachers in this regard?
5. Jenny feels she "needs to say something" about Pedro's situation. What should she say, and who should she say it to?

2.3.3 Research Topics

Evaluating a Special Educational Needs Policy at a Language School
Does a language school have a policy for learners with special educational needs? What are school administrators' views about the implementation of such a policy? What support does a school offer teachers for working with language learners with special educational needs?

1. Identify a language school or a language program within a larger institution.
2. Inquire if it has a policy regarding language learners with special educational needs. If it does, locate the policy and read it carefully.
3. Prepare a set of *structured interview questions* (M9), that is, an interview schedule that does not allow much flexibility in the way or order the

questions are asked. The questions will vary if the school has a policy and if the school does not have a policy.
4. Conduct structured interviews with several managers or administrators in the school or program. Ask about their knowledge of language learners with special educational needs, the need for a policy for learners with special needs, the increasing prevalence of ADHD in schools, and their awareness of the need for support for teachers and other school staff.
5. After analyzing the data, produce some *descriptive statistics* (M4) of the main themes discovered, for example frequency counts and percentages, and summarize the findings in the form of tables and short paragraphs.
6. Interview the leader of the school or program about your findings.
7. What does the policy look like? Should it change? Should there be one if there isn't already one? What support should be offered to language teachers?

Surveying Special Educational Needs Vocabulary Awareness
What words do we use to talk about learners with special educational needs? Are we aware of different types of special educational needs? Are we afraid of mis-using words associated with these needs? Why?

1. Consult relevant *literature or search websites* (M6) on the internet that describe special educational needs in schools. Or consult with a knowledgeable person you may know.
2. Compile a list of up to twenty terms, concepts, or phrases that are commonly used in the field of special needs education or are increasingly used in discussions of these needs in the school context.
3. Design a spreadsheet listing the terms in the first column. In adjacent columns, ask a series of questions.
4. Distribute the list to language teachers in your school or program or beyond. In the columns next to the terms, ask them, for example, (a) to identify terms that they are familiar with, (b) to indicate how important it is for language teachers to know these terms, (c) if they know how to respond to learners with the particular special educational needs they are familiar with, and (d) if they feel they need professional development or any other support from the school. Collect as many responses as possible.
5. What is the level of the teachers' awareness? What should schools do about the outcome? Do you have enough information to present it at a faculty meeting or teacher conference?

2.3.4 Resources

Apriliyanti, D. L. (2023). Teachers' challenges in teaching English to students with special needs: How to cope with them? *Indonesian Journal of Community and Special Needs Education*, *3*(2), 131–140. https://ejournal.upi.edu/index.php/IJCSNE/article/view/56869 (Accessed October 28, 2024).

Csizér, K. & Kontra, E. H. (2020). Foreign language learning characteristics of deaf and severely hard-of-hearing students. *The Modern Language Journal*, *104*(1), 233–249. https://doi.org/10.1111/modl.12630

Debreli, E. & Ishanova, I. (2019). Foreign language classroom management: Types of student misbehaviour and strategies adapted by the teachers in handling disruptive behaviour. *Cogent Education*, *6*(1), 1648629. https://doi.org/10.1080/2331186X.2019.1648629

2.4 Disruption in a Multigrade Language Classroom

Keywords
- India
- Remote rural primary school
- Multigrade classroom
- Knowing school and community
- Researcher interference

2.4.1 Pre-reading Reflection

1. What problems might arise for teachers in language classrooms where there are widely varying levels of proficiency in the target language?
2. What are some features of rural schools as compared to urban schools? Think of actual examples of rural schools you might be familiar with.
3. How do teachers feel when they are being observed teaching by another teacher?

Devi Primary School is situated on the outskirts of a remote village in northern India. The school has about a hundred students and two teachers. There are two neatly painted classrooms, with the students divided about equally between the two rooms. Multiple grades are taught in the classrooms, as are multiple subjects, including English. The learners seldom hear any English outside the classroom, and very little in the classroom as well. The teacher of one of the classes, Miss Grover, is not a very proficient speaker of English, but she is able

2.4 Disruption in a Multigrade Language Classroom

to follow most of the lessons in the textbook that has been given to her by the educational leaders in the district. She is not too concerned that her group of multigrade learners do not get to learn much English. They are not motivated to learn the language, and in fact fear it when it is time for a focus on English in class. What they typically do each lesson is copy some sentences from the board into their notebooks and then read them aloud in choral fashion imitating the teacher. Perhaps they learn a new word or two each week.

Miss Grover believes that their other school subjects (i.e., basic literacy in their home language, numeracy) are more important for them, but more important still is the development of their communicative and social skills, their personal growth, and their ability to learn by teaching each other. She knows that many of her students will drop out of primary school before long, and so teaching these skills are more relevant to their future lives than acquiring knowledge of English. There is growing pressure, though, from both parents and other leaders in the village community for English to be taught and so she dutifully persists with the English lessons.

Recently, Miss Grover and her colleague were informed by written notice that the school had been selected to participate in a research project with a French university. The project, which aimed to understand and improve multigrade language teaching practices in rural schools in India, was being sponsored by an international non-governmental organization (NGO) working in parts of northern India. Soon after receiving the notice, a French researcher arrived at the school. She was introduced to the two teachers as Dr. Durand by one of the NGO officers. Dr. Durand was to spend two weeks at the school observing teaching and learning. Over the first few days, Dr. Durand mostly sat at the back of the classroom observing the action and taking notes. She and Miss Grover communicated occasionally about what was going on using the limited English they both had. Miss Grover found it refreshing to have another adult in the classroom and enjoyed showing off her teaching skills. During one of the English activities at the start of her second week, Dr. Durand unexpectedly stood up from her seat at the back of the room and joined a group of about eight students who were sitting on a mat near her seat. While the lesson continued, Miss Grover noticed Dr. Durand pointing to some of the students' notebooks and talking to them. These students engaged with Dr. Durand and did not pay attention to what Miss Grover was doing. Students from other groups also appeared interested in what Dr. Durand's students were up to. This distracted Miss Grover somewhat, but she continued with the lesson, calling the students back to attention.

After the lesson, Miss Grover approached Dr. Durand and, speaking in a quiet and polite way, asked her not to interact with the students during her lessons. She said she felt confident about what she was doing in her classes, and although she was happy having Dr. Durand observe her classes, she did not want her interrupting their flow.

2.4.2 Questions

1. What is your reaction to Miss Grover's attitude to her students' English learning? And their learning generally?
2. Members of the rural village community want the school to teach their children English. Why do you think this is so, and is it a reasonable demand?
3. Multigrade teaching is common in rural schools in India. Do you know of other contexts in which multigrade teaching and learning takes place? If so, describe them.
4. What is your view on the way Miss Grover managed the distraction caused by Dr. Durand interacting with a group of students in her class while she was teaching? Do you agree or disagree with her stance?
5. Perhaps Miss Grover missed out on an opportunity to learn something from Dr. Durand. Is this possible?

2.4.3 Research Topics

Exploring Language Learners' Perceptions of Multigrade Language Learning

What do language learners think about learning in multigrade classrooms? Do they enjoy it? Can they focus on their learning? Do they believe they would learn better in same-grade classrooms? What is their relationship like with learners from a different grade?

1. Locate one classroom consisting of multigrade language learning. These classrooms are quite common and are found not only in rural schools; for example, in open-plan classroom arrangements.
2. Design a *narrative frame* (M16) for the language learners of all grades in the classroom. When completed, the frame should tell a story of the learners' experiences of and reflections on learning language in the multigrade classroom.
3. The frame should not be too long, and the teacher could incorporate the frame into a writing lesson.
4. Analyze the learners' completed frames for common themes. Count the themes and compare the numbers.
5. How do the learners feel about having to learn in multigrade classrooms? Do they say anything about the teaching? Do different grades have different perceptions?

Discussing Parents' Reasons for Desiring English for Their Children
Why do parents demand English learning for their children? Is this demand the same in all contexts?

1. Recruit a small team of collaborators (four or five) for this study. The collaborators should be teaching or working in different locations across a region – or more ambitiously, across a country.
2. Design a *brief questionnaire* (M17) for parents, asking them about their attitudes toward the English language, its importance in their social world, its relevance to their lives, if it is important for their children to learn English, and why, and what schools should be doing about English teaching.
3. The questionnaire should require little writing, so construct closed-item questions or provide space for short written answers. But have options for longer responses in case some parents want to contribute more. The questionnaire may need to be translated into the language of the parents.
4. Invite your collaborators to distribute the questionnaire to parents of English learners within their educational networks, and then to return the completed questionnaires to you.
5. Why is the demand for English so high? Is it always high? Do the parents say anything useful about what schools can do to help their children learn English?

2.4.4 Resources

Jeyaraj, J. S. (2017). Challenges of teaching English in India. *Language Forum: A Journal of Language & Literature*, *43*(1–2), 59–81. http://dx.doi.org/10.2139/ssrn.3486395

Mishra, B. (2015). Innovative ways of English language teaching in rural India through technology. *International Journal of English and Literature*, *6*(2), 38–44. https://doi.org/10.5897/IJEL2014.0686

Naparan, G. B. & Alinsug, V. G. (2021). Classroom strategies of multigrade teachers. *Social Sciences & Humanities Open*, *3*(1), 100109. https://doi.org/10.1016/j.ssaho.2021.100109

2.5 Young Learners with Limited Class Time for Learning

Keywords
- Japan
- Elementary school
- Introduction of English learning
- Teacher professional development
- Assistant Language Teacher (ALT)

2.5.1 Pre-reading Reflection

1. In ideal conditions, how much time per week should be allocated to learning English as a foreign language in elementary schools?
2. What constraints in real contexts might restrict this amount of time?
3. What might the main two or three jobs of an Assistant Language Teacher or teacher aide be in a language classroom?

In 2020, English learning became compulsory in the early grades of elementary school in Japan. The aim was for students to know a few hundred words and expressions (600–700) in English by the time they finished elementary school. This was a significant policy decision, with major implications for schools, English teacher education, and language learning. Kato High School, located in a suburb of a small city, exemplifies many of the challenges associated with this language-in-education policy decision.

Kato High is a medium-sized elementary school with about 400 students. Before 2020, English had never been taught as a subject in the school and none of its teachers was a qualified English teacher. In fact, none would claim to be even remotely proficient in English. Most teachers teach the full range of subjects on offer, including Japanese language, and also take care of extracurricular activities. Some teachers felt that learning and then teaching the limited number of English words and expressions in the syllabus would be a manageable and enjoyable challenge, especially if they were released from some of their other teaching duties. However, this was only a very small group of teachers in the school.

The school management was ideologically supportive of the new English-teaching policy initiative but was unsure about how to implement it. Nevertheless, it took the policy seriously and began planning well before English lessons were scheduled to begin. The first step was to set up a committee (a sort of ad hoc English Department) that would be responsible for the following: (a) allocating work release hours to a sufficient number of teachers to ensure that the English teaching would be covered across the required grades in the school; (b) designing the timetable for English lessons – one hour per week for lower grades and two hours per week for higher grades; (c) organizing English learning for the teachers as part of their professional development so that they could cope with the level of English in the prescribed textbooks, and arranging workshops for them to practice some basic English teaching methods; and (d) looking into acquiring one or more ALTs (English-speaking Assistant Language Teachers hired through a Japanese government scheme) in the longer term.

Kato High School has been struggling now for two years. The school has not been able to hire an ALT, but has been placed on a waiting list. The teachers have made substantial progress with their English learning. They have not developed communicative skills but have done well to learn the basic material in the textbooks and are able to work on those materials with their students quite confidently. The school contracted a private English teacher to work with the teachers for the first six months of 2020 during a series of after-school professional development workshops. The teachers haven't made much progress beyond what is in the textbook and are looking forward to the arrival of an ALT who will continue to help them with their learning.

The teachers have observed that their students make almost no progress with English learning over the year. Typically, they are not interested in learning English, but do have fun during lessons, and there is a little evidence of learning, particularly in the short term during imitation and repetition activities. But by the next lesson they appear to have forgotten what they had previously learned. There is no formal assessment. The teachers believe that there is not enough time dedicated to English learning in the school timetable. They have discussed these issues with management, but there is nothing they can do. The hours and syllabus for English instruction are set by higher authorities. Teachers are losing interest and feel that their hard work is not producing satisfactory results.

2.5.2 Questions

1. What are the arguments for and against introducing compulsory English as a foreign language (EFL) learning to young learners in lower school grades?
2. What has Kato High School so far got right in its planning for and implementation of the new English learning policy?
3. What has the school got wrong?
4. What difference might an ALT make within the school? What could this assistant English teacher actually do and how effective would they be?
5. The teachers are losing interest, and they believe that the learners are not learning English. What solutions would you propose for dealing with these two significant problems?

2.5.3 Research Topics

Carrying Out an International Survey of English Learning Hours in Primary Schools

How many hours do primary school EFL or ESL learners spend learning English in the classroom each week? What do national or regional language-in-education policies stipulate regarding the number of English lessons and the number of hours to be spent each week learning English? What is the rationale for these decisions?

1. *National language-in-education policies* (M6) are usually available on the internet. Search for the policies of five countries or ask colleagues who work in these countries to help you locate them.
2. Scrutinize the policies to find out information about EFL or ESL teaching in the primary or elementary school sector.
3. Specifically look for information about when English is introduced into the curriculum and how much time is required to be spent each week learning English.
4. Do a comparison of the five policies.
5. What do the policies have in common? What are their main differences? What is the average time that primary school EFL or ESL learners spend learning English in the classroom each week?

Visiting a Primary School in an EFL Context

How much English is visible in a primary school in an EFL context? How much English is heard in such a school? What do teachers of other subjects say about English learning and teaching in the school? How do English teachers perceive their work in these schools?

1. Access to a primary school in an EFL context is needed for this research topic. Gain permission to visit the school, preferably with a host, who can arrange the visit and a tour.
2. Spend a day or two at the school. *Observe your surroundings* (M7) constantly while at the school. Look at the *objects, signs, and materials* (M13) in the school grounds and buildings.
3. If access is gained to English classes, take note of which grade classes they are, the age of the learners, and what happens during lessons.
4. Speak to as many people in the school as possible. Ask your host to introduce you to the principal, other administrators, English teachers, and teachers of other subjects. Talk to students.
5. After the school visit(s), write a *reflective journal* (M14) of your experiences at the school. Describe all your observations and reflect on what they might mean in relation to teaching EFL in the primary school context.
6. With the school's permission, post the journal entry on your professional social media and ask for comments.
7. Do learners spend enough time learning English? Do they enjoy it? Are the materials and facilities adequate? Does the school provide professional development support for EFL teachers?

2.5.4 Resources

Carreira, J. M. (2006). Motivation for learning English as a foreign language in Japanese elementary schools. *JALT Journal, 28*(2), 135–157. https://doi.org/10.37546/JALTJJ28.2-2

Christmas, J. (2014). Challenges with creating professional development workshops for Japanese elementary school teachers. *The Language Teacher*, *38* (6), 3–9. https://doi.org/10.37546/JALTTLT38.6-1

Fennelly, M., & Luxton, R. (2011). Are they ready? On the verge of compulsory English, elementary school teachers lack confidence. *The Language Teacher*, *35*(2), 19–24. https://doi.org/10.37546/JALTTLT35.2-2

2.6 Gender Identity in the Classroom

Keywords
- Uruguay
- High school
- EFL teacher
- Sexual orientation and gender identity
- Bullying

2.6.1 Pre-reading Reflection

1. Imagine that a student in your class writes in one of their compositions that they are confused about their sexuality and asks you for advice.
2. Do you think that students tend to reveal more about their personal identities in language classes than in the classes of other subjects?
3. Do you feel you are up to date with debates regarding gender identity in education?

Pablo is an English teacher with more than thirty years' experience. He has been working in a public high school in a poor neighborhood of Montevideo, Uruguay, for more than twenty years. He has also served as the Academic Coordinator of the EFL Department for many years. Pablo is held in high regard and is admired by his colleagues and students due to his professionalism, great communication skills, empathy, and patience. He is gay, and his sexual orientation has never caused any issues at work. He does not talk openly about his sexual orientation but does not hide it either. Only a few of his closest friends at work know that he has been married since 2013, when same-sex marriage was legalized in the country.

Because of his professional and personal qualities, Pablo has been asked to serve on the school's "wellbeing and bullying prevention committee" to reduce the high levels of mental abuse and bullying in the school. One day, he saw one of his students crying alone in the hallway while everyone else was in class. She looked sad and stressed, so he immediately invited her to his office to talk about her problem. The student, Fabiola, told Pablo that she felt lonely in her class and that for quite a while some of her classmates had been bullying her. She also said she did not want her classmates to be punished for this, she only wanted to be left in peace. Fabiola was a quiet student and she had very good grades; however, she often spent time alone and during breaks she would normally be seen with her ear-pods in, listening to music and reading a book. Although she had been bullied by some of her classmates for quite a while, she did not want to disclose this situation to anyone.

Pablo tried to comfort Fabiola and told her that he was going to investigate the situation and find a solution to her problem. He went to her classroom and asked to see a couple of students (Carolina and Natalia, who were allegedly bullying Fabiola). In this meeting, he talked to them in a respectful and calm manner and inquired about the situation in the class in general and with Fabiola. After a while, the girls confessed that they had been calling Fabiola names and had been making fun of her because they were sure that she had feelings for Natalia, which they were not happy about. They acknowledged that their own behavior was not appropriate. After the conversation with Pablo, they promised they would apologize to Fabiola and would stop calling her names and making fun of her, but they did not promise to become friends with her.

Pablo was satisfied with this meeting and the next day had a follow-up meeting with Fabiola. In this meeting, Pablo explained to her what had happened in his conversation with Natalia and Carolina; that is, that they promised to change their aggressive behavior toward her. He also told Fabiola that it was not a crime to feel attracted to a person of the same sex, that he understood how she might be feeling, and that there was nothing to feel sad about or ashamed of. Fabiola replied tearfully that her main problem was not that she felt attracted to other girls, but that she did not like her own body; she looked at herself in the mirror and hated what she saw. She did not know how to feel about herself. She felt as if she had been given the wrong body, and felt more like a boy than a girl. Pablo felt lost for words. However, after he had had time to reflect on the situation, from all perspectives, he remained determined to help Fabiola. He just needed to figure out what to do.

2.6.2 Questions

1. Sexual orientation and gender identity are complex topics with political, social, cultural, psychological and emotional aspects. How should these be addressed in teacher education programs to prepare teachers to deal with them?
2. What kinds of mechanisms should schools put in place to support students like Fabiola, and their teachers?
3. Pablo is an EFL teacher. Should he be getting involved in helping Fabiola during this challenging time for her?

4. Why do you think Pablo does not know how to help Fabiola? What does he need "to figure out"?
5. Should the teacher seek support for Natalia and Carolina? Why? What might that support be?

2.6.3 Research Topics

Reflecting on Transgender Identities in the Classroom
What does having a transgender identity mean? Should language teachers be aware of transgender issues in education? How do schools work with transgender students?

1. Following a *duoethnography* (M7) approach, invite a teacher or student teacher colleague to have a discussion with you about transgender issues in language education.
2. Set aside an hour for the dialogue. Before meeting, plan a schedule of topics to be covered. These might include, broadly, your understanding of the term transgender, your experience with gender diverse students, colleagues' attitudes to transgender students and ideologies, and what school policies on facilitating the needs of transgender students should look like.
3. Record and then transcribe the dialogue.
4. Collaboratively, analyze the content of the transcript. What keywords, *metaphors* (M11), and ideas are salient in the dialogue?
5. Does the analysis raise any ideas for further research?

Investigating Language Learners Reflecting on Gender and Sexuality
How do adult learners feel about reflecting on their gender and sexuality in their language classrooms? Do they see the relevance of doing so to their language learning? What emotions do they experience during the reflection process?

1. Carry out the investigation in a class of adult language learners.
2. On their school-approved smart device, ask the learners to design a *multimodal collage* (M12) representing their own gender or sexuality, or both. The collage is for personal reflection only and is not to be shared.
3. The collage could consist of some of the following media: photographs, pictures, emojis, colors, shapes, speech bubbles.
4. When they have completed their collage, ask the learners to write a short paragraph, also on their smart device, describing their thoughts about the process of reflecting on their gender or sexuality. How did it make them feel? How do gender and sexuality relate to their language learner identity?
5. After asking the learners to delete both their collage and their paragraph, have a *class discussion* (M8) with the students about the reflection activity.

6. What did everyone learn about the process? Could this activity be used as part of a larger research project?

2.6.4 Resources

Bartholomaeus, C., Riggs, D. W., & Andrew, Y. (2017). The capacity of South Australian primary school teachers and pre-service teachers to work with trans and gender diverse students. *Teaching and Teacher Education*, *65*, 127–135. https://doi.org/10.1016/j.tate.2017.03.006

Knisely, K. A. & Paiz, J. M. (2021). Bringing trans, non-binary, and queer understandings to bear in language education. *Critical Multilingualism Studies*, *9*(1), 23–45. https://cms.arizona.edu/index.php/multilingual/article/view/237

Martino, W., Kassen, J., & Omercajic, K. (2022). Supporting transgender students in schools: Beyond an individualist approach to trans inclusion in the education system. *Educational Review*, *74*(4), 753–772. https://doi.org/10.1080/00131911.2020.1829559

2.7 An Immigrant Learner's Problems and Successes

Keywords
- New Zealand and Iran
- Immigrant learner
- Female adult learner
- Problems and successes learning English
- Imagining future learning and identity

2.7.1 Pre-reading Reflection

1. As a new immigrant in a country, would constructing a language identity be a priority for the immigrant?
2. Imagine arriving in a new country as an immigrant with little knowledge of the host-country majority language. How would you feel?
3. What is an "ethnic bubble" in a community? Are there any advantages of living in one for immigrants?

Sara lives in New Zealand. She is an immigrant from Iran. Below she tells her story of using and learning English in her new country. She reflects on her past

2.7 An Immigrant Learner's Problems and Successes

and present problems and successes, and she also imagines her future life as an English user in New Zealand.

"I come from Iran. I speak Farsi and Turkish. Now also English. My arrival date was 2 January 2010. We, my husband and my daughter, live in Hamilton. My daughter is seven years old. In Iran, lives my father and mother, three brothers and two sisters, and one nephew. My job in Iran, I was a dental nurse. Now in New Zealand I study English and take care of my family. Sometimes I take care of my friends' children. I have a small garden. My husband chose to come to New Zealand. My daughter likes New Zealand.

"When I first came to New Zealand my English was almost non-existent. I could only say some of the alphabet, and hello and goodbye. Soon after I arrived, a problem I experienced with English was everything. I couldn't understand or read or speak. I was worried about a lot of things. Another problem I had with my English was I wanted to understand, but I couldn't. I would like to work but I couldn't. After a while, however, I had been attending free ESOL classes. Fortunately, I had made a friend. She could speak Farsi well and I had an ESOL tutor. So gradually I began to understand. Also, my daughter helped me. I realized things were getting better when I was able to hear words and understand some of them, and I could talk a little. In those early days, another example of success with my English was going shopping, and to understand the name, the price, and which size, which country the product came from.

"Now my English is a lot better. I can read basic English, write, understand more than I can speak. I find I can more easily listen and understand people. What I can really do well when I use English is my pronunciation is very clear and reading is easier for me. Also, I remember once I bought my daughter some shorts, they were too small, so the lady explained to me to check the size, and small, medium and the age on the label. However, when I use English, I'm still having problems with my ability to express myself. I would like to be able to solve this problem but I think I need to talk more with different people. It is easier to talk with children, they use simpler words and sentences. In the future, I would like to use English to return to work as a dental nurse. I imagine that I will also be able to become a beautician, which I enjoy. I will know that I have learned enough English when I can understand and speak everything. Learning English is important for me because already I was thirty-three when I began studying English. Everyone speaks English here. It is important to learn this language.

"After about one year my daughter told me, 'Mum, your English is getting better.' Sometimes when I went out people wanted to talk to me, but I couldn't understand them, I just looked at them, and they would talk a lot and then get tired and go away. It made me feel sad. But now I say, 'please speak more.'"

2.7.2 Questions

1. How would you describe Sara's level of motivation to learn and use English in New Zealand? What factors in her environment contribute to her motivation?
2. How significant to Sara are the problems she has faced using English in her everyday life? How do you think these problems make her feel?
3. Sara mentions having an ESOL (English for Speakers of Other Languages) tutor. If this tutor worked one-on-one with Sara, what kind of material or content might they cover during their tutoring sessions?
4. How might the tutor, and Sara's friends, support her in maintaining her motivation to learn English? How could they support her emotionally?
5. How likely is it that Sara will achieve her goal of working as a dental nurse in New Zealand? What will she need to do to achieve this goal, and what might prevent her from doing so?

2.7.3 Research Topics

Recording Emotions Related to Language Learning Successes and Problems
How do language learners feel about the successes they experience in language learning? And how do they feel about their problems or failures? What *are* successes and failures in language learning?

1. Arrange a class of language learners into pairs. Select a level with which you are familiar or in which you are interested (e.g., primary or high school, adult learners).
2. Before collaborating in pairs, work as a whole class to design a *short interview schedule* (M9) consisting of a structured set of questions about language learning successes and problems experienced by the learners and their emotional responses to these successes and problems.
3. Ask the pairs to use their smartphones to interview and record each other, according to the schedule.
4. Interviews should last about ten to fifteen minutes. When the interviews are over, ask the students to send their recordings to you.
5. Analyze the data, listing all the successes and problems mentioned by the learners. You could do a *frequency count* (M4) of these.
6. What successes and failures are mentioned most frequently by the learners? What emotions are associated with these? Report the findings to the class.

Studying Adult Immigrants' English Learner Reflexive Identities
How do adult immigrants see themselves as English learners? What in their histories affects their learning today? How do they imagine their English learner and user identities in the future?

1. Gather a group of about eight to ten adult immigrant English learners, either through your professional networks or from an institution that you are familiar with.
2. Meet the group twice. The first time, introduce yourself and tell the learners about your background. Let them know you are interested in talking to them about their histories of English learning and their reflections on how they imagine themselves as English learners and users in the future. Have a general open discussion about English and immigration.
3. At the end of the meeting, ask the learners to bring to the second meeting two *artefacts (e.g., an object or a photo)* (M13), one from their home country, and one from their new country. Both artefacts should tell a story about their language knowledge and use and relate to their past, current, and future language-related identities.
4. At the second meeting, give each learner an opportunity to talk about their two artefacts. Open the floor like a *focus group discussion* (M8). Facilitate the discussion, ensuring it stays on topic and that everyone gets a turn to contribute.
5. Record and transcribe both meetings.
6. How do the learners describe their past language learner lives? What linguistic aspirations do the learners have? How do they see themselves in the future?

2.7.4 Resources

Everatt, J., Fletcher, J., Kim, J., & Subramaniam, Y.B. (2025). What do New Zealand teachers and principals perceive is happening for English as an additional language students with the changing architecture of New Zealand schools? *Educational Review*, 77(4), 1105–1124. https://doi.org/10.1080/00131911.2023.2263662

Gunderson, L. (2021). The consequences of English learner as a category in teaching, learning, and research. *Journal of Adolescent & Adult Literacy*, 64(4), 431–439. https://doi.org/10.1002/jaal.1116

Xiang, V., Parackal, S., Gurung, G., & Subramaniam, R. M. (2023). Asian migrants navigating New Zealand primary care: A qualitative study. *Journal of Primary Health Care*, 15(1), 30–37. https://doi.org/10.1071/HC22132

3 Teacher–Student Relationships

Cases in this chapter

3.1	Teacher as Friend	*page* 88
3.2	Knowing Students' Names	91
3.3	Respect for EMI Teachers	94
3.4	Privacy of a Gay Primary School Teacher	98
3.5	Working as a NNEST at University	101
3.6	University Policy on Student–Teacher Sexual Relationships	105
3.7	Being a Black Teacher in Japan	108

3.1 Teacher as Friend

Keywords
- Australia
- Polytechnic
- Changing professions
- Immigrant English teaching
- Favoring Muslim students

3.1.1 Pre-reading Reflection

1. Think of a teacher you've had who was very friendly with their students. In what ways did this teacher exhibit their friendly behavior? How did the students typically respond?
2. Who was your favorite teacher? What made them your favorite teacher?
3. Do you think there should be guidelines for teachers regarding their relationships with students? If so, who should issue these guidelines?

For several years, Fariq had worked as a social worker among the largely immigrant community in the city neighborhood where he lived. He was an immigrant himself. He moved to Australia when he was a teenager with his parents who had jobs in the business sector. Fariq was not business inclined and went to university to study law and liberal arts. He hated law but completed his BA degree, nevertheless. After completing a postgraduate qualification in social work and education he started working for an NGO that focused on supporting and settling new immigrants with a Muslim and predominantly Arabic-speaking background.

As a young social worker Fariq interacted with many families, visiting their homes, religious institutions, and cultural centers. Because of his own background, Fariq was familiar with their sociocultural practices and felt comfortable serving as a social worker in their midst. Early on in his work experience he became aware of the immigrants' limitations in English. Generally, children at school were making much better progress learning English than their parents, some of whom were struggling with their language transactions at work or with life in the community. Fariq tried to help them when he could by, for example, translating documents for them, making phone calls on their behalf, accompanying them to appointments, and even checking the English homework of the school children.

When Fariq was in his early forties, he decided to train to become an English teacher. He had learned a lot about the needs of immigrants and felt he could help them more if he had specialist knowledge of the English language and how to teach it. He resigned from his social worker job and enrolled full-time in a Master of TESOL program, which he completed in one year. After graduating, he immediately got a job at a local polytechnic that serves a large immigrant population from many different countries. Fariq was assigned adult English classes for both beginners and more advanced learners. Some students were planning on studying further at university, while others were hoping to gain language skills that would help them cope in their daily lives. Others were aiming to secure employment. There were also some older learners who were attending class for social purposes – to meet and interact with people outside the home.

Fariq got on very well with his students, particularly the older Muslim students. They often invited him out for coffee after class, and even hosted him in their homes for meals and social gatherings. He tried to resist their constant invitations because he felt it was unfair on students from other immigrant groups, with whom he often struggled to relate. In class he found himself gravitating toward the Arabic-speaking students during group work. He knew he was helping them more than the other students in the class.

Throughout Fariq's first year of teaching, the same pattern continued. He had multiple classes each term, all similar in terms of their multilingual, multicultural makeup of immigrant populations from around the world. Fariq believed he spent far too much time interacting with and supporting the Arabic speakers in class and socialized too frequently out of class with the Muslim students, particularly men of about his age (and their families). No complaints were made about his teaching or about his relationships with his students, but he suspected that students were aware of his behavior and spoke about it among themselves.

3.1.2 Questions

1. What are some similarities and differences between the work of a language teacher and the work of a social worker? When Fariq was working as a social worker, why could he only give limited language support to the people he was working with?
2. Is it unusual to become a language teacher later in life? What are some advantages and disadvantages of doing so, particularly in the environment in which Fariq worked?
3. Fariq felt his close friendships with his male Muslim students was unfair to other students in his class. Do you agree?
4. In what ways did the kind of institution that Fariq worked in enable his teacher–student friendships? How might these friendships be different in other kinds of educational institutions?
5. Do you think Fariq needs to change his ways of interacting with his students, both inside and outside his English classes? If so, what should he do?

3.1.3 Research Topics

Assessing Teachers' Preferences for Language Learners (Part 1)
Why do teachers prefer teaching some language learners more than others? How do teachers monitor their relationships with learners in their classrooms? Do they have favorites?

1. Design an anonymous *questionnaire* (M17) on Google Forms or Qualtrics (or similar). Include in the questionnaire a list of about twenty language learner characteristics for teacher respondents to rank in terms of their preferences, such as: dedicated, enthusiastic, disinterested, smart, talkative, friendly, punctual, unmotivated, high achieving.
2. Have a separate list of identity categories associated with learners, such as: culture, religion, ethnicity, sexuality, gender, nationality. Ask teacher respondents to indicate on *rating scales* (M17) how important these are for their professional relationships with their learners.
3. Make the questionnaire link available to language teachers in an institution or a region that you have access to. Ensure anonymity.
4. What characteristics of their language learners do teachers prioritize in developing relationships with them? Are their relationships visible and equitable in the classroom?

Exploring Teachers' Preferences (Part 2)
Are teachers aware of their preferences and potential prejudices in developing relationships with their learners?

3.2 Knowing Students' Names

1. As a Part 2 to the previous research topic, include at the end of the Google Forms, Qualtrics or similar questionnaire an invitation asking teacher respondents to supply their email contact details if they would be willing to be interviewed about their questionnaire responses and to explore the research topic further.
2. Select appropriate and accessible teachers to *interview* (M9).
3. Retrieve each respondent's questionnaire from the online database and work through it during the interview, asking for clarification of any answers and elaborating further on selected questions.
4. Design a brief semi-structured interview schedule that asks fresh questions about this topic, including teachers' awareness of their preferences and potential prejudices in working with their learners and developing relationships with them.

3.1.4   Resources

García-Moya, I., Moreno, C., & Brooks, F. M. (2019). The "balancing acts" of building positive relationships with students: Secondary school teachers' perspectives in England and Spain. *Teaching and Teacher Education, 86,* 102883. https://doi.org/10.1016/j.tate.2019.102883

Rezai, A., Namaziandost, E., Miri, M., & Kumar, T. (2022). Demographic biases and assessment fairness in classroom: Insights from Iranian university teachers. *Language Testing in Asia, 12*(8), 1–20. https://doi.org/10.1186/s40468-022-00157-6

Rodriguez, T. L., Mahalingappa, L., Evangeliste, M., & Thoma, L. (2018). Educators must be activists: Advocating for Muslim students. *The European Educational Researcher, 1*(2), 117–131. https://doi.org/10.31757/euer.123

3.2   Knowing Students' Names

Keywords
- Indonesia
- Private language school
- US English teacher
- Remembering names
- Fear of appearing racist

3.2.1   Pre-reading Reflection

1. Teaching abroad for the first time requires some significant cultural adjustments. Can you think of any examples?

2. What are some potential consequences of a teacher not knowing their students' names?
3. What are some useful strategies for remembering students' names in the classroom?

After twelve years teaching English as a second language at her high school in the Midwestern USA, Dorothy Mutch was finally granted a period of sabbatical leave from her school, the only school where she has been employed. Over the years she has participated in many professional development courses and workshops, has read widely, and has conducted several action research projects. She loves her job, her students, and her school. Dorothy believes she has a growth mindset, since she is always looking out for opportunities to do things differently, to be innovative, and to develop as a teacher. She wants her students to learn. However, in recent years she's had to admit to herself that she's been feeling a little stale in her current position. And so, she decided that taking sabbatical leave for one year, teaching English in another country, would open her eyes to new cultures, educational systems, and ways of learning and teaching English, and therefore rejuvenate her motivation and enthusiasm for teaching.

A couple of years ago Dorothy met a university English teacher from Indonesia who was part of a group of teachers visiting Dorothy's school district. She maintained contact with the teacher via social media and when it came time to look for a teaching position overseas during her sabbatical, the Indonesian teacher was very helpful in securing a placement for her as a part-time general English teacher at a friend's private English school in Jakarta. Dorothy settled quickly into her new neighborhood and the school, and also her job. Her new colleagues were very helpful and the students, she said, were "delightful." Dorothy can't speak Indonesian (Bahasa Indonesia). In fact, English is the only language she can speak. Even though many of her learners in the US are Spanish speakers, she has not learned the language herself. She has, however, become quite good at Spanish pronunciation, and feels confident about pronouncing the names of her Spanish students in her US classes – when she can remember them! Remembering names has always been a challenge for Dorothy, not only at school, but in everyday life too. She claims she is good with faces, but not with names. Now in Indonesia she has the twofold concern of not only pronouncing her students' Indonesian names correctly but also remembering them.

Dorothy was determined to try. She believes that using names in the classroom is a way of connecting with students, respecting them, and developing good relationships with them. She also feels that it creates a sense of belonging for students and reduces their learning anxiety, enabling them to be more effective language learners. Her classes are small – about fifteen students per class. In the first week she asked an Indonesian teacher to go over the names of her students

3.2 Knowing Students' Names

with her to check her pronunciation, and she seemed to do well. She practiced at home. Students placed name cards in front of them on their desks; Dorothy explained that this was to help her learn and remember their names. The students didn't seem to mind, but as time wore on, she observed a few giggles when it was obvious that Dorothy was looking down at the cards before saying their names, sometimes pausing and still saying the names incorrectly too. Classroom talk seemed stilted and artificial. When Dorothy discontinued using the name cards, she only remembered the names of the more vocal, extroverted students. She is thinking about asking students to wear name tags on their tops but after so much time is afraid that this might make it appear that she is disrespecting their culture, or has some sort of racist tendencies, which is the last thing she would want her students to think. Saying "you" and pointing to students is really not the way she wants to continue engaging students in classroom activities.

3.2.2   Questions

1. Dorothy seemed ready for a period of sabbatical leave from her teaching situation in the US. Do you think going to Indonesia was a good choice for her?
2. Dorothy appears to be a dedicated, hard-working language teacher. Why do you think, then, she struggled so much with learning and remembering names?
3. Dorothy lists several benefits of using students' names in the classroom. Do you agree with these, and can you add any others to the list?
4. Do you think Dorothy is exaggerating when she says the students might think she is being "sort of" racist if she asks them, after so long, to put on name tags? Should she go ahead with the name tags idea?
5. Dorothy seems to be at a bit of a loss. What should she do next?

3.2.3   Research Topics

Analyzing Classroom Interaction for Patterns of Name Use
How and when do teachers use names in the language classroom? Why do they use names? What are alternatives to the use of names?

1. Record two or three language classroom lessons.
2. Listen to the recordings and select one that includes a lot of interaction between the teacher and the students.
3. Transcribe the interaction in full.
4. Analyze the interaction using basic *discourse analytical* (M5) procedures such as noting who is talking, when they are talking, and who they are talking to. Note explicit use of names – why are names being used at that moment of the talk? How frequently does the teacher use names? Do learners use names?

5. Identify instances in the talk where the teacher addresses students or refers to them (e.g., calling on them to answer a question, asking them to keep quiet, praising them to other students) and does not use their name. What does the teacher do instead?
6. What patterns or trends of name use do you find in the classroom interaction?

Monitoring the Effect of Using Names in the Classroom
What effect does using names in the classroom have on classroom interaction? Do teachers notice a difference when they use names more in the classroom?

1. Collaborate with a teacher to plan several strategies to increase the use of names in classroom interaction.
2. Names could be used, for example, to nominate a learner to contribute an answer, to request a learner to follow a command, to ask a learner to help with a classroom management issue, and to call on a student with a raised hand.
3. Implement the strategies in one lesson and record the interaction, preferably on video.
4. Listen closely to the recording or watch the video together with the teacher, and pay particular attention to the interaction when names are used. Stop the recording at selected places when names are used and *discuss with the teacher* (M15) what they notice about the interaction.
5. Is there a noticeable difference to the atmosphere in the classroom? Are learners more engaged in classroom interaction?

3.2.4 Resources

Cooper, K. M., Haney, B., Krieg, A., & Brownell, S. E. (2017). What's in a name? The importance of students perceiving that an instructor knows their names in a high-enrollment biology classroom. *CBE–Life Sciences Education*, *16*(1), 1–13. https://doi.org/10.1187/cbe.16-08-0265

Jepson, K. K. (2020). Commentary: Learning students' given names benefits EMI classes. *Frontiers in Psychology*, *11*, 1625. https://doi.org/10.3389/fpsyg.2020.01625

Tutyandari, C. (2022). English language pre-service teachers' sense of preparedness for teaching: An Indonesian case. *TEFLIN Journal*, *33*(2), 367–385. https://doi.org/10.15639/teflinjournal.v33i2/367-385

3.3 Respect for EMI Teachers

Keywords
- China
- University

3.3 Respect for EMI Teachers

- Teachers from Hong Kong and Brazil
- English medium instruction (EMI)
- Careful not to disrupt relationship

3.3.1 Pre-reading Reflection

1. In your context, is teaching a respected profession? How do you know?
2. How did or do you get along with your lecturers at university?
3. What is your reaction when students ask the same questions over and over again?

Dr. Huang is a mathematics teacher at a large university in Southwest China. She comes from Hong Kong, where she obtained her PhD. She is well-published for an early career academic. This is her first job, and she has been at the university for about four years. During this time, she has become good friends with Dr. Souza, who teaches physical science. He is from Brazil and trained in the UK, completing his PhD part-time while working as a laboratory technician at a university in London. He took on the job in China because he felt he needed more teaching experience to further his academic career. He has been at the university for three years now. Dr. Souza and Dr. Huang meet regularly for lunch to talk about how things are going with their teaching, with their departments, and with their academic careers generally. They both use English – an additional language for them – as medium of instruction (EMI) in their teaching at the university, and this is often a topic of conversation too. Today when they meet for lunch, EMI comes up again, but this time in relation to how they get along with their students.

DR. SOUZA: You won't believe it, but it happened again. Remember I was saying that with my second-year group I have to keep explaining the English instructions for their weekly online task. It is so simple. But each week I go over the instructions and tell them exactly what to do. I'm sure they understand because they do the tasks well.

DR. HUANG: They must be anxious because, aren't the tasks graded?

DR. SOUZA: Yes, they are, but I have gone over the meaning many times. I have even given them Chinese translations of the key English words. The tasks are basic and what they have to do should be obvious by now.

DR. HUANG: Yeah, maybe to you, but they're trying to figure out physics and must do it in English. And they need to get good grades all at once. That's tough.

DR. SOUZA: I know, that's why I try to be patient with them. But it's not only with the online task instructions. They worry all the time about all the English they come across.

DR. HUANG: Actually, it's the same with my classes, as I've said before. I'm doing a group activity tomorrow and have already prepared some translations of the main content, just to get them going. They'll be fine. These are good students. I really like them.

DR. SOUZA: Me too. They do what I say and seem to appreciate what I do for them in class. I still can't believe how nice they are at this university.

DR. HUANG: What do you mean?
DR. SOUZA: I don't know, they just seem nice. When I was at university, we didn't really pay much attention to the lecturer – who the person was. Just got the information in class and left. Sometimes we'd even challenge them about what they were doing or ignore them in class. I feel a bit embarrassed about it now.
DR. HUANG: No, I don't think we did that. Sounds distressing. For all, but especially the teacher!
DR. SOUZA: True, maybe that's why I'm trying to be so patient and caring with my students. They drive me crazy with all the questions and requests to repeat the English and explain the English. It never stops. But I don't want to show my frustration, or worse, get angry in class. I don't want to spoil what we've got going. I think I'm lucky that we get on so well.

3.3.2 Questions

1. As can be seen in Dr. Huang and Dr. Souza's conversation, teaching in an EMI environment can be challenging. How could it affect a teacher's relationship with their students?
2. Referring to his students, Dr. Souza says, "they just seem nice." What does he mean by this?
3. Why do you think Dr. Huang's and Dr. Souza's university experiences as students are so different in terms of their relationships with their lecturers?
4. Dr. Huang says that challenging lecturers and ignoring them in class "sounds distressing." What does she mean? What could the reasons behind this distressing behavior be?
5. What could Dr. Souza do that might "spoil what we've got going"? Consider first what he and his students currently have "got going."

3.3.3 Research Topics

Inquiring into EMI Lecturers' Translingual Identities
What linguistic identities do content subject lecturers construct in EMI settings? What languages do they use during lessons and how does this affect how they reflexively see themselves as teachers?

1. Arrange to conduct an *interview* (M9) with a content subject (i.e., not a language) lecturer in an EMI university context. The lecturer should have a first language other than English and different from the language of the students, who are also not English first language speakers. The medium of instruction is English.
2. Plan a semi-structured interview schedule that examines the teaching experiences of the lecturer in this EMI context. Ask about how they take language into account when they plan lessons, if they use multiple languages in the classroom (and how they do so), what challenges they

experience lecturing in an EMI context, what successes they have, and how they identify as language practitioners.
3. Record and then listen to the interview very carefully. Select interesting and relevant passages and transcribe them.
4. Take these to the lecturer in a *second, focused interview* (M9) and ask them to talk more about their translingual lecturer identity in relation to the extracts.
5. What is a translingual lecturer identity? How do translingual lecturers practice in the classroom? How do they feel about who they are?

Assessing Students' Respect for EMI Teachers

What do university students think about their EMI content subject teachers? Do they respect the work they do? Do they value their teachers' language abilities and their use of multiple languages or translanguaging in the classroom?

1. Collaborate with a colleague who works in a different EMI context to the one you have access to. Both contexts should be EFL contexts, with the teachers being non-native speakers of English.
2. In each of these contexts, select one or two teachers who teach content subjects.
3. Together with your collaborator, design a *survey* (M17) that investigates the students' perceptions of these teachers.
4. In the survey, ask the students to rate their teachers according to their teaching expertise, language(s) proficiency, classroom practices, professionalism, content subject knowledge, English proficiency for academic purposes, and effective use of multiple languages in the classroom.
5. Compare student survey responses from the two EMI contexts.
6. How do they differ in terms of their respect for their teachers? Do the students appreciate their teachers' language use in the classroom?

3.3.4 Resources

McKinley, J., Rose, H., & Lan Curdt-Christiansen, X. (2023). EMI in Chinese higher education: The muddy water of "Englishisation." *Applied Linguistics Review*, *14*(6), 1475–1481. https://doi.org/10.1515/applirev-2022-0015

Shao, L. & Rose, H. (2022). Teachers' experiences of English-medium instruction in higher education: A cross case investigation of China, Japan and the Netherlands. *Journal of Multilingual and Multicultural Development*, *45*(7), 2801–2816. https://doi.org/10.1080/01434632.2022.2073358

Xu, X., Rose, H., McKinley, J., & Zhou, S. (2021). The incentivisation of English medium instruction in Chinese universities: Policy misfires and misalignments. *Applied Linguistics Review*, *14*(6), 1539–1561. https://doi.org/10.1515/applirev-2021-0181

3.4 Privacy of a Gay Primary School Teacher

Keywords
- Canada
- Elementary school
- Gay teacher
- Teacher near retirement
- Private life exposed by new teacher

3.4.1 Pre-reading Reflection

1. What are your thoughts about keeping a teacher's personal life private at school?
2. Being a gay teacher is not easy in some parts of the world. Can you think of examples?
3. At about what age level is it appropriate to begin teaching about gender and sexuality issues at school? In what ways could the topic of gender and sexuality be incorporated into language instruction?

James Start has worked at the same elementary school in a small city in British Columbia, Canada, for many years. He is about five years away from retirement and plans to see out these final years of his career "without any drama," as he puts it. He is a dedicated English as a second language (ESL) teacher for recent immigrant and refugee arrivals, and he also teaches reading and writing for the higher grades in his elementary school. He is busy and loves his job. He cares about his students and gets on well with his colleagues. Mr. Start is popular with the parents too – the young learners report to them that he is kind and patient and funny.

Mr. Start is gay and lives with his long-term partner a short bus ride away from the school. He prefers to keep his personal life private at school, although he is certainly not secretive about being gay. His teaching colleagues at school know he's gay and many have met his partner at social events. As far as the children go, they either know or don't know, or are too young to understand same-sex relationships. No one asks any questions, or says anything, and Mr. Start likes it that way. Over the years, there has been the odd question from students about his wife or about whether he has any children. But Mr. Start has well-practiced strategies for batting them off and there has never been any uncomfortable follow-up.

One recent morning in class, however, an eleven-year-old boy asked him what the name of his husband is. They were doing a reading activity that involved pair work, with subsequent reporting back to the whole class – about twenty-five students. The question from the boy came when it was time to report back. Mr. Start was floored by the question. He wasn't sure what to say and mumbled some sort of response before moving the discussion on to the next pair. But the boy came back with a second question, asking Mr. Start how long he and his husband had been married. This time Mr. Start quietly and with humor explained that his private life was not appropriate for classroom discussion. But he did ask the boy why he was asking these private questions. The boy explained that in another class, their teacher had been talking about issues related to boys and girls and gender, and used Mr. Start as an example of someone, close to them, who is in a same-sex relationship.

The teacher is a new teacher who joined the school only a few months ago, and teaches subjects related to social studies, including, it appears, gender. Mr. Start thought he should visit her classroom to talk about what happened. He had met her when she arrived at the school, and they had shared a couple of coffees together at local cafés. They got on well, but he hadn't expected her to talk about him to her students. When he entered her classroom, the first thing he noticed was a huge rainbow Pride flag hanging on the front wall of the classroom. He didn't know what gender she identified as, and he didn't care, but the flag certainly signalled to him her political stance on gender issues, and possibly the content of her social studies lessons. They had a congenial conversation; the teacher said she didn't think Mr. Start would mind her using him as an example. He politely asked her to refrain from doing so again, especially because he didn't want his students confused or his relationship with them upset in any way. Later, Mr. Start discovered from other teachers that parents had complained about the teacher because their children had started talking at home about matters relating to sex and gender that they felt uncomfortable about. The school had not acted on the complaints because, they argued, its diversity and inclusion policies had not been violated.

3.4.2 Questions

1. For many years Mr. Start lived a quiet, professional life as a gay primary school ESL teacher. What environmental conditions allowed this to be the case?
2. Mr. Start had previously been asked by students about his wife and children, and he was able to routinely deflect these questions. How do you think he did this? What did he say?
3. Should Mr. Start have answered the eleven-year-old boy's questions about his partner's name and the length of their relationship?
4. Has Mr. Start's relationship with his students now changed in any way? Consider both his and the students' perspectives.
5. Did the school follow up appropriately regarding the parents' complaints about the social studies teacher? What are some reasons for your answer?

3.4.3 Research Topics

Discovering What Language Teachers Are Willing to Share About Their Private Lives

How much are teachers willing to reveal about their private lives to their students? Are they willing to share some aspects of their private lives more than others? Does teaching *language* students make a difference to what they are willing to share?

1. Gain access to an elementary or high school and invite a group of four to five language teachers to meet for a *focus group discussion* (M8).
2. Start the discussion by talking about issues of privacy and teacher professionalism in the workplace.
3. Be prepared with a list of topics for further discussion – for example, teaching younger learners, teaching language learners, the aspects of one's life one would want to keep private (e.g., sexuality, marital status, first name, nationality, family details, recreational activities).
4. Facilitate the discussion by staying on topic and ensuring that all participants have an opportunity to contribute. Record the focus group discussion.
5. Listen to the recording and highlight the main themes that emerged from the discussion.
6. Invite the four or five teachers for *one-on-one semi-structured interviews* (M9) to explore the main themes further. Record and analyze those interviews.
7. What aspects of their lives do teachers want to keep private? Why? Does working with language learners make a difference to their views about privacy? Does the age of the learners matter?

Inquiring into What Language Learners Would Like to Know About Their Teachers

Why do young language learners like their teachers? Why might they not like their teachers? What would they like to know about their teachers? Why?

1. Design a *narrative frame* (M16) that, when completed, will tell a story about a language learner's perceptions of their teacher and what they would like to know about them.
2. Include in the frame sentence starters like the following: "My English teacher is .... I like my teacher because .... But sometimes I don't like my teacher because .... What I would like to know about my English teacher is .... This is because .... My teacher never talks about .... I would like to know more about this because ...."
3. Leave a space at the end of the frame and invite respondents to write freely about what more they would like to know about their teacher.

4. Distribute the frame to as many young language learners as feasible in an institution, either in paper form or digitally. Collect the frames and analyze them thematically.
5. What common aspects of language teachers' lives are young learners interested in? Why is this the case?

3.4.4   Resources

Brett, A. (2024). Under the spotlight: Exploring the challenges and opportunities of being a visible LGBT+ teacher. *Sex Education*, *24*(1), 61–75. https://doi.org/10.1080/14681811.2022.2143344

Llewellyn, A. & Reynolds, K. (2021). Within and between heteronormativity and diversity: Narratives of LGB teachers and coming and being out in schools. *Sex Education*, *21*(1), 13–26. https://doi.org/10.1080/14681811.2020.1749040

Weng, Z., Troyan, F. J., Fernández, L., & McGuire, M. (2024). Examining language teacher identity and intersectionality across instructional contexts through the experience of *Perezhivanie*. *TESOL Quarterly*, *58*(2), 567–599. https://doi.org/10.1002/tesq.3237

3.5   Working as a NNEST at University

Keywords
- New Zealand and India
- University
- Non-native English-speaking teacher (NNEST)
- Reading and writing course
- Receiving poor student evaluations

3.5.1   Pre-reading Reflection

1. What do you understand by the concept "native-speakerism"? Can you give an example?
2. What are some ways of ensuring good attendance at university-level English classes? What can teachers do?
3. How important is a teacher's accent in the language learning classroom? Explain your answer.

Rakesh is an Applied Linguistics PhD student at a university in New Zealand. He was born in India and speaks Gujarati as his first language. Rakesh went to a university in Mumbai where he completed both his BA and MA through the medium of English. After completing his MA, he taught academic English at the same university on a part-time basis while also doing some private English tutoring for school students in the neighborhood where he lived. His desire is to eventually move into a full-time academic position at a university in India. But he realized a PhD was required for this type of university job. He also knew he needed to build up his research portfolio. Doing a PhD would equip him with the necessary research knowledge and skills, and he aimed to publish a few articles while still a PhD student. Rakesh worked hard and was ambitious.

He chose New Zealand as a study destination because of the reputation of the doctoral supervisors at the university he wished to attend. When he arrived and started his studies, he indicated to his supervisor that he intended to apply for a position as a GTA (Graduate Teaching Assistant) so that he could gain some teaching experience in another country and earn some money for living expenses. His supervisor recommended that it would be preferable to start working as a GTA in his second year of study, once he had settled down and made a solid start with his research. When the second year came around, Rakesh was appointed GTA on a large first-year academic reading and writing course. He would teach one of several streams of twenty-five students – all materials and lessons being designed by the lecturer in charge of the course.

The students were mostly international students from China. A handful of students came from Bangladesh, Brazil, and some of the Pacific Islands, for example. Rakesh enjoyed his classes. He found the assigned material easy to navigate – it was quite similar to what he had taught in India. He worked through the coursebook lesson by lesson, in line with what the other GTAs were doing. They met weekly to discuss progress and to plan ahead. Classroom interaction was satisfactory, although not as lively as Rakesh would have liked. After a few weeks he noticed that class attendance started to decline, but he had heard that this was typical of undergraduate classes at the university, so he was not too worried. Toward the end of the semester, however, only about seven or eight students showed up to class. Nevertheless, he pushed on till the end of the semester, working hard preparing and teaching all classes and grading assignments. On the whole, he felt reasonably pleased with how his first semester as a GTA turned out.

That is, until the students' teaching evaluations came in. Ratings on a range of teaching variables on Likert-type scales (e.g., preparedness, content knowledge, grading reliability) were about average, not particularly unusual for these types of academic English, skills-focused courses. But it was the open-ended comments section that both surprised and disappointed Rakesh. Three main criticisms were targeted at his teaching: (a) the students struggled to understand his accent, (b) they blatantly stated that they would have preferred a "native English speaker" as their teacher, and (c) they felt they were wasting their time attending class and decided to rely on the detailed coursebook instead. Some students commented that they liked Rakesh, that he had a good sense of humor, and that they could see he was a dedicated teacher, so there were certainly some positives in the student evaluations.

Like the other GTAs on the course, Rakesh has a one-to-one meeting planned with the course lecturer to review the evaluations. He is not entirely sure what the outcome will be, but one thing that concerns him is his continuing employment as a GTA.

3.5.2 Questions

1. Do you think Rakesh was qualified to teach the reading and writing course as a GTA?
2. Rakesh felt satisfied with his teaching at the end of the semester. Was he justified in feeling this way?
3. In the comments section of the teaching evaluations, the students had three main criticisms. Which of these represents most explicitly "native-speakerism"?
4. How do you think Rakesh responded emotionally to the students' teaching evaluations? Could his response affect his development or identity as a teacher?
5. What do you predict will be the outcome of Rakesh's meeting with the course lecturer? Give reasons for your answer.

3.5.3 Research Topics

Asking Language Learners About Their Perceptions of NNEST Characteristics

What specific NNEST characteristics are learners aware of in the classroom? Which of these characteristics do they believe make a difference to their learning? Which present challenges to them in their classroom learning?

1. Devise a list of about ten NNEST characteristics frequently discussed in the literature on this topic, such as accent, knowledge of grammar, teaching style, race, nationality.
2. Ask one or more classes of university-level language learners who have a NNEST as their English teacher or EAP (English for Academic Purposes) teacher to write a two-part *reflective journal* (M14) of about 400 words. In the first part (200 words), they write a reflection on their ideal NNEST, incorporating the ten characteristics on the list. Ask them to add and underline a further five. In the second part of the reflective writing (also 200 words), they describe, using the same fifteen words, a NNEST that presents challenges to their learning in the language classroom.

3. Collect the reflective journals and analyze them. An optional extension is to have a discussion with the students about the outcomes of the analysis; record the discussion.
4. What are the main characteristics of an ideal NNEST from the perspective of these students? What are the most significant challenges that a NNEST presents to their learning?

Examining Teachers' Responses to Student Evaluations

How do teachers respond to students' evaluations of their teaching? How seriously do they consider the students' comments? Do they act on what the students have to say by changing their practice?

1. Recruit up to five language teachers who teach EAP or any language at university level. Invite them to be *interviewed* (M9) individually about their experiences of being evaluated by their students in formal end-of-semester evaluation processes. The focus of the evaluation will be their teaching.
2. If they agree, ask them to bring along to the interview copies of any recent student evaluations for discussion during the interview.
3. Prepare a *semi-structured interview schedule* (M9) that examines the nature of evaluations the teachers typically undergo, their immediate emotional responses when receiving evaluation feedback, the way they reflect on the feedback, and how the feedback affects their future teaching practice.
4. Record the interviews and transcribe extracts that are relevant to the topic. Analyze the extracts in detail and compare any emerging themes across the five interviews.
5. What are some examples of the feedback students give in the evaluations? How seriously do the language teachers take this feedback and do they act on it? Do they respond emotionally to the students' comments?

3.5.4 Resources

Collins, J. (2021). Navigating the Contact Zone: Postcolonial graduate teaching assistants' experiences in a UK higher education institution. *Teaching in Higher Education*, *26*(3), 404–421. https://doi.org/10.1080/13562517.2021.1881774

Gibson, M. J. et al. (2022). Where's the harm? Screening student evaluations of teaching for offensive, threatening or distressing comments. *Australasian Journal of Educational Technology*, *38*(2), 35–48. https://doi.org/10.14742/ajet.6133

Ramjattan, V. A. (2023). The accent work of international teaching assistants. *TESOL Quarterly*, *57*(4), 1256–1281. https://doi.org/10.1002/tesq.3190

3.6 University Policy on Student–Teacher Sexual Relationships

Keywords
- Scotland and Malaysia
- Higher education
- Head of department manager
- Professor and PhD student
- Inappropriate sexual relationship

3.6.1 Pre-reading Reflection

1. Are sexual relationships between students and their teachers at university ever acceptable?
2. How should universities manage such relationships in the workplace?
3. When you think of a professor and a student being involved in a sexual relationship, what gender dynamics come to mind?

Professor Croburg is head of a teacher education department at a medium-sized university in a city in Scotland. The university is located downtown and has a large number of international students. There is a curriculum studies section in the department that focuses on multilingual and multicultural education, as well as several other sections including educational technology. The department is part of a larger school with disciplines that cover subjects like physical education and educational psychology. Over the years, Professor Croburg's department has shifted from being undergraduate heavy, with high numbers of students eager to become teachers, to being a department with a growing postgraduate student population.

Unexpectedly, Professor Croburg received an anonymous email about one of the PhD students in the educational technology program. It was long and allegedly written by the father of the student. It was quite difficult to follow the argument in the message, lacking as it was in coherence and grammatical accuracy. Professor Croburg suspected that it had been written by someone in a distressed emotional state. Exclamation marks and words written in CAPS were scattered throughout the message. The email message named Professor Morales in the curriculum studies section, and it appeared to be accusing him of having a sexual relationship with the email writer's daughter, the educational technology PhD student. The Chinese student was from Malaysia, and the "father" was writing from there.

Professor Croburg was shocked, and he did not know what to do next. He wasn't one hundred percent sure he understood the email message correctly. He could hardly confront Professor Morales about the situation if it were not true. And he certainly couldn't talk to the student. What he decided to do, immediately, by himself, and without telling anyone at this stage, was to consult the university policy on faculty–student (sexual) relationships: Were they allowed? He didn't know. What were managers to do if the relationships were exposed? He was sure there would be appropriate guidelines. To his dismay, he could not find any such policy. There were policies to do with respect and pastoral care for students, relating to their diversity, cultures, and wellbeing. He could also find nothing about how to approach accused faculty and what disciplinary outcomes might result if indeed they were found to have breached any code of conduct.

Professor Croburg knew that at some stage he would probably have to consult human resources (HR), but in the meantime he decided to speak confidentially to another senior member of the school, Dr. Shirley Manner, who had been at the university for a long time. Dr. Manner was in educational psychology and so not connected to either educational technology or curriculum studies, although she knew Professor Morales well, having worked on a number of committees with him. She had spent some time in Malaysia on a recent sabbatical and might therefore be able to provide some relevant cultural input. They met in Dr. Manner's office and as soon as Professor Croburg began talking about the email he had received, Dr. Manner interrupted him and said she had received the same message from the anonymous writer. She had not known what to do but was planning to talk to Professor Croburg in the next day or so. As far as she knew, sexual relationships were indeed allowed at the university, as long as both parties consented and there was no obvious conflict of interest – a student–supervisor relationship, for instance, which was not the case here. Professor Croburg and Dr. Manner wondered if anyone else had received the email message but had no idea how they would proactively find out.

3.6.2 Questions

1. Since the email message Professor Croburg received was anonymous, should he have paid any attention to it at all?
2. Professor Croburg decided it would not have been a good idea to approach the PhD student about the message. Do you think this was the right decision?
3. If in fact the student was having a sexual relationship with Professor Morales, and her father in Malaysia somehow found out about it, what is the moral dilemma in all of this?
4. How do you suggest Professor Croburg goes about finding out if other members, including students, of the department received the anonymous email?
5. Issues of power are evident in multiple ways in these various relationships – student, father, curriculum studies professor, head of department. Who do you think HR should focus on when trying to resolve the situation?

3.6.3 Research Topics

Analyzing Policies on Sexual Harassment in an Educational Institution
What happens when it is revealed that a teacher is stalking or sexually harassing a student in an educational institution? How is it investigated? Who investigates? What policies guide the investigation and the consequences?

1. Gain access to an institution that is willing to have its human resources policies reviewed. Read the catalog of policy documents and select those that are applicable to teacher–student relationships including stalking, sexual relations, sexual harassment, and bullying.
2. *Critically analyze the documents* (M6) in detail, aiming to understand the implications of the policy statements for both teachers and students. Consider the meaning of key words and phrases in the document. Are the policy statements equitable? Are students' safety and wellbeing considered? Are teachers protected?
3. After analyzing and understanding the relevant policy statements, arrange *an interview* (M9) with a senior member of human resources management. Verify your understanding of the policy statements with them, and ask them if they are willing to share any experiences of dealing with stalking or sexual harassment in the institution.
4. How do institutions manage issues of stalking and sexual harassment involving a teacher and a student? Are their policies equitable, unambiguous, and effective?

Exploring Language as Subject as a Catalyst for Intimate or Sexual Teacher–Learner Relationships
(1) Does language as subject make the teacher–learner relationship more conducive to developing into a sexual or intimate relationship? (2) Does language, more than other subjects, have something to do with it?

1. Using an *informal research approach* (M7), ask the above two questions (1–2) to language teacher colleagues, language learners, student teachers, and school administrators. Approach people that you feel comfortable talking to.
2. Focus on doing so as you go about your professional life over a specified period of time (a few weeks). Broaden the scope to as many educational workplaces as you have access to.
3. Each time after you talk to someone, write brief notes about the content of the conversation, outlining the main points discussed. Don't record the conversations.
4. Compile your notes into one document, with different sections for the different categories of respondents (teachers, learners, student teachers, administrators).

5. What are the respondents' answers to the two questions? What are the similarities and differences between the categories of respondents? Does the nature of language teaching and learning play a part in developing intimate or sexual learner–teacher relationships?

3.6.4 Resources

Bull, A., Bradley, A., Kanyeredzi, A., Page, T., Shi, C. C., & Wilson, J. (2023). Professional boundaries between faculty/staff and students in UK higher education: Students' levels of comfort with personal and sexualised interactions. *Journal of Further and Higher Education, 47*(6), 711–726. https://doi.org/10.1080/0309877X.2023.2226612

Lerman, L. G. (2006). First do no harm: Law professor misconduct toward law students. *Journal of Legal Education, 56*(1), 86–105. https://www.jstor.org/stable/42893958

Page, T. (2022). Sexual misconduct in UK higher education and the precarity of institutional knowledge. *British Journal of Sociology and Education, 43*(4), 566–583. https://doi.org/10.1080/01425692.2022.2057924

3.7 Being a Black Teacher in Japan

Keywords
- Japan and Jamaica
- Company-based school
- Business English teacher
- Black teacher's perceptions of workplace
- Unsure how to act on perceived racial barrier

3.7.1 Pre-reading Reflection

1. Think of a workplace or another setting where you stood out as different. How did it make you feel?
2. What is the most "monolingual," "monocultural" environment you have ever been in? Describe it.
3. Reflect on what you know about Japan or the Japanese educational system.

Elliot Sparrow, a Black male teacher, comes from Jamaica where his family has always lived. He now teaches English in a company-based school in Tokyo, Japan. He was recruited to Japan via an organization to teach in the elementary and secondary school system but after a very short time withdrew from his lower secondary school job due to what he considered to be poor treatment by the school's administration. The case revolved around pay and working hours, and his request to cancel his contract, especially since he further argued that his mental health was on the brink of being negatively impacted, was accepted. When he left his secondary school job, he didn't want to return to Jamaica because he had loved his short time living in Japan. He had only been in the country for about six months and felt he wanted to stay longer. He has now been teaching in the company-based school for one year. The company is a large technology business, and his job is to teach its employees business English. Most of his students are college graduates and early career businesspeople. With one or two exceptions, his classes are made up of male students. Mr. Sparrow has a BA in English and Psychology and a Postgraduate Diploma in Education. He taught in a Jamaican primary school for three years before moving to Japan.

During his first year of teaching in the company, Mr. Sparrow quickly acquired knowledge about teaching business English; he accessed materials from the internet, and other teachers at the school were very helpful with sharing resources. He likes the idea that his teaching is specifically focused on the work of his learners, in their actual workplace. With permission, he observes them working and he attempts to engage with them outside the classroom to talk about their work. This, however, does not happen very often. Even though the workers, his students, seem friendly enough, they do not appear keen to move beyond a very formal relationship. Mr. Sparrow is aware that this is not the case with some of the other teachers, who often join the students for drinks after work. He is never invited. Those teachers are typically white men from the US and Australia who are around the same age as he is.

In class, the students also seem somewhat distant. They are never impolite or badly behaved, and he hasn't yet experienced any of the micro-aggressions that some of his Jamaican colleagues have experienced in the school system, such as students asking them if they have buildings in their country, or if they have seen an elephant before, and then sniggering before they get an answer. Mr. Sparrow never feels threatened or racially abused in any way, but he does feel that his race is both "noticed" and a barrier to a more productive teaching and learning environment. He's not sure if his perceptions are justified and is therefore uncertain about whether he should say anything to his students or to his colleagues. Overall, he is satisfied with his job; the conditions are good, the students come to class, they are well behaved, and they do learn. He doesn't mind missing out on socializing with his colleagues but does believe that his teaching and his students' learning could be much better if their relationship was better. Mr. Sparrow is also wary of raising a racial issue if there isn't one in the first place, and he is worried about what the consequences of that might be.

3.7.2 Questions

1. Mr. Sparrow learned about teaching business English on the internet, and he received useful materials from his colleagues. What other types of induction might have been helpful for him for this specific company-based job?
2. What role could Mr. Sparrow's White colleagues play in helping him to integrate better into his school? Do you think they should play any part in doing so? Why don't they appear to be doing anything already?
3. Are there any obvious signs that Mr. Sparrow's students are being racist toward him?
4. Do you think Mr. Sparrow should talk to his students about his perception of the race relations that concern him? If you do, how should he go about doing so? If not, why not?
5. Considering Mr. Sparrow's overall teaching experiences in Japan so far – including withdrawing from the secondary school job and being concerned about possible "racial issues" in his current job – do you think there might be other things going on in his life?

3.7.3 Research Topics

Creating a Climate for Talking About Race and Identity in the Language Classroom

What prevents teachers of color and their learners from talking about race in the language classroom? How could teachers go about pedagogizing race and identity in the language classroom?

1. Collaborate with a language teacher who identifies as a teacher of color and who appears to be a person of color to others, including their learners. They should work in a context where their learners are not primarily students of color.
2. Together with the teacher, design an *action research* (M1) project that aims to establish a climate in the teacher's classroom where issues of race can be more openly and safely discussed, and where race and identity are incorporated into learning activities.
3. Begin by exploring what the current situation is regarding ideas about race and identity. In a writing lesson, ask the learners to write a paragraph about their experiences of using and observing vocabulary associated with race at school.
4. The teacher's personal observations of race and identity in their classroom can be included.

5. Drawing on the analysis of the writing and the teacher's observations, develop one activity, to be included as part of a larger lesson, that gently introduces talk about race.
6. After the activity, ask the teacher to have a whole-class discussion with their students about the activity, and their willingness to engage in similar activities about race and identity in the future.

Analyzing Job Advertisements for Signs of Racial Prejudice
Do international job searches discriminate against people of color in their job advertisements? In what ways might the design and word choice of job advertisements for private language schools discourage English teachers of color from applying?

1. Select multiple international ELT (English Language Teaching) or TESOL websites that have job advertising pages for private English language schools and universities (not elementary or high schools).
2. Search the job lists and download English teacher advertisements that show signs of discrimination against English teachers of color.
3. Categorize the advertisements by country.
4. Now do a close *critical discourse analysis* (M5) of the selected advertisements. Pay careful attention to the text – for example, requirements for first or native language speakers, or particular countries (e.g., US, UK, Australia).
5. Look at images of people and places, and the use of colors, objects, and spaces in the advertisements. How are they arranged? How do they interact with the text?
6. Are there common or blatant discursive methods for discriminating against English teachers of color in the advertisements? Are there national differences?

3.7.4 Resources

Cushing, I. (2023). "Miss, can you speak English?": Raciolinguistic ideologies and language oppression in initial teacher education. *British Journal of Sociology of Education*, *44*(5), 896–911. https://doi.org/10.1080/01425692.2023.2206006

Egitim, S. & Garcia, T. (2021). Japanese university students' perceptions of foreign English teachers. *English Language Teaching*, *14*(5), 13–22. https://doi.org/10.5539/elt.v14n5p13

Wong, W. & Ortega, Y. (2023). Addressing anti-Black racism in English language teaching: Experiences from duoethnography research. *TESOL Quarterly*, *58*(4), 1428–1459. https://doi.org/10.1002/tesq.3291

4 Language Assessment

Cases in this chapter

4.1	Pressure of External Public Examinations	*page* 112
4.2	Too Much Internal Assessment	115
4.3	Post-entry University Language Assessment	119
4.4	Immigration English Language Requirements	122
4.5	Deliberately Underperforming on University English Language Tests	126
4.6	Using AI in a University EAP Course	129
4.7	Students Copying Off Each Other and Learning	133

4.1 Pressure of External Public Examinations

Keywords
- Pakistan
- Higher secondary school
- English teacher
- Washback of external examinations
- Resistance to creativity in pedagogy

4.1.1 Pre-reading Reflection

1. What does "creativity" in language teaching and learning mean?
2. Have you been a student or worked in a school system that did external public examinations? What are your thoughts about such an examination process?
3. How powerful is the phenomenon of "washback" in language testing? Do you know what washback is?

Ms. Dania Lasi has been teaching English in a large urban higher secondary school in Karachi, Pakistan, for more than ten years. She loves it. The school is always busy – lots of students running around, special events taking place all the time, new teachers arriving in the English Department, professional development sessions, and occasionally visitors from other regions, even from overseas. Ms. Lasi always feels inspired; she is willing to learn, and lead workshops, she is constantly reading about English teaching, and she puts her hand up to take on new professional tasks in the department. Her colleagues often tell her to slow down – "relax and smell the roses," they jokingly say.

When the Covid-19 pandemic hit in 2020, further opportunities arose for Ms. Lasi to direct her energy toward new endeavors, particularly related to online teaching and learning. She did this with her usual enthusiasm and worked through the pandemic months with relative ease. During those same months, emerging technologies such as Zoom enabled language teachers around the world to meet online and share their experiences of classroom practices, both old and new. High-profile scholars, researchers, and teacher educators were also invited to present online webinars to global audiences, and these were typically free – all one needed was the internet and the time. Social media was awash with announcements, and Ms. Lasi made the most of her time at home to participate in as many of these sessions as she could. Anticipating a return to the classroom post-pandemic, she was particularly interested in webinars that focused on "creativity" in language teaching and learning. She had come across this concept in one of her online readings and wished to explore it some more. By the time schools re-opened she had attended several presentations on creativity-related topics and felt ready to implement some new ideas in her classes.

Ms. Lasi knew this would be challenging because of the examination-focused pedagogy prevalent in her school and her own classroom, and the phenomenon called "washback." Students put a lot of pressure on teachers to stick to what might be coming up in the external public examination, an examination very important for their futures. Ms. Lasi taught senior grades where this pressure from students (and parents) was even more intense. Nevertheless, she was determined to incorporate, in small portions, creative activities that she hoped would maintain her students' interest and also lead to better learning. Of course, she could not stray too far away from the examination content and topics because the students would notice immediately. And this turned out to be the case. Students, like their teachers, are very familiar with past exam papers and have scrutinized their contents. They expect this content to be taught in class. When Ms. Lasi introduced any variation, however small, in the form of a creative activity, students asked, "What does this have to do with the exam?" or "Will this be in the exam?"

Ms. Lasi tried to explain to the students that the activity was contributing to their English learning and developing new language skills, but they were not particularly interested in hearing that explanation. She could literally see the concerned, almost fearful, expression on their faces. The power of the external exam hanging over their heads is evident in everything the students do. This attitude is something that really displeases Ms. Lasi. She decided to pull back somewhat from slowly introducing creativity into her lessons. The last thing she wanted was for her students to be emotionally upset at this important stage of their school careers, or to receive complaints from their parents or the school administrators.

4.1.2 Questions

1. Ms. Lasi is clearly an energetic, enthusiastic teacher who is willing to learn and who wants her students to learn. How do you feel about her experience after reading this case?
2. Was Ms. Lasi's approach to introducing some "creativity" into her post-Covid lessons appropriate? Could she have gone about it differently?
3. Do you blame the students for reacting the way they did?
4. Was Ms. Lasi's response to their reaction the right one? Should she have persevered, or tried an alternative approach? What could she have done, for example?
5. What makes external English language examinations so powerful in the lives of high school students?

4.1.3 Research Topics

Gathering Ideas for Countering Examination-Focused Pedagogy
How can teaching activities or tasks that are not obviously examination-focused be incorporated into classroom language lessons? What might these activities or tasks look like?

1. Recruit a group of about ten language teachers who work in a context or institution (e.g., high school or university) that rigidly teaches an examination-focused language syllabus.
2. Ask the teachers to design a creative or communicative activity that might be incorporated into a traditional grammar, exam-oriented language lesson.
3. Create a WhatsApp (or similar) group for the ten teachers and ask them to voice message (about two to three minutes) a brief description of the activity.
4. Give all teacher participants a few days to listen to the messages.
5. Organize a *Zoom* (or similar) *focus group* (M8) with the teachers to *discuss the activities* (M13) – what they look like and how they might be used. Record the meeting.
6. What do the activities have in common? What chance do they have of being used successfully in an exam-oriented language lesson? What advice could be passed on to other teachers working in similar contexts?

Discovering Learners' Perceptions of Enjoyment in Grammar-Focused English Lessons
Do learners enjoy grammar-focused teaching and testing activities in traditional English classrooms? Do they believe these activities teach them how to speak English?

1. Work with a class of English learners that follows a traditional grammar-focused approach to teaching and testing.
2. Confirm through observation, document analysis, or a short interview with their teacher that this is indeed the case.
3. Design a *questionnaire* (M17) that lists ten to fifteen traditional grammar-focused activities, such as sentence transformation, fill-in-the-gap activities, translation, sentence error correction, and choosing the correct option. Include two or three communicative activities as well.
4. For each activity listed, provide two Likert-type scales; one that asks the respondents to rate their level of enjoyment of that activity, and the other that asks them if they believe the activity helps them learn to speak English.
5. Analyze the questionnaires by *counting the responses* (M4) to each option on the two rating scales. Convert to percentages.
6. Which activities do the learners enjoy the most? Generally, do they believe the grammar-focused activities help them to learn English? How do the communicative activities compare with the grammar-focused activities?

4.1.4   Resources

Rind, I. A. & Mari, M. A. (2019). Analysing the impact of external examination on teaching and learning of English at the secondary level education. *Cogent Education, 6*(1), 1574947. https://doi.org/10.1080/2331186X.2019.1574947

Tin, T. B. (2013). Towards creativity in ELT: The need to say something new. *ELT Journal, 67*(4), 385–397. https://doi.org/10.1093/elt/cct022

Yung, K. W.-H. (2023). Engaging exam-oriented students in communicative language teaching by "packaging" learning English through songs as exam practice. *RELC Journal, 54*(1), 280–290. https://doi.org/10.1177/0033688220978542

4.2   Too Much Internal Assessment

Keywords
- South Africa
- High school
- Teachers of English and Sesotho
- Proposed change to internal assessment
- Choosing different approaches

4.2.1 Pre-reading Reflection

1. Should teachers be given the opportunity to debate proposed curriculum changes in their schools?
2. How much language assessment is too much assessment?
3. Are end-of-course examinations appropriate for language learning?

Naledi and Jono are two language teachers at a high school in Bloemfontein, a city in central South Africa. Jono, who has been at the school for about three years, teaches English – most of his students speak a home language other than English but they follow the English Home Language curriculum. Naledi, who has been at the school for over twenty years, teaches Sesotho Home Language, a regional African language and home language to many students at the school. Both these languages are taught as additional languages too, but not by Naledi or Jono. Their school is a very good public school funded by the state. In their time at the school both Naledi and Jono have seen curriculum changes come and go, especially Naledi. The most recent proposed change is a scaled-down, non-official re-introduction of frequent and regular internal assessment associated with the outdated and abandoned outcomes-based education curriculum prevalent in the 1990s and early 2000s. The proposal is the idea of the head of the Languages Department and comes in the form of a discussion document, with a decision to be made within a month, after consultation. Naledi and Jono have a conversation about the proposal one day while driving to a professional development (PD) workshop in the city.

JONO: Too much work. Too much marking. Too much lesson interruption. Honestly, what are they thinking?

NALEDI: I remember this approach to assessment from years ago. Yes, yes, yes. A lot of work, but it meant the students were constantly monitored. We were ...

JONO: Outdated. I'm sorry, I've read about it, and the research shows that it does not really improve the language learning of students. In fact, it slows learning down!

NALEDI: Ah, where does it say that? I remember in my classes we used to have regular tests after every unit of work. The learners got to expect it and prepare for it. The process just became routine.

JONO: Well, I think routine is the problem. Assessments should be more than "routine." They should be timed appropriately and designed to fit the tasks and goals of the curriculum.

NALEDI: That's exactly what the proposal is trying to achieve – you've just come over to my side, hahaha.

JONO: No, I don't think you understand what I mean. Besides, it's not only about the tests or the assessments, it's about the whole curriculum, which means teaching methods as well, and the materials we use, and student motivation. It's also about how the learners feel, their emotions and their identities.

NALEDI: What are you saying now, identities?

JONO: Yes, in my MA we did a course on learner identity and how important it is to take identity into account in the classroom. We should consider who they are as learners, what their goals and needs are, where they come from, and who they want to be.

NALEDI: What on earth does all that have to do with assessment? If they want to pass and go to the next grade, they must study hard and focus on all the assessments. The more assessments the better. It gives them practice, right? Especially for the end-of-year exam. Of course, we must get to know our students – we learned that in college years ago, and I do. I try to learn all their names.

JONO: I still think we need to have fewer tests and other types of assessment, and to plan for them carefully. We don't want to over assess. I'm definitely not going to vote for the change back to the old-fashioned outcomes-based type of curriculum. I know it's not full-scale implementation they want but I think things are working pretty well at the moment. None of my students have failed in the past three years. So, I must be doing something right.

NALEDI: We're going to be late for the PD, Jono. You'd better drive faster.

4.2.2 Questions

1. Why do you think the head of department is wanting to go back to a previous approach to assessing languages in the school? What reasons might make sense in that particular context?
2. Naledi has fond memories of the proposed approach. What does she like about it?
3. Jono is clearly opposed to the proposal. What is his main objection? How could he be convinced to support the proposal?
4. Whose side are you on – Naledi's or Jono's? Give reasons for your answer.
5. Too much internal assessment is a complaint often directed at outcomes-based forms of education by teachers. List some of the problems with "too much assessment" and consider how teachers like Jono and Naledi could overcome them in their classrooms, while still achieving the goals of the curriculum.

4.2.3 Research Topics

Reflecting on Personal Experiences of Classroom Language Assessment

How were you assessed in the classroom as a learner of an additional language? What approaches did you prefer? Which of these approaches do you believe were most effective for your language learning?

1. Draw a *timeline* (M12) of your classroom language learning experiences, starting with when you first began learning an additional language and work through key moments of your language learning career.
2. Indicate on the timeline what assessments you underwent at these key moments (e.g., elementary school).

3. Write notes attached to the timeline about when the assessments took place, what approaches to assessment were used by your teachers, and how effective you believe they were. Which assessments did you prefer doing? Did some help you learn your additional language(s) more than others?
4. Meet with a language teacher and share your timeline and your ideas about classroom additional language assessment, based on your experience.
5. How does the teacher respond to your timeline and related ideas, according to their experience? Now, with this teacher, meet one more language teacher, and share both your timeline and your co-constructed ideas. What patterns of understanding are emerging about language assessment in the classroom?

Evaluating a School's Internal Language Assessment Policies and Practices
Do schools have internal language assessment policies and common practices? What is their rationale for having or not having them? What are teachers' attitudes to language assessment practices in their school?

1. Design a small-scale *ethnographic study* (M7) to be carried out in one language teaching program in a high school, a private language school, or a university language department.
2. Spend time in the school or language department, learning about its language assessment policies and practices, both at the program level and at the individual classroom level. Assign a definite period for the study (e.g., one month) to focus the data collection activities.
3. During this time, consult and review available *documentation* (M13), such as syllabus statements, program policies, exam papers, and teacher lesson plans.
4. Observe language classrooms as a participant observer to learn about what assessment takes place. Talk to the teachers after class about what you observed. Do they independently design assessments or are they following prescribed school guidelines?
5. Interview other language teachers to discover their attitudes to school-wide assessment requirements, if any, and their own assessment practices.
6. Analyze and triangulate the document, observation, and interview data.
7. What's going on with assessment in the school? Are the teachers free to assess as they see fit? Do the assessment practices in the school appear to be sound?

4.2.4 Resources

Lewkowicz, J. & Leung, C. (2021). Classroom-based assessment. *Language Teaching*, *54*(1), 47–57. https://doi.org/10.1017/S0261444820000506

Mufanti, R., Carter, D., & England, N. (2024). Outcomes-based education in Indonesian higher education: Reporting on the understanding, challenges, and support available to teachers. *Social Sciences & Humanities Open, 9*, 100873. https://doi.org/10.1016/j.ssaho.2024.100873

Schmidt, M. J. (2017). The perils of outcomes-based education in fostering South African educational transformation. *Open Journal of Political Science, 7*(3), 368–379. https://doi.org/10.4236/ojps.2017.73030

4.3 Post-entry University Language Assessment[1]

Keywords
- New Zealand
- University
- English language needs assessment
- English support at university
- Discriminatory policies

4.3.1 Pre-reading Reflection

1. Many universities globally are shifting to English medium of instruction (EMI). Why do you think this is so?
2. What is the most important kind of English language support EMI universities should offer their students?
3. Should students be screened based on their English proficiency *pre*-entry to EMI universities?

Aotearoa University is a large urban university in New Zealand. English is the medium of instruction for all subjects. The majority of the 20,000 students at the university would claim to be English first language speakers, but many others are international students or immigrant-background students who speak first languages other than English.

In recent years, there has been growing discontent with the English proficiency of these latter groups of students. This has come from two directions: (1) The students do not feel supported. They struggle to understand the English they hear in lectures, they do not feel confident enough to contribute to small-group discussions, they believe they are being penalized for their poor academic writing, and they do not know who to go to for English language support.

---

[1] This case draws on the research of Read and von Randow (2013). See the full reference in the Resources below the case.

(2) The lecturers complain about the poor quality of these students' writing. They claim they are there to teach content, not to correct English mistakes, or to teach grammar and spelling. The lecturers say students do not engage in classroom discussions. They too do not know who to send the students to for help with their English.

Academic authorities at Aotearoa University started to listen to the concerns of both students and lecturers, and decided they needed to do something about it. Their first thoughts turned to testing – testing the English skills of international and immigrant-background students entering the university, particularly those who identified as speakers of English as an additional language (i.e., not English first language speakers). Initially, they thought of testing students prior to accepting them; a kind of gatekeeping exercise. But this was very soon changed to post-acceptance "assessment." Assessment was considered a better term to use since it did not mean assigning students a grade or passing/failing them. Instead, the assessment would measure what type of English help students needed (e.g., reading, writing). Based on the assessment, students would be directed to appropriate support.

An English assessment unit was established at the university, staffed with a manager, qualified assessors, and language support personnel. Appropriate workshops, courses, a self-access center, and online English language learning materials were developed over time. Depending on the outcome of students' assessments, they would be offered the appropriate kind and level of support. Not long after the assessment program got going, a few concerns began to emerge. The main one had to do with who was required to do the English assessment. All students who had not previously studied in an English-medium setting (at high school for incoming undergraduates and at university for postgraduates) were already required to show evidence of an approved level of English proficiency – for example, results on the IELTS (International English Language Testing System) or TOEFL (Test of English as a Foreign Language) tests – before acceptance into programs at Aotearoa University. But now, on acceptance, they were required to take the university English assessment as well. Students who had previously studied in English (i.e., mostly English first language speakers) were not required to undergo further English assessment at Aotearoa University. This was perceived to be unfair.

A second major, unresolved concern relates to the perception of the status of the assessment. Even though students do not receive a grade for the assessment – it is not a test with a score that appears on the student's academic record – there remains some uncertainty about the goals of the assessment and the consequences of being diagnosed as needing support. Students feel threatened by the obligatory nature of the assessment and do not all fully understand why they are required to do it while some other students do not, especially since they have met all the entry requirements of the university.

4.3.2 Questions

1. What did the university get right and what did it get wrong when planning for and establishing the assessment regime?
2. Why do you think the university decided not to test students before admitting them to the university? That is, why did they not measure their English language skills to determine if they would be accepted into the university?
3. If you were working as an English language adviser in the assessment unit, what do you imagine your job would entail?
4. How might terms such as "English first language" and "English as an additional language" be variously interpreted by students and lecturers in the university?
5. Regarding English language assessment at Aotearoa University, what do you feel is the next major decision the university has to make?

4.3.3 Research Topics

Exploring Potential Alternative and Innovative Post-entry Diagnostic English Language Assessments for University

How innovative are post-entry English language assessments at university? Do they include virtual simulations or gamification in their battery of tests? What constraints prevent such innovation?

1. Contact both the manager and test developer in the language assessment unit of a university that conducts post-entry diagnostic English language assessments. Connect with another type of institution that conducts post-entry English assessments if more easily accessible.
2. Obtain their permission to examine samples of the diagnostic English language assessments that are used in the institution. Ask the manager and the test developer about the testing principles that are considered when designing these assessments. Do they consider the assessments to be relatively traditional or innovative?
3. *Interview* (M9) the manager and test developer together to discuss any recent and potential innovations in their assessment development, and ask specifically about, for example, virtual interactive simulations, gamification, and adaptive challenges (tasks that adjust in difficulty based on the test-taker's performance).
4. Have they considered such innovations? Have they implemented any innovations similar to these? What are possible institutional or testing-related constraints that might prevent these innovations?

Investigating Postgraduate University Students' Emotions About Pre-entry Testing

How do current postgraduate university students feel about having been required to take pre-entry, gatekeeping English tests such as IELTS and TOEFL? What emotions did they experience before and after taking the test? What were the reasons for their emotions?

1. Recruit five postgraduate students at an EMI (English medium instruction) university who were required to take a pre-entry English test (e.g., IELTS or TOEFL) as a condition of acceptance.
2. Design a *structured interview schedule* (M9) of about ten questions and conduct the interview orally with each of the participants. Ask the same questions in the same order, and elicit only brief answers.
3. The questions should cover topics such as: why they were required to do a pre-entry English test, their feeling about having to do it, how they felt afterwards, their attitudes toward the university pre-test requirements, and how they feel now.
4. Drawing on the answers, construct an *anonymous questionnaire* (M17) on Google Forms or Qualtrics (or similar) to explore these topics in further depth and with a wider group of postgraduate student respondents from the same institution (or beyond).
5. Do the students agree with the university pre-entry English language testing policy? How did doing the test make them feel? Do they now believe that the test served its purpose?

4.3.4 Resources

Green, J. H., Davis, C., Harmes, M., Judith, K., & Weideman, A. (2025). Using a five-phase applied linguistics design to develop a contextualized academic literacy placement test for pre-university pathway students. *Literacy Research and Instruction*, *64*(2), 229–255. https://doi.org/10.1080/19388071.2024.2340031

Read. J. & von Randow, J. (2013). A university post-entry English language assessment: Charting the changes. *International Journal of English Studies*, *13*(2), 89–110. https://doi.org/10.6018/ijes.13.2.185931

Ruegg, R., Hoang, H., & Petersen, N. (2024). The influence of English language proficiency test scores on the academic success of ESL undergraduate students. *Educational Research and Evaluation*, *29*(3–4), 111–129. https://doi.org/10.1080/13803611.2024.2314533

4.4 Immigration English Language Requirements

Keywords
- New Zealand
- Private language lessons
- Immigrant learners
- Residence and working visa requirements
- Classroom friendship dynamics

4.4 Immigration English Language Requirements

4.4.1 Pre-reading Reflection

1. Are you aware of any English language proficiency requirements as a condition for obtaining a visa to live or work in a country?
2. What do you think is the most difficult part of living in a country for immigrants who have limited proficiency in the majority language of that country?
3. What situations might lead language teachers to give informal lessons to friends or members of their family?

George worked as an English teacher in Asia for five years when he was in his late twenties and early thirties. In 2015, he returned to his home in Auckland, New Zealand, and decided to pursue a PhD in applied linguistics at one of the local universities. During this time, he actively took part in football games with a group of people from the former-Yugoslav community, to which he also belonged, having emigrated to New Zealand at the age of twelve with his family.

Knowing about George's experience in English teaching, some of his football friends approached him about giving them evening English lessons. They were all recent immigrants who needed high IELTS test scores to secure their residence or work visas. They also wanted to improve their English for business purposes. All were tilers who were either self-employed or they worked for other members of the former-Yugoslav community in the city. The group was made up of six learners, most of whom were in their late thirties and early forties, with their English level ranging from beginner to intermediate. They paid George to teach them twice a week for two hours after work. The group particularly enjoyed having George as their teacher because of their existing personal relationship, and because they shared the same native language, which came in handy when pedagogical explanations in English were too difficult. The shared language was also useful when it came to interrupting lessons to tell jokes and boost the morale of the group when they found the lessons too difficult.

Despite finding satisfaction working with this group, George felt ambivalent about several aspects related to teaching and learning. He strongly desired to help the group as much as possible, knowing that their English proficiency would greatly impact their quality of life and their future personal and career goals in New Zealand, but the lessons did not always go according to plan: some of the students often sabotaged George's attempts to encourage an English-only policy during lessons; the informal nature of the lessons prevented George from holding the students to account for their learning habits; and the previous lack of formal education of some of the students held back the rest of the class.

George sympathized with the group's challenges. The required high IELTS score weighed heavily on their minds, as most of them desperately wanted to remain in New Zealand with their families. He thought it unfair that they were initially granted work visas based on their trade skills, but in order to remain in the country were expected to improve their English proficiency beyond what their jobs required. They were, furthermore, set unrealistic time limits in which to achieve the required test scores. In addition, their day-to-day exposure to English in the real world was minimal since they gravitated toward their local diaspora community in their free time and at work, where their time on building sites consisted of physical work that afforded them very few opportunities to participate in English conversations.

The private lessons with George continued for over a year. The students insisted on continuing, despite George feeling increasingly worried that their slow progress may set them up to fail. He was very aware that the stakes were high for the learners and their families.

4.4.2 Questions

1. What is your opinion of countries, like New Zealand and Australia, requiring high scores on standardized English tests as a prerequisite for obtaining work or residence visas?
2. Where do you think immigrant workers might voice their concerns if immigration policy regarding language assessment suddenly becomes unjustifiably harsh? Do they have a voice in this situation?
3. How might the lack of prior formal education affect this immigrant group of learners when learning English? How could George address this issue?
4. Should George have taken on the task of teaching this group? What are some of the ethical dilemmas associated with his decision?
5. Knowing that students are under pressure to learn a language, with real-life plans and ambitions at stake, can also put pressure on teachers. How do you think George feels about continuing as this group's teacher? For his own good, should he continue?

4.4.3 Research Topics

Investigating Prospective Immigrants' Perceptions of English Proficiency Test Requirements

How do prospective (pre-departure) immigrants feel about having to take an English proficiency test as part of their visa application process? What do they know about such a test? How do the language requirements impact their aspirations and integration prospects?

4.4 Immigration English Language Requirements

1. Locate prospective immigrants who are planning to move to an English-speaking dominant country that requires an English proficiency test such as IELTS as part of their visa application process.
2. *Interview* (M9) those that are available and willing to talk about their pre-test expectations and perceptions.
3. Prepare a semi-structured interview schedule that asks about their attitudes, feelings, and their perceptions of the test and about its relevance to their future lives as immigrants. Engage in open conversation and explore their pre-immigration journey and post-immigration expectations in depth.
4. What role does the test play in their personal and professional aspirations? Do they believe it is fair or necessary? Have they tried to avoid being tested?

Reviewing Language Test Requirements and Examining Immigrants' Perceptions of These
What are the English proficiency requirements for entry to English dominant countries? What is the countries' rationale for these requirements? What do settled immigrants think of the requirements and their rationale?

1. *Review* (M6) the English proficiency requirements of two or three English dominant countries, such as Canada, Australia, and the UK. These are available on the internet. Note what English tests are required. What is the rationale behind the English language testing requirements?
2. Write a brief statement about common requirements from the two or three countries, and then compile a composite list of reasons for the testing.
3. Present this list to about ten recent immigrants who have settled in English dominant countries. This can be done face-to-face or virtually. Ask them to comment on both the requirements and their experiences of taking the English test. Work through the composite list one by one and ask for their response.
4. What was their experience of taking the English test? Do they see any value in taking the test for their post-immigration lives?

4.4.4 Resources

Byrne, B. (2017). Testing times: The place of the citizenship test in the UK immigration regime and new citizens' responses to it. *Sociology, 51*(2), 323–338. https://doi.org/10.1177/0038038515622908

Wardrip, P. & Gomez, L. (2024). Exploring teachers' knowledge of students' friend networks: What do they know and how do they use it for instruction. *Journal of Research in Innovative Teaching & Learning, 17*(1), 83–99. https://doi.org/10.1108/JRIT-08-2022-0052

Yao, D. & Wallace, M. P. (2021). Language assessment for immigration: A review of validation research over the last two decades. *Frontiers in Psychology, 12*, 773132. https://doi.org/10.3389/fpsyg.2021.773132

4.5 Deliberately Underperforming on University English Language Tests

Keywords
- Bangladesh
- University
- Mandatory English learning
- Placement testing
- Strategic underperformance

4.5.1 Pre-reading Reflection

1. Are you aware of any universities where successful study of an additional (second or foreign) language is a requirement for graduation?
2. Some students under-report their language proficiency level when enrolling in language courses at university. Why would they do this?
3. Imagine being in your third year at university and suddenly being told you have to complete your degree with your second language as medium of instruction.

At a university college in Bangladesh, new entrants are required to sit an English language placement test so that they can be placed at the appropriate proficiency level in an English language course. The course consists of five proficiency levels. Once a student is placed at the appropriate level, they are required to attend classes regularly, complete all assessments, and obtain a pass mark for that level in order to qualify for their degree at the end of their tertiary education. Students are also encouraged by the university to enroll in the remaining higher levels once they have completed the mandatory level. As an incentive, the university offers a certificate to those who complete the fifth level.

The course aims to improve the English language proficiency of students by the time they graduate. The university has made it mandatory for students to complete the level at which they are placed because it believes some level of English language proficiency is required for graduates to compete in the job market and to secure well-paid employment. However, it has made only one level compulsory to ensure that students are not pressured too much since they are already burdened with heavy workloads in their main subjects, which they follow in the Bangla medium of instruction.

The course has been running for five years and during this time English language teachers have realized that some students may be deliberately underperforming on the placement test held at the time of university entrance. For example, teachers have observed that the majority of students placed at the lowest proficiency level often score very high marks on the assessments. Also, a few students have admitted to their teachers that they did not do their best on the placement test because they wanted to be placed at the lowest level possible. When teachers inquired about the reason for this, some students told them that they wanted to reduce their study workload at the university, and being placed at a lower proficiency level than their actual proficiency meant they had to work less hard in the English course. Others stated that it is because they are guaranteed a pass mark in a class which is at a level below their actual proficiency. Teachers have noticed that every year around seventy to eighty percent of students fall into the two lower proficiency levels while the rest are distributed among the three higher proficiency levels. They also noticed that only about 10 percent are motivated to go on to complete the higher levels that are not mandatory. However, the university does not know how many students tend to underperform on the placement test and how serious this problem is.

Teachers feel that the course objectives are not achieved if students underperform on the placement test. The reasons provided by the students also indicate that they are not motivated to improve their English language proficiency. Instead, they merely wish to pass the mandatory level to obtain their degrees. Some teachers believe that, to resolve the issue, more than one level should be made mandatory. Others feel that none of the levels should be mandatory and that this would ensure that only students who are truly motivated to learn English would take the course.

4.5.2 Questions

1. Should English language courses be mandatory at a university such as this one in Bangladesh?
2. Do you think the university should investigate the problem of students underperforming on the placement test? Give a reason for your answer.
3. The university is keen to improve the English language proficiency of its students so as to ensure good employment opportunities for them once they graduate. However, the English language learning objectives of the students, as revealed to their teachers, do not align with the university's goals. Why do you think this is the case?
4. What are your views about the two solutions offered by the teachers to solve deliberate underperformance on the placement test?

5. If the university finds substantial evidence of widespread underperformance, it would immediately begin work to solve the problem. What could the university do to stop students from underperforming on the placement test?

4.5.3 Research Topics

Investigating Imagined Language Identities of EMI Students at University
How do non-native English-speaking students at an EMI university perceive their identities? Are they primarily content subject students or English language learners? How do they imagine their professional identities in the future after university?

1. Select a group of up to twenty non-native English-speaking students at an EMI university. They should be nearing the end of their studies (e.g., final year).
2. Gather the students together in one setting. Provide them with two blank *body outline silhouettes* (M2) on two separate pieces of paper. Have available a range of colored pens.
3. Invite them to use different colors to represent different languages on the silhouettes, and to include shapes, drawings, and words on or near the bodies.
4. One of the silhouettes is how they currently perceive their identities as EMI students at university. Which languages are important to them? What do they use those languages for? What is the purpose of English in their student lives?
5. The second body silhouette is to show, again using colors, shapes and words, how they see themselves in their imagined future lives after university.
6. What changes from the first silhouette? What role does English play in their lives pre- and post-graduation? How do they see their future selves?

Probing Lecturers' Language Use Strategies When Setting Assessments in EMI Contexts
In what ways do EMI university lecturers consider the English language proficiency of their content subject students when they design assessments?

1. Meet with a content subject lecturer (e.g., science, history) who teaches in an EMI university with non-native English-speaking students.
2. Before the meeting, ask them to bring along samples of their assessments such as class tests, assignments, and end-of-course examinations.
3. *Interview* (M9) the lecturer, focusing on whether and, if so, how they consider the English language skills of their students when they plan, design, and conduct class assessments.

4. Together *analyze the sample assessments* (M6) for evidence of the lecturer's claims. Ask the lecturer to point to how their design takes into account the English ability of their students.
5. Repeat the interview and assessment analysis with a lecturer of another content subject in the same university.
6. Are the lecturers more interested in their content subject than in their students' English language use and learning? How do their awareness and attitudes relate to their assessment practices?

4.5.4   Resources

Alam, M. R., Ansarey, D., Abdul Halim, H., Rana, M. M., Khan Milon, M. R., & Mitu, R. K. (2022). Exploring Bangladeshi university students' willingness to communicate (WTC) in English classes through a qualitative study. *Asian-Pacific Journal of Second and Foreign Language Education*, *7*(2), 1–17. https://doi.org/10.1186/s40862-022-00129-6

Chowdhury, R. & Kabir, A. H. (2014). Language wars: English education policy and practice in Bangladesh. *Multilingual Education*, *4*(21), 1–16. https://doi.org/10.1186/s13616-014-0021-2

Liao, Y.-F. (2022). Using the English GSAT for placement into EFL classes: Accuracy and validity concerns. *Language Testing in Asia*, *12*(31), 1–23. https://doi.org/10.1186/s40468-022-00181-6

4.6   Using AI in a University EAP Course

Keywords
- United Kingdom
- University
- English for Academic Purposes course
- ChatGPT incorporated into instruction
- Resistance from experienced teachers

4.6.1   Pre-reading Reflection

1. Artificial intelligence (AI) is having a big impact on teaching and learning in higher education. In what ways?
2. Describe how you have engaged with AI in your professional life? If you haven't, do you plan to in the future?
3. Should students be allowed to use ChatGPT (or similar) in examinations?

Introduction to English for Academic Purposes (IEAP) is a general EAP course offered to undergraduate and coursework postgraduate students at a medium-sized university in England. It is credit bearing and runs for a full semester. The course focuses on all four language skills (reading, writing, speaking, and listening), although writing tends to be emphasized more. The skills are typically integrated into lessons and course materials, and various multimodal and mobile technologies such as Zoom, Canvas, social media, and YouTube are also used for teaching and managing the course. The course has been offered for many years and continually undergoes curriculum development. It is popular with students and thus has several streams running each semester, each consisting of about twenty students. It is available only to speakers of English as a second language, who are mainly international students.

There is no final examination. Students are assessed regularly throughout the course on multiple assignments, from summarizing tasks, to writing notes after listening to a lecture, reading comprehension exercises, writing from sources tests, and oral presentations. The assessment regime has always been successful; assessment tasks and grading systems are evaluated by students every semester and moderated by professional academics at other universities on an annual basis. These smooth-running assessment practices were suddenly unsettled when the AI tool ChatGPT became "a thing," as one of the teachers put it. From not knowing anything about ChatGPT, within a few months teachers became aware of multiple versions of similar AI tools, and realized that they could have an effect on their teaching, particularly on how they assess their students. Sure enough, it didn't take long for the IEAP teachers to suspect that work submitted for assessment was being generated by ChatGPT. Not only writing tasks, but the way some project proposals had been formatted, for example, appeared different from the usual submissions.

Teachers were forced to re-think how they were going to continue assessing their students in the future. Their immediate reaction was to absolutely forbid them from using any form of AI in their assignments. This rule was clearly stated in course documentation, and teachers of all streams were told to speak to their students in class and online about the issue, including both learning and moral implications. Students seemed to accept the new assessment processes, with many admitting that they did not know much about ChatGPT, although they had heard about it. Changing the assignment tasks, however, started to involve a lot of work for the teachers – assignments across all the streams had to be aligned and so much consultation was involved even for the smallest change. Bit by bit the assignments changed, and it took some creativity to ensure that ChatGPT could not be used in any way to help students with the assignments. At the same time, perhaps at a faster pace, the students began to learn more about AI tools, and it was clear to the teachers that they were now using them regularly in their work, not only for assessed assignments. The team of IEAP teachers over time realized that their approach was probably not the right one, and so decided to investigate ways in which they, too, could use ChatGPT in their teaching, and even allow students to constructively make use of it when doing their assignments. This would take further professional development on their part, and they called in experts to advise them in a series of workshops.

However, not all were happy with these changes. Some of the more experienced teachers, who had been teaching the IEAP course for many years, felt strongly that it was not appropriate in an academic English course to use anything "artificial" to replace genuine skills development. "We wouldn't be teaching them to function in their other university courses," they argued. They maintained that students should use their own knowledge of academic reading, writing, listening, and speaking.

4.6.2 Questions

1. What might some of the "moral implications" be of using AI tools for assessed assignments without permission?
2. Was the teachers' later change in approach to allow the use of ChatGPT in assignments in the IEAP course a good one?
3. Do you agree with some of the teachers who commented, "We wouldn't be teaching them to function in their other university courses"? Give a reason for your answer.
4. Is the dilemma regarding the use of AI tools for assessment the same for *language*-oriented learning and the learning of other subjects at university (e.g., history, biology)?
5. Does the fact that the students in the IEAP course are speakers of English as a second language have any bearing on your answers to the questions above? How would your answers be different if the course students were speakers of English as a first language?

4.6.3 Research Topics

Exploring Writing Teachers' Challenges with AI in Assessments
What challenges have university writing teachers (or language teachers who also teach writing) recently experienced with AI in their classroom assessments? How have they tried to address them?

1. Engage with five writing teachers. Ask them to list up to five challenges they have recently experienced with students using AI in their writing assessments (e.g., creating text, editing text). For each challenge, ask them to describe briefly how they have attempted to address that challenge.
2. Collect the responses from the teachers and analyze them for common themes. Compile a list of common challenges and common ways to address them.
3. Invite the teachers to *meet in-person or virtually* (M8) for an hour to discuss the common themes. Facilitate the discussion in such a way that all participants contribute equally. Record the discussion.
4. How are writing assessments being affected by AI? What are the teachers' major concerns? How are they responding?
5. Can the outcomes of the discussion be used to make recommendations to teachers, or to a program? Can they be presented at a seminar or conference?

Identifying Academic English Writing Students' Awareness of the Potential of AI

Are writing students aware of how AI could help them improve their writing? Do they know when and how to use AI in their writing courses? Have they considered ethical issues when it comes to writing assessments?

1. Consult the web pages of three or four of the many AI writing assistance tools now freely available. If you are unsure about where to begin, ask an expert in the field about which tools are the most popular with writing teachers and students.
2. *Review* (M6) the capabilities of these tools that are most relevant to an academic English writing course or program that you are familiar with.
3. Compile a list of features that the tools claim help writers improve their writing, such as brainstorming, composing, editing, summarizing, and proofing.
4. Design a *survey* (M17) to be distributed to the writing students in a class or program that you have access to.
5. List each feature on the survey and for each of them ask students on Likert-type scales (a) to indicate how aware they are of that feature being helpful for improving writing, and (b) the extent of their use of that feature in their writing course.
6. In an open-ended question, ask the respondents to comment on any ethical issues which might arise when using AI assistance for writing assessments.
7. Do students use AI assistance in academic English courses? Do they believe it helps them improve their writing? Do they reveal any ethical concerns about using (or potentially using) AI in their assessments?

4.6.4 Resources

Barrot, J. S. (2023). Using ChatGPT for second language writing: Pitfalls and potentials. *Assessing Writing*, *57*, 100745. https://doi.org/10.1016/j.asw.2023.100745

Wise, B., Emerson, L., Van Luyn, A., Dyson, B., Bjork, C., & Thomas, S. E. (2024). A scholarly dialogue: Writing scholarship, authorship, academic integrity and the challenges of AI. *Higher Education Research & Development*, *43*(3), 578–590. https://doi.org/10.1080/07294360.2023.2280195

Yang, H., Gao, C., & Shen, H.-Z. (2024). Learner interaction with, and response to, AI-programmed automated writing evaluation feedback in EFL writing: An exploratory study. *Education and Information Technologies*, *29*, 3837–3858. https://doi.org/10.1007/s10639-023-11991-3

4.7 Students Copying Off Each Other and Learning

Keywords
- Zimbabwe
- Lower secondary school
- Teacher of Shona language
- Students copying written homework
- Revising and learning while copying

4.7.1 Pre-reading Reflection

1. Why do writing and grammar rather than listening and speaking get so much more attention in language learning classrooms?
2. How might a student benefit from copying writing assignments off another student?
3. Does it make a difference if the writing is a graded assessment?

Mrs. Onai teaches Shona, a major Zimbabwean language, to lower secondary grades at a private school in Harare, the capital city of the country. Her students are first-language speakers of Shona, and they study the language as a school subject. They find it very difficult, for a number of reasons; dialectal variation means that there are vocabulary differences, phonology can also vary between dialects, some vocabulary and idioms in textbooks and other written materials represent older forms of the language unfamiliar to young users, and, as many students say, "the grammar is complicated." Mrs. Onai hears complaints about the language from students all the time. They believe it is hard to study and they don't enjoy it. Most are doing the subject because they have no choice. Mrs. Onai is aware of this and tries to make the classes as interesting as possible. She explains the linguistic variation and builds discussion of the differences into her lessons, even though it is not required in the syllabus.

All skills are covered in the syllabus, but the emphasis is on writing and grammatical knowledge, reflecting the content of the end-of-year examinations. The study of literature also makes up a large component of the syllabus. To prepare for the exams, Mrs. Onai sets her students quite a bit of writing to do during the year. This is usually assigned as homework, although some class time is also set aside for writing work. The pen and paper written homework is typically assessed and given a mark. The marks are added up to produce an average coursework mark that counts toward the overall grade for the subject at the end of the year. Sometimes the homework writing is connected to the literature being studied (e.g., a character description, or a review of a poem), or it consists of short paragraphs, or more usually, a short composition.

The quality of writing in the students' compositions, not surprisingly, varies over the year, indicating either improvement in writing skills, or, in a negative direction, disinterest in a topic or lack of trying very hard. This is to be expected, and Mrs. Onai is used to seeing such swings over the course of her teaching career. With one class, however, she noticed a different pattern emerging. The content of some of the students' compositions was remarkably similar, and she suspected that they may be copying off each other, or at least sharing their ideas about what to write. This only happened with a few pairs of students but enough for her to become suspicious. Were they collaborating to produce one composition and then varying their own before submitting it to make it look different from the other? Was one student's composition copied by another without their knowledge? Did they discuss what to write and then write independently? These questions worried Mrs. Onai, and although she was pretty sure that some form of cheating was going on in this class, she felt she couldn't make accusations without any proof.

She noticed one other thing that made her hesitate about acting too soon. Where students were making changes to the writing to conceal any copying (if they were), they were, besides other changes, targeting the vocabulary and grammatical forms that represented dialectical or stylistic variation (old versus modern usage). Mrs. Onai thought this showed some initiative, and also some learning. It meant that if they knew how to make the changes to the writing, they must know about the variations and what they mean. The students were actually doing something constructive to produce their compositions, even if they did work "collaboratively" with another student. Mrs. Onai decided not to intervene at this point, and rather to observe what happened the next time homework compositions were submitted for marking.

4.7.2 Questions

1. Compulsory language study at school can lead to attitude problems with learners. Is Mrs. Onai's approach to dealing with the students' attitudes appropriate? What more could she do?
2. Should the homework compositions always be assessed, i.e., given a mark or grade?
3. How might Mrs. Onai productively use collaborative writing as an approach in her classes? What would this achieve?
4. Do you agree with Mrs. Onai's view that her students are learning by copying?
5. Do you think Mrs. Onai should have investigated possible cheating?

4.7.3 Research Topics

Understanding Students' Perceptions of Required Collaborative Writing Assessments

How do students react to compulsory collaborative writing assessments? What do they perceive as their benefits? What pressures do they feel when required to collaborate?

1. Identify a language learning class at senior high school or undergraduate university level.
2. Check with their teacher that the students do collaborative writing assessments, that is, where pairs or groups of students work together (e.g., peer drafting, peer editing) to produce a joint or individual piece of writing for assessment purposes.
3. Select five students or ask for volunteers who are willing to share digitally their experiences of collaborative writing for assessment. The focus will be on their feelings about having to do compulsory collaborative assessments, and what they believe their benefits are.
4. Arrange to meet each of the five students individually on a digital platform such as Zoom.
5. Before the meeting, ask them to prepare a *multimodal story* (M12, M16) consisting of one or more of PowerPoint (or similar), text, photos, visuals, and writing products, for sharing on screen during the meeting.
6. When you meet, talk briefly about the purpose of the investigation, and then let the students share the screen. Record their presentation.
7. What do they like and dislike about compulsory collaborative writing assessments? What benefits and tensions do they experience.

Probing Language Teachers' Attitudes to Cheating on Class Assignments

How do language teachers try to prevent cheating on class assignments? What do they do when they discover cheating? What do they understand by "cheating"?

1. In a language teaching school, department, or program, contact the team of language teachers and ask to meet with them as a group.
2. Explain to the group the topic to be probed, that is, their attitudes to students cheating in their language classes, what they understand by cheating, how they prevent it, and what they do when they discover cheating.
3. Before the meeting, design a lengthy, multi-part *narrative frame* (M16) that covers these areas in detail. At the start of the frame, insert a blank space for the teacher respondents to introduce themselves, and at the end of the frame, insert another blank space for the teachers to add comments that might not have been covered in the frame.
4. At the meeting with the teachers, give clear instructions for how to complete the narrative frame, and after the meeting ask the teachers to return the digital frame to you.
5. Invite them to attach any assignments that illustrate points they raise in the frame.
6. Analyze the frames thematically, sentence starter by sentence starter, and by overall trends.
7. What does cheating mean for these teachers? Do they try to prevent it in the design and implementation of their assignments? What happens when they discover cheating?

4.7.4 Resources

Arellano, W. M. B., Galarza Parra, J. N., Villavicencio Reinoso, J. M., & Quito Ochoa, J. F. (2024). A study on academic dishonesty among English as a foreign language students. *Heliyon, 10*(13), e33876. https://doi.org/10.1016/j.heliyon.2024.e33876

Sevnarayan, K. & Maphoto, K. B. (2024). Exploring the dark side of online distance learning: Cheating behaviours, contributing factors, and strategies to enhance the integrity of online assessment. *Journal of Academic Ethics, 22*, 51–70. https://doi.org/10.1007/s10805-023-09501-8

Waltzer, T., DeBernardi, F.C., & Dahl, A. (2023). Student and teacher views on cheating in high school: Perceptions, evaluations, and decisions. *Journal of Research on Adolescence, 33*(1), 108–126. https://doi.org/10.1111/jora.12784

5 Classroom Management

Cases in this chapter

5.1	Expat Novice Teacher and Pre-primary Student	*page* 137
5.2	Planning Too Much Lesson Content	141
5.3	The Student Leader in the Classroom	144
5.4	Using Canvas (LMS) Pre- and Post-Covid-19	147
5.5	Classroom Management for First-Year Teachers	151
5.6	A New Student in Class	154
5.7	The Field Trip (That Never Happened)	158

5.1   Expat Novice Teacher and Pre-primary Student

Keywords
- Thailand
- Private pre-school
- Expat first-year English teacher
- A problematic student
- Teacher stress and exhaustion

5.1.1   *Pre-reading Reflection*

1. "Backpacker English teachers" travel the world teaching English. They have limited experience and stay in jobs for short periods of time. Do you know any "backpacker teachers"?
2. Why do you think "backpacker teachers" often don't have success teaching their classes?
3. What are your thoughts about a school having an English-only policy?

Bryan is an American expat English teacher working in Thailand. He is in his mid-twenties and in his first year of teaching. He arrived in Thailand shortly after finishing his BA degree in French Language and Literature. His plan was to try English teaching and travel through Asia. He was hired by a private pre-school in Phuket, where children aged five to seven were taught English in English. There was a strict English-only policy in the school. He co-taught his group of nineteen children with a Thai co-teacher.

Shortly after starting his role, he was warned by his co-teacher that he may face some difficulties with his group. He was told that his predecessor had employed a fairly liberal classroom management style and that this group might therefore be difficult to discipline. In particular, one boy (Niran), who was six years of age, was known to be experiencing a hard time at school. He often seemed to ignore teachers completely and would not talk to them or listen to them when he was issued with instructions. He also didn't appear to engage effectively in classroom lessons and activities. At times Niran behaved aggressively toward other students in the classroom. Bryan quickly learned that managing Niran would become both time-consuming and demanding and that doing so would likely interfere with his work on a daily basis.

Bryan's co-teacher advised him that Niran's behavior was most probably influenced by his family circumstances, which the school had limited information about. Bryan soon learned that the boy was living with his grandparents. They were the only ones regularly seen at drop-offs and pick-ups before and after school. He was also informed that Niran might have been exposed to family harm incidents involving his parents, who had separated. Bryan expressed his concern about these matters to school management and suggested that Niran should be given additional support, or even transferred to a school better suited to meet his needs and with more suitably qualified teachers. The school manager told him that the school owner had a personal relationship with the grandparents and had promised them to accept the boy in one of the school's classes and take good care of him.

Bryan constantly felt anxious about having Niran in his class because he believed he was not qualified to diagnose and address his needs. He also strongly believed that Niran's struggles and behavior were negatively affecting the other students' learning and wellbeing in the classroom. He was very sympathetic about Niran's difficulties and the negative effect they were having on his development and ability to learn, and he genuinely wanted to help Niran, but he was concerned that his lack of appropriate experience and skills would prevent him from doing so.

Reflecting on this situation, Bryan soon realized that given the status of Thailand's education sector, with many regions having under-resourced schools in terms of both facilities and professional staff, many children like Niran would simply have to go without the specific support they needed. He also learned through his experience that at times it can take only one student to significantly change the dynamics of the teaching context. On the days when Niran was absent, for example, he found the class to be more engaged and productive, and he felt that more learning took place.

For the remainder of his one-year contract with the school, Bryan struggled to deal with Niran's disciplinary problems, and although things improved marginally over time, he never really found a way to help Niran participate

5.1 Expat Novice Teacher and Pre-primary Student

successfully in class activities and to control his disruptive behavior. Bryan enjoyed teaching at the school and would have considered accepting a contract extension that was offered to him but felt exhausted by the classroom challenges that so constantly confronted him, and thus opted to leave the school.

5.1.2 Questions

1. Do you think an English-only policy is appropriate for learners as young as those in Bryan's class? Whether you support this policy or not, what alternative language medium policies might be appropriate at this particular school?
2. Should students' personal information, such as family background and history of criminal activity, be shared with their teachers?
3. What role could Bryan's Thai co-teacher have played in managing Niran?
4. It is unlikely that Niran is the main reason Bryan did not extend his contract at the school. What other factors might have contributed to Bryan not renewing his contract?
5. What is your image of a "backpacker" English language teacher? What are some of the characteristics of such a teacher? Is Bryan one?

5.1.3 Research Topics

Learning About the Management Coping Practices of Early-Career Language Teachers

How do novice language teachers cope with classroom management issues during the first few months of their teaching careers? What challenges do they experience and how do they overcome them?

1. Arrange to observe one lesson per week or every two weeks of an early career language teacher during the first few months of their teaching career. The teacher could be working at any level, including primary or secondary school, or as a graduate teaching assistant at university.
2. During each lesson, take notes of the classroom interaction, including the behavior of the learners, miscommunications and unusual classroom talk, and how the teacher copes with any disruptions.
3. Briefly *interview* (M9) the teacher after each lesson, perhaps over tea or coffee, to discuss how the lesson went from the perspective of the teacher. Refer to any specific disruptive incidents or unusual student behaviors that you observed and ask the teacher *to comment on* (M15) the coping strategies they employed to manage them.
4. Over time, collate a list of classroom disruptions and related teacher coping strategies.

5. Are these disruptions typical of an early-career teacher's classroom? What coping strategies appear to be successful? Does the fact that the classroom is a *language* learning classroom make a difference?

Evaluating Induction Programs for New Language Teachers
What kind of induction do schools offer new language teachers to prepare and support them when they start teaching at the school? How much focus is given to classroom management? What aspects of management are covered?

1. Make formal contact with three language school managers or heads of language departments in different educational institutions.
2. Arrange to meet them individually and let them know before the meeting that you wish to inquire about their induction programs for new teachers. Invite them to ask another manager, human resources worker, or senior language teacher to join the meeting.
3. Before the meeting, request that they bring along any formal policy statements the school has regarding induction programs for new teachers.
4. Also before the meetings, prepare a set of *semi-structured interview questions* (M9) for the manager and colleague. Ask them if their schools or departments hold induction programs for new language teachers, and if so, how long they last and what content they consist of. What emphasis is given to classroom management? If they don't have induction programs, ask them why not. What other means of support do they offer new teachers?
5. Work through any of the policy statements that the managers provided. Ask them to comment specifically on classroom management clauses.
6. After analyzing the three interviews, evaluate the commonalities and shortcomings of the schools' induction programs.
7. What alternatives do they have in place? What classroom management skills or strategies do they focus on? Are new teachers left to sink or swim?

5.1.4 Resources

Ningsih, B., Fauziati, E., Prastiwi, Y., & Rahmawati, L. E. (2023). Teacher's strategy in dealing with disruptive behavior from a student's perspective. *Al-Ishlah: Jurnal Pendidikan, 15*(4), 4481–4491. https://doi.org/10.35445/alishlah.v15i4.3173

Jiwasiddi, A., Schlagwein, D., Cahalane, M., Cecez-Kecmanovic, D., Leong, C., & Ractham, P. (2024). Digital nomadism as a new part of the visitor economy: The case of the "digital nomad capital" Chiang Mai, Thailand. *Information Systems Journal, 34*(5), 1493–1535. https://doi.org/10.1111/isj.12496

Wangdi, T. & Namgyel, S. (2022). Classroom to reduce student disruptive behavior: An action research. *MEXTESOL Journal, 46*(1), 1–11. https://doi.org/10.61871/mj.v46n1-16

5.2 Planning Too Much Lesson Content

Keywords
- Miami, USA
- Private English language center
- English teacher
- Time management
- Never finishing lessons

5.2.1 Pre-reading Reflection

1. Preparing too much or preparing too little for a lesson – which is worse?
2. Do you think students in class pay attention to teachers managing time during a lesson?
3. Is it possible to be taught better time management skills?

Jake has been teaching English to adults for three years. He works in a private English language center in Miami, Florida, and this is his first job. He started teaching at the center immediately after completing his BA and MA degrees. While studying, Jake worked various short-term, part-time English teaching jobs at his university and at language schools in the city. In only a few years he has built up considerable experience teaching a range of different courses to students with diverse backgrounds. In his current job at the center, he teaches general English courses that aim to provide learners with language skills for employment and further study in the US. The general English courses run from anywhere between one or two weeks to up to fifteen weeks. Students have twenty one-hour lessons per week. The center has a very good reputation. Its teachers all have qualifications in English teaching, and there is a spread of early-career and experienced teachers (representing a wide range of ages). The management of the center is excellent – regular reviews show it is a sound business with good quality teaching. The center charges high fees, and students have equally high expectations.

Besides general English classes, the center offers courses in business English and courses to prepare for international standardized tests such as IELTS and TOEFL. Jake would like to teach on these courses at some point in the future, but he feels that he is not yet ready. He has one nagging teaching issue that has plagued him since he did his teaching practicum during his MA teacher preparation. And he needs to sort it out before he can teach on courses with inflexible lesson plans, tight schedules where all teachers keep pace and in step with each other, and strict deadlines for meeting unit completion and assessment targets. The general English course allows for more flexibility in course content and independence on the part of the teachers.

The problem Jake has is that he always over-prepares. He includes way too much content in his lesson plans and embeds too many activities into the classroom action. He has a fear of finishing the lesson before the class time is up and then not knowing what to do or say for the remainder of the time. And so, he includes as much material as possible in every lesson. It is always too much, and he can never finish. Although he tries. Sometimes he cuts pair and group work short to move onto the next section of the lesson, even though he can clearly see that students are engaged in the activity, speaking English, and that they are enjoying themselves. Ironically, he is worried he won't finish what he has prepared.

Jake finds this ongoing issue very frustrating, and so do the students, he suspects. He can sense they find the lessons rushed. Jake often says that the next day they will continue with the lesson content or complete an activity they started, but then they almost never do, and if they do, the students have forgotten where they were, or have lost interest in the task. The students haven't complained about this aspect of Jake's teaching yet in their course evaluations, but he is waiting for it to happen. When Jake did his practicum as a component of his MA a few years back, he experienced the same problem, and his supervisors offered him advice; they said he should work on his time management skills. They referred Jake to a time management workshop offered to graduate students by the university academic development program and pointed him to online materials available for free in the university library. Jake had a look at the online materials but thought they didn't look particularly useful. He skipped the workshop.

5.2.2 Questions

1. What is ironic about the way Jake prepares and conducts his lessons?
2. Do you think it is possible for Jake to change? Can he sort out this problem? What help might his apparently good language school offer him?
3. Would teaching on the tightly structured business English and IELTS/TOEFL courses be helpful to Jake's professional development? Give reasons for your answer.
4. What might be holding the students back from complaining about Jake's timing problem?
5. Should Jake have taken up the help offered to him when he was an MA student at university? Would this type of support really have helped?

5.2.3 Research Topics

Identifying and Explaining Time-Related Decisions in a Language Lesson
What decisions are made about timing during a lesson? When are they made? What moments and actions in the lesson prompt the decision-making?

1. Work with an experienced language teacher who has been teaching for over ten years.

2. Explain to the teacher that you are interested in time management during language lessons. Arrange to observe and video-record one of the teacher's lessons.
3. Record the lesson. After the class, watch the video-recording and note any time transitions (i.e., moving from one event to another), time-related instructions by the teacher, class opening and closing, and words used by the teacher or students that refer to time.
4. Then, meet with the teacher to observe the video-recording of the lesson together. In a *stimulated recall* (M15) process, ask the teacher to explain their decision-making at the times you identified when you first analyzed the video.
5. Why did they make those decisions? Did they feel any time-related anxiety during the lesson? Did they have a Plan B if things didn't go according to the lesson plan?
6. Ask the teacher if they have advice about time management during lessons for early-career language teachers.

Investigating Pre-service English Teachers' Anxieties About Finishing Future Lessons Early
Are pre-service English teachers anxious about finishing their future lessons early? What makes them anxious? What will they do to prevent finishing early?

1. Plan to meet with a class of pre-service English teachers in a teacher education program for one to two hours.
2. Start the meeting by having an open twenty-minute discussion about lesson planning and time management. If the class is large, work in small groups.
3. Present the class with a scenario or case where a teacher finishes an English lesson early and doesn't know what to do with the remaining time. In the scenario, the learners become restless, and the teacher grows anxious and embarrassed.
4. Ask the students to write down five *keywords* (M10) that describe how they feel after reflecting on the scenario. Instruct them to write one or two sentences after each keyword, explaining their choice of keyword.
5. Finally, ask them to write a short paragraph describing what they would do to prevent such a dilemma if they were the teacher.
6. Spend the rest of the meeting *discussing as a whole class* (M8) a selection of teachers' keywords. Record the discussion. Collect their keywords and paragraphs after the meeting.
7. What emotions do the pre-service English teachers experience? How do they manage them? What are their strategies for preventing lessons ending early?

5.2.4 Resources

König, J., Krepf, M., Bremerich-Vos, A., & Buchholtz, C. (2021). Meeting cognitive demands of lesson planning: Introducing the CODE-PLAN Model to describe and analyze teachers' planning competence. *The Teacher Educator, 56*(4), 466–487. https://doi.org/10.1080/08878730.2021.1938324

Makuru, L., Pato, M., & Mashauri, M. M. (2024). Time management in an EFL lesson room: An analysis of challenges faced by senior school teachers at Bunia in the Democratic Republic of the Congo. *European Journal of Linguistics, 3*(2), 1–14. https://doi.org/10.47941/ejl.2020

Tan, R., Djonov, E., & Chik, A. (2024). Time matters: A critical multimodal study of an English learning app for children in China. *Learning, Media and Technology*, 2384857. https://doi.org/10.1080/17439884.2024.2384857

5.3 The Student Leader in the Classroom

Keywords
- New York City, USA
- High school
- ESL teacher
- Student leader in the classroom
- Student discipline problems

5.3.1 Pre-reading Reflection

1. Some students, even young ones, can be quite powerful in the classroom. Can you think of examples?
2. In what ways, besides English language proficiency, are ESL students different from so-called mainstream students?
3. For what reasons would students stay in high school when they are clearly older than their fellow students?

Mr. Corfield teaches in a large inner-city school in New York: Cityside High School. He is a member of a very active and hard-working ESL Department. At his school, students (called English Language Learners or ELLs) take ESL courses for credit toward their high school diploma. The syllabus loosely follows state guidelines, but teachers have considerable freedom to be creative and to use their own materials or choose their own textbooks. The ESL courses are general, with an overall focus on communicative language teaching, and on the skills of speaking, reading, and writing. Usually, teams of teachers work together, particularly within any one grade, to decide on a common textbook. They also share materials and assessments. Generally, there is much collaboration among teachers in the department; they get along well and a strong collegial spirit is evident.

The school is located in a low socioeconomic area of the city. Most of the students have an immigrant background, meaning they are first- or second-generation immigrants, mainly from South America or the Caribbean. The majority are enrolled in the ESL program. Mr. Corfield, who is in his early forties, is well known as an excellent teacher. He has been teaching for nearly twenty years, about ten of those at Cityside High School. He is African-American and has lived his whole life in the same neighborhood as the school. He understands his students well and knows their needs and ambitions. Most will finish high school, but few will go on to study further. His aim is to teach them as much English as possible every year and to foster a love of learning.

Maintaining discipline has always been difficult in the ESL classes at the school. There are no serious problems; mainly a lot of talking and moving about the classroom. Concentration levels are low. Mr. Corfield experiences the same discipline issues, but he is tolerant, and with his quiet talk and calm manner usually achieves the aims of his lessons. One Grade 11 class (students about seventeen years old), however, is particularly challenging. There are twenty-five students in the class, about half boys and half girls. One boy, Diego, aged nineteen, is older than the other students. Diego is clearly the leader in the class. If he does some work, the other students do too. If he is in a rowdy mood, the class is especially noisy. Sometimes he walks around the room while Mr. Corfield is teaching; at other times he sits at the back and plays on his digital device, not paying any attention whatsoever to what is happening. Diego dictates the mood of the class, and whether he knows it or not, has an effect on the learning of all the students in the class.

Mr. Corfield is aware of Diego's power, both inside and outside the classroom. He has seen him in the schoolyard, always with a group of students around him, and he has also seen him around the neighborhood, where his companions are certainly not high school students. In private conversations, Diego has told Mr. Corfield that he is staying in high school because he needs a high school diploma to join the armed forces.

5.3.2 Questions

1. Do you believe Mr. Corfield is an effective ESL teacher? Give specific reasons for your answer.
2. What do you predict Diego's chances are of graduating from high school? Why?
3. How could Mr. Corfield work with Diego to establish and maintain more productive classroom management?

4. Do you think Mr. Corfield needs further professional development? If so, what might it entail? If not, why not?
5. Mr. Corfield has observed Diego interacting with others outside the classroom. Should he get involved in what he sees going on?

5.3.3 Research Topics

Identifying Characteristics of a Classroom Student Leader from the Students' Perspective

What positive and negative characteristics does a classroom student leader possess? How do students describe their leaders?

1. Focus this study on a language classroom at the middle or high school level.
2. Prepare a paper or digital *questionnaire* (M17) to be distributed to all learners in the classroom.
3. Design the questionnaire so that respondents are first asked to think of a student leader they are familiar with, perhaps in their current language learning classroom.
4. Ask them to list five characteristics of that student that make them a good leader – how their leadership contributes to class cohesion, a community spirit, and student learning, for example.
5. Then ask them to list five characteristics of that same or a different student that make them a leader who has negative influences on other students in the class – bullying, disrupting classroom activities, for example.
6. On the questionnaire, clearly instruct the respondents not to name or identify the student leaders.
7. Leave a blank space at the end of the questionnaire for the respondents to write a short paragraph to explain their two lists.
8. Collect the questionnaires and analyze them to identify the most common leadership characteristics, both positive and negative.
9. How do students describe their leaders? Would language teachers find these characteristics helpful for managing their classes?

Understanding Teachers' Attitudes Toward Inquiring About Students' Personal Lives

How do teachers feel about inquiring into their students' personal, private lives? What would prompt them to do so? What would they want to know?

1. Interview four language teachers who work in different contexts – for example, primary school, high school, university, or private language school.
2. Prepare a *semi-structured interview* (M9) schedule that asks a series of questions about why language teachers would want to know about their

students' personal, private lives. What are their attitudes toward making such inquiries? What would they want to know, and what would prompt them to make such inquiries?
3. Do not cover family life (that might be better left to a school or university counselor). Focus the questions on other aspects of their personal lives, such as friendships, social activities, or relationships.
4. Conduct the interviews for about one hour, either face-to-face or on a virtual platform such as Zoom or WhatsApp. Record the interviews.
5. Transcribe the interviews and analyze them for main themes. Collate common themes and then invite the four teachers to a *virtual focus group meeting* (M8) to discuss the themes in relation to the teachers' attitudes and experiences.
6. Under what circumstances would teachers feel the need to inquire into the personal lives of their students? How would doing so make them feel?

5.3.4 Resources

Holquist, S. E., Mitra, D. L., Conner, J., & Wright, N. L. (2023). What is student voice anyway? The intersection of student voice practices and shared leadership. *Educational Administration Quarterly, 59*(4), 703–743. https://doi.org/10.1177/0013161X231178023

Martínez-Carrera, S., Sánchez-Martínez, C., Martínez-Carrera, I., & Díaz Dieguez, M. A. (2024). Teachers' perceptions and position regarding the problem of bullying and its socio-educational prevention. *Behavioral Sciences, 14*(3), 229. https://doi.org/10.3390/bs14030229

Shinde, N. & Bamber, C. (2023). The role of leadership in promoting student centred teaching and facilitating learner's responsible behaviour. *Management Dynamics in the Knowledge Economy, 11*(3), 208–231. https://doi.org/10.2478/mdke-2023-0014

5.4 Using Canvas (LMS) Pre- and Post-Covid-19

Keywords
- Ireland
- University
- Applied Linguistics MA program
- Using Canvas during Covid-19
- Post-Covid-19 communication on Canvas

5.4.1 Pre-reading Reflection

1. How did you change your teaching or learning during the Covid-19 pandemic? Think of one significant change.

2. How efficient are you at using learning management systems such as Moodle, Blackboard, and Canvas?
3. What are some differences between teaching and learning *languages* and *content* subjects (e.g., applied linguistics subjects) on an LMS?

Garet University, a technological university in Ireland, offers a very successful MA program in Applied Linguistics. The program attracts a large number of international students who come to the university because of the program's strong reputation, and also because of the opportunities to combine their applied linguistics courses with other applied subjects on offer at the institution. Students also enjoy the university's close proximity to excellent, and well-known, natural attractions, which offer opportunities for walks, cycling, overnight camping, and relaxed sightseeing. Small villages, with interesting pubs and museums, are also close by. Some university students live in these villages, which might be called satellite suburbs of the university city, and commute to campus for lectures. In short, besides the good applied linguistics program and the possibility of innovating its structure by incorporating other subjects, international students desire the full Irish living experience.

The MA in Applied Linguistics is a coursework and dissertation degree and offers a range of core and elective courses, mainly geared towards language teacher education to cater for the type of students who enroll, that is, pre- and in-service language teachers. And of these, most are or plan to become English teachers. A few domestic (i.e., Irish) students are in the program, but the majority are international students. The university campus blends nicely into the urban landscape, with plenty of coffee shops and restaurants and retail outlets to meet the needs of students. Like at universities around the world, things changed drastically when Covid-19 came along in 2020. Not only did the campus and classrooms empty out, but the way courses were taught and managed also changed. The MA in Applied Linguistics program suddenly started to use Canvas (a learning management system) much more than before. It had been available at the university for several years, but in applied linguistics courses it was under-utilized, mainly used by course lecturers for record-keeping and sending out announcements to class members. Covid-19 changed all that. The lecturers quickly developed Canvas into a teaching and learning platform, interfacing it with online video-conferencing platforms, recording facilities, and other technologies that made emergency remote teaching and learning achievable under pandemic circumstances. The lecturers' and students' new online skills developed quickly, and good learning was sustained throughout the Covid-19 period. Surprisingly, students didn't drop out, and although the lecturers found the new teaching approach exhausting, it was also rewarding.

Covid-19 seemed to end as quickly as it started. It was announced that lecturers would resume on-campus teaching at the start of the new term. Students returned slowly. Classes were not as full as they were pre-pandemic. Requests started to come in from students for lectures to be recorded and posted on Canvas. There was some resistance to this request, mainly because recording equipment was not readily available and setting up a video-conferencing link (and then still having to find in-classroom recording equipment) was awkward and time-consuming. Lecturers felt they would be doing lectures twice, thus doubling their workload. There was some small attempt by lecturers of some of the courses to do recordings for a limited time, but others refused. This caused several issues. One was that students in different courses had different experiences in the same program – and they noticed. They complained to the program coordinator. Another was that those students who did come to class received current and necessary information about what was going on in their courses, information not always received by those who did not attend. There was thus a call from the latter students for better communications via Canvas. Again, some lecturers felt that they should not be spending extra time and effort communicating twice about the course, especially since students had been instructed to return to class, where information certainly was shared. They complained that students had become "too comfortable in their little villages" to return to campus.

5.4.2 Questions

1. The Applied Linguistics MA program at Garet University appears to be ideal. What makes it so?
2. Why do you think the Canvas LMS was under-utilized by the applied linguistics lecturers pre-Covid-19?
3. Why would the lecturers have found the new approach to using Canvas during the pandemic "rewarding"?
4. What did the *lecturers* get wrong with regard to Canvas use post-Covid-19? What did the MA *program* get wrong?
5. What did some of the lecturers mean by students becoming "too comfortable in their little villages"? What should they do now to get the students back on campus?

5.4.3 Research Topics

Discovering Teacher Educators' Strategies for Managing Communications on an LMS
How do language teacher educators monitor and control the amount and type of communications between themselves and their student teachers on an LMS? What are their reasons for implementing these strategies?

1. Identify a language teacher education program that uses an LMS such as Canvas, Google Classroom, or Blackboard.
2. Invite teacher educators who work in the program to meet with you one-on-one at their computer. Select up to five participants.
3. When you meet, ask the teacher educator to open the LMS and explain how they manage communications with their student teachers. Ask them to show you examples of how they limit messages and requests. What instructions about communicating with the teacher educator do they give at the start of the course, and during the course? What do they do when communications become overwhelming?
4. Make extensive notes during and after the meeting about what you discover. After meeting with the five teacher educators, compare their strategies. Compile a list of successful strategies – what works well and why is it effective.
5. What advice could be passed on to other teacher educators teaching on an LMS?

Outlining the Benefits and Disadvantages of Making Lecture Recordings Available After Face-to-Face Classes

In teacher education contexts where face-to-face class meetings are (or could be) recorded, should the recordings be made available to the students on an LMS after class? What are the benefits and disadvantages of doing so?

1. Locate a language teacher education class that typically has its meetings recorded.
2. Interview the lecturer. Prepare a *semi-structured interview* (M9) schedule, which includes questions about how the lectures are recorded, who requires them to be recorded (if anybody), what the benefits of recording the classes are for both the lecturer and student teachers, and what the disadvantages are.
3. To obtain the students' views, invite all students from the same class as the lecturer to complete a brief, *anonymous questionnaire* (M17) on Google Forms, Qualtrics, or similar. Ask the lecturer to distribute the link to the form via the class LMS.
4. On the questionnaire, ask the student respondents to indicate whether they watch the recordings, why or why not, and if they do, how they benefit from doing so.
5. Do the lecturer and the students have similar perspectives on sharing class recordings? What are the disadvantages of sharing the recordings on the class LMS? How do the students benefit, and the lecturer?

5.4.4 Resources

Alosaimi, M. (2023). Language teachers' identity development post COVID-19: A transformative learning perspective. *Frontiers in Education, 8,* 1275297. https://doi.org/10.3389/feduc.2023.1275297

Khong, H.-K., Chuah, K.-M., & Ahmad Sanusi, S. N. (2023). Is work from home (WFH) feasible for university language educators in the post COVID-19 era? *Journal of University Teaching & Learning Practice, 20* (6), 21. https://doi.org/10.53761/1.20.6.21

Porter-Szucs, I. & DeCicco, B. (2022). TriHy: Teaching an MA TESOL class face-to-face, synchronously online, and asynchronously online. *SN Social Sciences, 2,* 143. https://doi.org/10.1007/s43545-022-00434-4

5.5 Classroom Management for First-Year Teachers

Keywords
- Poland
- Primary school
- English teachers
- Identifying management issues for a workshop
- Reflecting on two management issues

5.5.1 Pre-reading Reflection

1. What's a good teaching strategy to get young learners to settle down in class? What works?
2. As a teacher, do you prefer a lively or a quiet class?
3. What do you think the top five classroom management issues are for novice or early-career teachers?

Krystyna and Joanna are from Poland. They studied together at university, where they met. They did the same language teacher education courses, graduated at the same time, and ended up getting jobs in the same primary school in a large city. They both teach English in the upper grades of the school and are in their first year of teaching. They have been teaching for six months and are getting along well at school, although both are experiencing some classroom management issues. These are not serious and are probably common to all first-year teachers adjusting to a new profession after training. But they are distracting, and both Krystyna and Joanna are annoyed that they can't seem to shake them off. They realize, of course, that they are still inexperienced language teachers, and that they will probably eventually learn to deal with these problems, but they are getting impatient. They want to focus on their teaching and their students' learning. Krystyna and Joanna will soon be attending a workshop on classroom management at a regional teachers' conference in the city, and attendees have been asked to submit prior to the workshop one burning issue for discussion on the day. Over morning coffee before school one day, Krystyna and Joanna reflect on what issue they will choose.

KRYSTYNA: Have you sent in your issue? I think they want something from us by next week. The facilitator says she will be collating all the issues and then listing them at the start of the workshop so we can see what they are and if there are any in common. Do you know what you will choose?

JOANNA: Where do I start? I suppose one is just keeping general control of the class. My students aren't bad or very disruptive, but it would be great if there was more peace and quiet. But that may be too much to expect with young children.

KRYSTYNA: Absolutely, but I think the workshop facilitator wants something more specific.

JOANNA: I know, and I do have something in mind, and it relates to my general point.

KRYSTYNA: What's that?

JOANNA: Something to do with the first few minutes of class – the opening of the lesson. It seems to take me ages to settle the class down. By the time we get down to work, ten minutes have already gone by. It's such a waste of time. I just can't seem to settle them – running around, talking, coming in late, taking out books, pushing and shoving. I read somewhere to play soft music when they enter the room, to bring the vibe down and calm the students as the lesson begins. Didn't work!

KRYSTYNA: Hahaha, sounds fun, maybe I should try it, although I don't seem to have the same problem. Maybe I am stricter with the kids. My problem is somewhat the opposite of yours. I find the students too quiet. I can't seem to get them to engage with the class work. I've tried getting them into pairs and small groups to do activities, but they seem rather mechanical and disinterested. Not sure if it's me or the material, or maybe it's them. I don't know.

JOANNA: That's weird. All my kids are so lively, I can't get them to sit down. They want to be involved in everything. Even when I do eventually settle them down after the lesson opening, they tend to want to jump up and move about. I often let them because I like to have an active class with chatter. It feels like they are working then.

KRYSTYNA: I think that would make me feel uncomfortable. I prefer to see them sitting down and paying attention to the lesson. That looks like work to me!

JOANNA: But then you say it looks like they are not enthusiastic and engaging? Good luck sending that issue to the workshop facilitator.

5.5.2 Questions

1. Are Krystyna and Joanna being too impatient about wanting to "shake off" their classroom management issues? Give a reason for your answer.
2. Joanna tried playing music to settle her learners down when they entered her classroom. What other strategies can you think of that might quickly settle the learners and allow the lesson to begin?
3. Joanna complains about not being able to start the lesson quickly and wishes for "more peace and quiet," but she also says, "I like to have an active class

5.5 Classroom Management Issues for First-Year Teachers

with chatter." What classroom management issue is she experiencing and what can she do about it?

4. How different is Krystyna from Joanna, and how does this show in their management styles? If you were a primary school student, whose classroom would you prefer to be in? Why?
5. If you were running the conference workshop that Krystyna and Joanna are going to attend, what advice would you give them?

5.5.3 Research Topics

Analyzing Language Lesson Openings

How do language teachers open their lessons? What interaction patterns are used by teachers in the first few minutes of the lessons? Are their openings effective for settling the class?

1. Engage three language teachers and request permission to observe one of their classes. Select teachers who work in a primary or high school setting.
2. Video-record on your smartphone the opening three to five minutes of the lesson or until the students have settled down to work.
3. Do a detailed transcription of the recorded opening, capturing all talk-in-interaction between the teacher and learners. Make notes of their physical movements and locations in the classroom.
4. Conduct a *discourse analysis* (M5) of the talk-in-interaction in each of the three transcripts. Align the analysis with your notes of the physical mobility arrangements in the classroom.
5. What type of language did the teachers use to open the lessons – instructions, questions, demands? What linguistic strategies appear to be most effective? Where did the teachers stand? How and where were the students moving? What patterns of interaction were common among the three teachers?

Discovering Language Teachers' Perceptions of an Ideal Classroom Atmosphere

What is an ideal language classroom atmosphere? How quiet would it be? How much bustling activity would be desired? What is the most appropriate atmosphere for learning?

1. Select language teachers who work in different educational contexts and with different levels of students.
2. Design a digital *narrative frame* (M16) that requires respondents to construct a story about the atmosphere in their ideal language classroom – for example, quiet, lively, energetic, noisy, learners silently working, little or lots of movement. Ensure the sequence of sentence starters form a story when completed. Starters might include: "In my ideal class learners would

have the freedom to … "; "I would like to keep control by … "; "I find it more relaxing when … "; "My learners always learn better when …."
3. At the end of the narrative frame, leave space for teachers to *draw* (M12) their language classroom, depicting an ideal atmosphere.
4. Distribute the narrative frame to the selected teachers electronically and request that they submit the frames in the same way when completed.
5. Analyze the written frames for salient themes related to classroom atmosphere.
6. What is the most popular ideal classroom atmosphere? What are the major contrasts? What reasons do teachers give for their ideal classroom atmosphere? Is there an ideal atmosphere for language learning? Do teachers working in different contexts perceive different ideal classroom atmospheres?
7. Do the drawings of ideal language classrooms reflect the findings from the narrative frames?

5.5.4 Resources

Karasova, J., & Nehyba, J. (2025). Novice teachers' classroom behaviour management: Situations, responses and impact on student behaviour. *British Educational Research Journal*, https://doi.org/10.1002/berj.4166

Sánchez Solarte, A. C. (2019). Classroom management and novice language teachers: Friend or foe? *HOW*, 26(1), 177–199. https://doi.org/10.19183/how.26.1.463

Woodcock, S. & Reupert, A. (2024). First-year primary teachers' classroom management strategies: Perceptions of use, confidence, and effectiveness. *Journal of Education for Teaching*, 50(1), 90–106. https://doi.org/10.1080/02607476.2023.2219218

5.6 A New Student in Class

Keywords
- Chile
- Primary school
- EFL teacher
- Inappropriate behavior in class
- New student struggling to adjust

5.6.1 Pre-reading Reflection

1. Imagine being a new student in a new school in a new city. What would some of your emotions be on day one?

2. How would you suggest teachers introduce new students to their class? What should they say?
3. Some new students struggle to engage in their new setting. What might some causes be?

Emilia is a recently graduated EFL teacher. She has two years' teaching experience at a small private school in a very affluent neighborhood in Santiago, Chile. Her classes range from Year 1 to Year 4 (children between six and nine years old). She teaches each class for two hours a day, every day. In Chile, primary school teachers of subjects like English, music, physical education, and art normally visit their classes for the scheduled hours or take them to the corresponding labs or gym. The rest of the time, the students would be with their class teacher in the same classroom. As an EFL teacher, Emilia visits her classes in their own classroom.

Emilia gets along with the students and her colleagues very well. She enjoys her teaching and feels particularly satisfied with the quality of her classroom management. From the very first day of the term, she establishes, together with her students, a small set of rules or expected behaviors along with corresponding rewards if students follow them. She is very motivated to work with primary school children as she finds them enthusiastic and eager to engage in the activities she plans. Children seem to like her and her classes. However, in Year 4, there is one student who does not always abide by the classroom rules. His name is Tomás. He constantly interrupts Emilia's classes and does not seem to respond to any of her warnings. He is reluctant to engage in any activities and when he is encouraged to do so or reminded of the class rules, he defiantly responds that he does not care. On occasions, when Emilia enters the classroom, he makes snide remarks. This is the first time Emilia has been required to deal with such challenging behavior.

Normally when a student behaves inappropriately, the observed behavior is recorded in a class book and then uploaded to the school intranet so that parents can be informed at the time of their child's misconduct. If the inappropriate behavior continues, parents are requested to attend a meeting with the head teacher and on some occasions with the subject teacher involved. The school also has a multidisciplinary team of professionals, including an educational psychologist, a Special Education Needs coordinator, and an occupational therapist, to support students with behavioral and or learning difficulties. They also work closely with the teachers involved in any particular case. If an issue is beyond the team's capacities, the school authorities and parents discuss the need to seek further professional help, such as with therapists, neurologists, or psychiatrists.

One day Emilia was teaching a lesson and Tomás refused to do any tasks. He was also disturbing some of his classmates sitting near him. She warned Tomás that if he continued with that behavior, she would have to call his parents for a meeting. He replied that he did not care. Then she said to him, "You may even get expelled from this school!" He replied, "That is exactly what I want! I don't want to be in this school anymore." Emilia did not know what to do or what to say.

After class Emilia decided to look further into the background of Tomás. She thought that knowing more about him would help explain some of his behavioral issues. She soon discovered, on talking to the head teacher, that Tomás and his family were from a small city in the south of Chile and that they had only recently moved to the capital, Santiago. Tomás was thus also a new student in the school. That was all the information Emilia could gather about Tomás. She was not satisfied with this information. She was determined to find out more, and to work closely with Tomás in order to overcome this potentially destructive situation.

5.6.2 Questions

1. What is your view of Emilia's practice of establishing a set of classroom rules together with her students at the start of the school term?
2. What might Tomás be trying to communicate through his classroom behavior?
3. On the whole, Emilia has good classroom management skills. What has she done right and what has she done wrong in the case of Tomás? Are the constant in-classroom warnings and annotations in the class book adequate tools to deal with students like Tomás?
4. Do you feel that the resources in the school are sufficient and appropriate to support both students and teachers when this sort of case arises?
5. What do you think Emilia's next move should be?

5.6.3 Research Topics

Surveying Primary School Language Students' Perceptions of Classroom Misbehavior

What do primary school students perceive to be bad behavior in the classroom? What are some examples? Why don't they like bad behavior?

1. Work with a teacher to engage a class of senior primary school language learners.
2. Talk to them briefly about good and bad behavior in the classroom.
3. Give each student a piece of paper and ask them to *draw an example* (M12) of a student behaving badly in a classroom. They can draw people and objects, and use words, shapes, and colors on their drawings. Invite them to talk to each other while drawing and ask questions about each other's drawings.
4. Collect their drawings. Are there any that stand out as particularly interesting or revealing about the topic?

5. Select four or five of these drawings and *meet one-on-one* (M9) with the students who produced them. Ask the students to describe their drawing in detail.
6. Why is the behavior bad? How do they respond to bad behavior in the classroom? How does it make them feel? What do their teachers do about the bad behavior?

Discovering Language Teachers' Approaches to Welcoming New Students to a Class

Do language teachers have procedures for welcoming new students to a class? Or do they leave them to settle in on their own? How do they monitor new students' ongoing integration into the class environment?

1. In a primary or high school workplace environment that you have access to, engage in *informal conversations* (M9) with language teachers about welcoming new learners to their classes.
2. Ask them if they have routine procedures for welcoming newcomers, and if so, what these procedures are. Are they successful? How does the teacher know? How are languages – the target language and the language of the new learner – taken into account? How long do they monitor the settling in of the learner?
3. If they don't have any specific procedures for introducing and welcoming new students, why don't they? What do they do instead?
4. Aim to have conversations with about five different teachers. After each conversation, write detailed notes of the content of the talk.
5. Do the teachers describe effective welcoming practices that can be passed on to new teachers?

5.6.4 Resources

Cabaroğlu, N. & Altinel, Z. (2010). Misbehaviour in EFL classes: Teachers' and students' perspectives. *Ç.Ü. Sosyal Bilimler Enstitüsü Dergisi, 19*(2), 99–119. https://dergipark.org.tr/en/pub/cusosbil/issue/4384/60190

Debreli, E. & Ishanova, I. (2019). Foreign language classroom management: Types of student misbehaviour and strategies adapted by the teachers in handling disruptive behaviour. *Cogent Education, 6*(1), 1648629. https://doi.org/10.1080/2331186X.2019.1648629

Metaxas, M. J. (2021). Are the most effective approaches towards helping students with Emotional Behavioural Disorders (EBDs) predisposed and trait based? *Psychiatry International, 2*(1), 85–107. https://doi.org/10.3390/psychiatryint2010007

5.7 The Field Trip (That Never Happened)

Keywords
- Canada
- Private school
- Part-time ESL teacher
- Planning a field trip
- Parents' queries and concerns

5.7.1 Pre-reading Reflection

1. Do you have memories of going on a school field trip when at elementary or secondary school? How was it?
2. What health and safety risks might apply to day trips off school grounds?
3. What are some of the language learning benefits of going on short field trips? Imagine one specific type of trip.

Xiaoming Chen is an ESL support teacher at a private school in a small city on the east coast of Canada. Her job is part-time, and she works with students from elementary through to secondary level. For only a part-time position, she has considerable responsibility, including: developing the ESL curriculum; preparing, administering, and grading assessments; attending staff meetings; reporting on students' progress; and leading some extracurricular activities. Two other ESL teachers share these responsibilities in the school. They have been at the school much longer than Xiaoming and have full-time positions. Having recently qualified as an English teacher in Canada, Xiaoming has been at the school for about eight months.

Xiaoming loves her job, and the hours suit her. She has two young children and having a full-time job would mean not spending enough time with them during the week. She obtained her BA degree in China about ten years ago before moving to Canada with her husband. She had her children after settling in the same city where she now lives and works. When her children got a bit older, she decided to continue her studies, finishing her MA in English Language Teaching, and immediately afterward taking up the job at her current school. Now, halfway through her second semester at the school, Xiaoming feels comfortable enough to take one of her small ESL classes on a field trip, and with the Spring weather improving day by day, she has a plan. The ten-year-old students have recently started working on a climate change project and have been developing a weather-related vocabulary. The aim of the project is for each student to produce their own multimodal poster on which a selection of these new words is to be used appropriately. They will then share and review (in writing) each other's posters on the class learning management system.

5.7 The Field Trip (That Never Happened)

Planning the field trip turns to be harder than Xiaoming anticipated. What she wanted to do was quite simple. She and the group of twelve students would walk to a park three blocks away from the school and spend an hour there (a) "observing nature," such as the sky, the grass, any breeze, birds, the weather, sounds; and (b) describing "how you feel about what you observe." They would write notes on a worksheet while observing and then come together for the last few minutes of the hour to share their experiences. The walk back to the school would take about five to eight minutes. Xiaoming consulted the two other ESL teachers, who thought the plan sounded reasonable. She then began preparing the paperwork – the most important part of which was the parents' consent form, which included information about what the field trip would entail, the dates with departure and return times, the destination, what the students should wear, and any element of risk. One of her colleagues reviewed the form and said it looked fine, and the school principal thought that the trip sounded like a great idea. It had to be signed by parents and returned to the school.

Although the trip was short and uncomplicated, there were a surprising number of queries from parents, who requested answers before signing the form. In fact, only four signed forms were returned. Four other parents refused to sign and would not allow their children on the trip, citing the following reasons: "Ms. Chen's inexperience as a teacher at the school," a recent protest held in the park (mentioned by two parents), and the project could be done on the school grounds. The remaining parents wanted to know if Xiaoming knew what she was doing, if more than one teacher would be accompanying the children, and why students couldn't stay in the classroom where they belong. With only four certainties, Xiaoming decided to abandon the field trip. The questions were too hard to answer (and quite offensive, she thought), and the group was getting too small to justify the effort.

5.7.2 Questions

1. One query raised by the parents has to do with Xiaoming's experience. Do you think she is experienced enough to lead her planned field trip? Why or why not?
2. Can you think of an alternative way of handling the parental consent form process?
3. How do you feel about some parents' attitude regarding students remaining on the school grounds and in their classroom instead of going on the field trip? Was a field trip justified to successfully complete the climate change project?

4. Did Xiaoming make the right decision to abandon the field trip? What would you have done?
5. How could the school have supported Xiaoming both before she sent out the forms to parents and when they were returned?

5.7.3 Research Topics

Researching the Place of Field Trips in Language Education
What are the benefits of "getting out of the classroom" in language learning? Are there lessons to be learned on field trips that can't be learned in language classrooms? What are they?

1. Spend a few hours *searching the internet* (M6) for information about the benefits of field trips for language learning. Websites such as the following offer useful suggestions: https://www.readingrockets.org/topics/english-language-learners/articles/successful-field-trips-english-language-learners
2. After reviewing several websites, compile a list of (a) benefits. Categorize them according to age of learner and level of proficiency, if available. Do the same with lists for (b) risks, (c) recommendations for planning, and (d) evaluating field trips.
3. Present the lists to language teachers who teach young learners and those who teach adults. *Ask them to comment* (M9) on the (a) – (d) lists and how they apply to their own contexts and practices. Focus mainly on the benefits of field trips.
4. Do they obviously promote language learning? How do field trips contribute to learner identity development? Do they raise political or cultural awareness?
5. What risks do the teachers fear? Do the potential risks stop them from taking their learners on field trips?
6. Are the benefits and risks different for adult learners and young learners?

Investigating the Roles and Responsibilities of Part-Time Language Instructors
What roles and responsibilities are appropriate for part-time language instructors? How is their workload monitored and protected? What support do they get in their schools?

1. In one school or institutional language department, meet with the administrator (e.g., human resources manager, principal) who is responsible for appointing part-time language instructors.
2. *Interview* (M9) the administrator to inquire about the process of appointing part-time language instructors, and ask about: how they

are appointed, their teaching workload allocations, their teaching and administration responsibilities, what support they get for classroom management issues, and how their work is evaluated and their well-being monitored.
3. Now conduct *semi-structured interviews* (M9) with the part-time instructors in the school or department. Ask them the same set of questions.
4. Compare the instructors' and the administrator's answers to the questions.
5. Do part-time language instructors feel that they are exploited? Are they over-worked? Are they assigned responsibilities for which they do not feel qualified? Do they feel supported and protected?

5.7.4 Resources

DeWitt, J. & Storksdieck, M. (2008). A short review of school field trips: Key findings from the past and implications for the future. *Visitor Studies, 11*(2), 181–197. https://doi.org/10.1080/10645570802355562

Garcia, M. B., Nadelson, L. S., & Yeh, A. (2023). *"We're going on a virtual trip!"*: A switching-replications experiment of 360-degree videos as a physical field trip alternative in primary education. *International Journal of Child Care and Education Policy, 17*, 4. https://doi.org/10.1186/s40723-023-00110-x

MacCallum, K., & Parsons, D. (2022). Integrating mobile mixed reality to enhance learning before, during, and after physical field trips. *International Journal of Mobile and Blended Learning, 14*(2), 1–11. https://doi.org/10.4018/IJMBL.304456

6 Professional Development

Cases in this chapter

6.1	Presenting at First International Conference	*page* 162
6.2	Conducting Workshops for Teacher Colleagues	165
6.3	Doing a PhD Part-Time	169
6.4	Going on a Short-Term Study-Abroad Exchange	172
6.5	Developing as a Teacher-Researcher	176
6.6	Being Active in a Language Teacher Association	179
6.7	Introducing Translanguaging in the Classroom	183

6.1 Presenting at First International Conference

Keywords
- Venezuela and USA
- International TESOL conference
- Language teacher educator
- Presenting classroom research
- Technical issues and poor presentation

6.1.1 Pre-reading Reflection

1. Have you presented at a conference before? What is your best and worst memory? If you haven't, what do you fear?
2. What do teachers and teacher educators gain from attending conferences?
3. Why do some teachers and teacher educators never attend conferences?

Luis Pérez is an English teacher and teacher educator at a university in a major city in Venezuela. He completed his undergraduate studies in the same city and a few years later his MA in TESOL at a US university, which he was fortunate to do on a scholarship. He then returned to Venezuela to begin his current university teaching job. That was five years ago. He plans to enrol for a PhD within the next year or two. Since starting work, he has continuously been engaged in small-scale exploratory action research projects, and has generated enough interesting findings, he believes, to share at a conference. He submitted a proposal to present at a large international conference in the US. It was

6.1 Presenting at First International Conference

accepted. His expenses were partly covered by a national professional association that annually sponsors a small group of teachers to attend the same conference. This was his first trip back to the US since he left after graduating. The following is extracted from Luis's reflective journal, which he wrote after his return to Venezuela.

"My conference experience was both successful and not successful. Firstly, let me briefly comment on the successful parts. All the travel went well, and the hotel was comfortable. The conference venue is amazing. I have never seen such a huge convention center before. This was my first big international conference that I have attended. The many rooms are large – I kept thinking about who would attend my session. How many people are interested in language learner identity construction in Venezuelan university classrooms? Our group of six from Venezuela, including the association president, stuck together quite a bit, but we also agreed that we must talk to as many different people as possible. I was keen to explore topics for my PhD, especially those related to learner and teacher identity.

My presentation was on the third of four days. I was very well prepared. I had practiced presenting my PowerPoint slides with colleagues and knew the content well. On the first day I went to find my room. It was big – too big for my presentation, I thought. I went to other presenters' talks in the same room and it was never more than half full, about twenty to thirty people each time. I had twenty-five minutes for my presentation, with five minutes of questions and answers. When I walked into the room to set up for my talk, no one was there. There was no presentation before mine. I struggled to connect my USB to the laptop provided. Somehow, my file wouldn't show on the computer. I tried multiple different ways to connect but had no luck. I had taken my own laptop with me and tried to connect it to the data-projector, but the systems were not in sync. By this time about five people had entered the room, including two of my colleagues from Venezuela. I called one of them to help me. I was flustered. We went back to trying to use the USB in the conference laptop. Another member of the audience (now numbered eight) also came to help and eventually we got the presentation up and running. But this had eaten into my presentation time by five minutes. When I finally got started, I looked up to an audience of eight people in this vast room, and I could feel my composure disappearing! I couldn't think straight. I mumbled my way through the presentation. I could see my two colleagues nodding in support, but they looked tense. I eventually finished in what seemed liked ages. No one left during the talk and there were one or two questions afterward, which I was able to answer. Later, having a glass of wine with my whole group of Venezuelan colleagues, I was almost in tears, but they gave me love and support. One of them then asked me, 'But did you learn anything?' This got me thinking."

6.1.2 Questions

1. Do you think Luis was qualified enough to present at a major international conference?
2. Could Luis have been better prepared or supported? If so, how and by whom?
3. In his journal entry, Luis appears to be concerned about "space." In what ways do his perceptions and encounters with space play a part in his conference experience?
4. How did you feel reading about Luis's presentation experience? If you were the presenter, would you have done anything differently at the time?
5. Luis ends his journal entry by saying, "This got me thinking." What did he possibly think about, and for how long?

6.1.3 Research Topics

Discovering Conference Keynote Speakers' Preparation and Presentation Strategies

How do experienced conference keynote speakers plan and prepare for their presentations? What strategies do they use to ensure a successful presentation? What advice do they have for novice presenters?

1. Attend a relevant language education conference that has two or three keynote or plenary speakers.
2. With the permission of the conference organizers, invite the keynote speakers individually to have coffee with you for thirty minutes after their presentations.
3. Design a short, *structured interview* (M9) with the same set of questions, in the same order, for the two or three keynote speakers. Include questions about their preparation for the presentation they delivered, the content and technology they selected, the presentation technique they preferred, what they aimed to achieve, and if they thought it was successful.
4. When you have asked the keynote speakers the structured interview questions about their presentation at this conference, engage in informal conversation with them about their experiences presenting at other conferences, and ask them for any advice they have to offer those new to conference presenting. Record the interviews and the follow-up conversations.
5. Compare the presenters' answers and advice. What are the similarities and differences?
6. How did the keynote presenters feel about the effectiveness of their presentation? Did it turn out as they planned? Did you discover any useful advice for new presenters?

Critiquing Teacher Conference Presentations
What makes for a good teacher conference presentation? In what ways can teacher presenters improve their presentations?

1. Before attending your next teacher-focused conference, determine who of your teacher (or student teacher, teacher educator) colleagues will be attending the same conference.
2. Agree to work together as a team (of about four or five) to observe each other's presentations at the conference.
3. Collaboratively, develop an *observation sheet* (M3) that records descriptions and ratings of various aspects of the presentations, including: relevance and interest of content, time management, choice and use of appropriate technology, engagement with audience, voice and hand gestures, handling of questions.
4. Commit to attending and carefully observing each other's presentations. As a group, attend a few other teachers' presentations and record your observations.
5. After the conference, collate the group's observation records and analyze them together as a team.
6. How did the members of the team perform? Were there any surprises in the way the presentations unfolded? What did the presenters learn by doing the presentations? What went noticeably wrong? How did the non-team presentations compare?
7. Compile the answers into a guide-sheet that can be distributed to other teacher presenters. Could the results become a conference presentation?

6.1.4 Resources

Inal, S., Tunaboylu, O., & Kazazoglu, S. (2023). The rise of webinars as professional development modality: Investigating the opinions of teacher educators of English. *Shanlax International Journal of Education*, *12*(1), 1–12. https://doi.org/10.34293/education.v12i1.6870

Salas, A. (2016). Attending a convention as professional development for EFL teachers. *MEXTESOL Journal*, *40*(1). https://mextesol.penamiller.com/static/indexaace.html?page=journal&id_article=1331

Tanaka, J. & Díez-Ortega, M. (2021). The impact of attending second language teaching conferences. *MITESOL Journal: An Online Publication of MITESOL*, *3*, 3. https://scholarworks.gvsu.edu/mitesol/vol3/iss1/3

6.2 Conducting Workshops for Teacher Colleagues

Keywords
- South Africa
- High school

- Head of Afrikaans Department
- Workshops for language teachers
- Lack of motivation and commitment

6.2.1 Pre-reading Reflection

1. What do you like and dislike about school-based workshops? If you are a teacher, do you find them helpful for your professional development?
2. How does going to conferences lead to professional development for teachers? Think of actual examples.
3. Who do you think should oversee professional development in schools?

Henk Prinsloo is head of the Afrikaans Language Department at a large, well-established school in the Eastern Cape region of South Africa. The department is small, but Henk is a powerful figure in the school. Now in his mid-forties, he has taught Afrikaans for many years and has held various leadership roles in several schools in the region. He has a doctorate in school administration but has remained teaching in the language classroom where he feels he belongs. Henk is motivated and liked by teachers across the school; he is also a coach of boys' rugby and cricket teams, and so he's a favorite with the students as well. Henk is loyal to the school, where he has been for over ten years now. He's passionate about it doing well, whether in the classroom or on the sports field.

English and isiXhosa are two other language departments in the school, both bigger in terms of teacher numbers and students studying the languages. During the mid-year break, some of the language teachers from all three departments traditionally go to regional and even national language education conferences. They are sponsored by the school because the principal believes that teachers need to keep up to date with recent developments – including research – in the field. They do not need to present any of their own research, although they are encouraged to. When they return to school after the break, all the language teachers (including those who did not attend conferences) meet for an hour-long debriefing and to share conference experiences and anything useful they had learned. Henk typically found these sessions to be a waste of time. Teachers chatted more about social events and their travel and about teachers from other schools than about the presentations they attended or what they had learned. He believed that these meetings needed to be formalized in some way.

In consultation with the principal, Henk proposed that in the school term following the conferences, those teachers who had attended collaborate in pairs or threes to present a series of workshops around themes relevant to language teaching and learning in the school (all three languages). At the most recent round of conferences, for example, a number of topics caught the teachers' attention, and Henk felt these could be the focus of at least three or four workshops; mobile language learning, translanguaging, and decolonizing the textbook. These were new ideas to the teachers, as far as Henk was aware, and would therefore make excellent areas to explore in workshops.

Henk was very excited about the idea of workshops; in fact, he thought that they didn't need only to follow conferences, they could be organized throughout the year, perhaps one a month. This, he believed, would maintain some sort of professional development momentum for the language teachers on an ongoing basis. He wrote down his ideas in the form of a proposal and showed it to the Afrikaans teachers, who supported it. He then took it to the principal, who also approved. But when he distributed the proposal to the other language teachers, they showed far less enthusiasm. They felt they had enough on their plates without having to organize workshops. They said participating in them would probably be acceptable, especially those following conferences, but they weren't too pleased about having also to plan and deliver workshops, and then all year round. Henk was bitterly disappointed with this outcome but was determined not to give up. With his Afrikaans colleagues, he decided he would reflect on his plan for year-round workshops and see what he could come up with for the good of their learners, their professional development, and the school as a whole.

6.2.2 Questions

1. What was the language teachers' overall attitude to post-conference debriefings and the proposed continuous professional development?
2. How might have Henk's program of workshops enhanced the teachers' professional development?
3. Henk's plan for regular, continuous workshops throughout the year for language teachers and conducted by them was not successful. What went wrong?
4. Henk was "determined not to give up." What could he do next? What might he still achieve?
5. If you were the school principal, would you continue to sponsor the language teachers to attend conferences? If so, how would you decide on budget and allocation of funds?

6.2.3 Research Topics

Assessing the Level of Participant Engagement in Language Teaching Webinars
What makes a webinar engaging for participants? Why do they stay connected online? What activities do they engage in? What presenter characteristics keep them engaged?

1. Since the Covid-19 pandemic there are literally thousands of YouTube (or similar, such as Youku) webinars freely available that cover content relevant

to language teacher education, from teaching methods, to teacher research methodologies, to approaches to maintaining teacher wellbeing.
2. Find one webinar that is relevant to a group of pre-service language teachers that you have access to. The webinar should be no longer than thirty to sixty minutes and be applicable to the work they are doing in their teacher education program. It should show all webinar content and activities.
3. Prepare a short *survey* (M17) for completion by the pre-service teachers after they have viewed the webinar. In the survey, ask them to rate and rank various aspects of the webinar, such as: clarity of presentation, method of participant activities (e.g., open discussion, group work in break-out rooms), time management, participant videos on or off, use of technology.
4. Watch the video in class and then ask the teachers to complete the survey. Then have an open discussion about their opinions on the webinar. What kept the participants engaged?
5. Collect the survey responses and make notes on the discussion.
6. What makes the webinar a good one? How active are the participants? What are its shortcomings?

Measuring Enthusiasm for Professional Development (PD) Workshops in a Busy Language School
How eagerly do teachers in a school welcome notice of forthcoming PD workshops? Why do or don't they look forward to them?

1. Visit a language school that regularly holds PD workshops for its teachers. Arrange to meet the organizer of the workshops. Inquire about the program of workshops, their purpose and content, who attends, and who usually facilitates the workshops. Ask if you can see any policy documents related to PD in the school.
2. Now meet with a *focus group* (M8) of teachers at the school. Invite all the language teachers and meet at the school for about an hour.
3. Before the meeting, plan a set of discussion topics similar to those addressed with the workshop coordinator, but add topics about teachers' willingness to participate, and their reasons for wanting or not wanting to participate.
4. Work through all the topics during the discussion, allowing free flow of interaction. Record the focus group discussion.
5. Listen to the recording of the discussion and transcribe those parts that most saliently focus on the issue of having to participate in school PD workshops.
6. Are the PD workshops worthwhile? Do they contribute to their professional development? Are the teachers' comments potentially useful for the coordinator, or for PD workshop coordinators in other contexts?

6.2.4 Resources

Hismanoglu, M. (2010). Effective professional development strategies of English language teachers. *Procedia – Social and Behavioral Sciences*, *2*(2), 990–995. https://doi.org/10.1016/j.sbspro.2010.03.139

Milton, C., du Plessis, S., & van der Heever, H. (2020). English as an additional language: Professional development needs of early childhood practitioners in historically disadvantaged contexts. *South African Journal of Childhood Education*, *10*(1), a804. https://doi.org/10.4102/sajce.v10i1.804

Sadeghi, K. & Richards, J. C. (2021). Professional development among English language teachers: Challenges and recommendations for practice. *Heliyon*, *7* (9), e08053. https://doi.org/10.1016/j.heliyon.2021.e08053

6.3 Doing a PhD Part-Time[1]

Keywords
- Austria
- High school
- EFL teacher
- PhD studies
- Attending a doctoral colloquium

6.3.1 Pre-reading Reflection

1. In an educational system that you are familiar with, is it unusual for secondary school teachers to study for a PhD?
2. What challenges do you think they would face while studying and teaching at the same time?
3. How might they benefit from having completed the PhD?

Verena Secondary School in southern Austria has a good reputation. Students do well and their parents are happy with their educational development and the school's impressive pass rate. Students enjoy life at the school; the teachers are dedicated, have good qualifications, and are keen to organize extracurricular activities. The leadership team is experienced. It manages the staffing and budget of the school appropriately and ethically and adheres to regional curriculum and assessment policies. It is also generally supportive of student

---

[1] This case was inspired by my participation as a visiting professor in a doctoral colloquium in Austria.

and staff initiatives that align with the mission of the school. On the whole, the school is a well-functioning institution.

Maria is an English teacher at Verena Secondary School. She's been working there for six years – her first job after graduating with an MA degree. She loves her job. She gets on well with her students and her colleagues, and she gets good results; her students learn English. Maria plans to teach English for a few years before becoming a language teacher educator. Her ambition is to become a university professor. For now, though, her focus is on her own professional development so that she can continue to learn and grow as an English teacher at Verena Secondary School. She therefore enrolled to do a PhD at a local university with a very good reputation in language education and applied linguistics. There she met fellow teachers who were also keen to enhance their teaching careers. Maria worked with a supervisor who was an expert in CLIL (Content and Language Integrated Learning), the topic of Maria's PhD research. Maria has been working on her PhD for just over a year. She is making slow progress, but this is not a concern for her. She has a busy life as a teacher and she considers the PhD work to be a part-time, yet exciting, addition to her professional workload.

The school, however, is not at all interested in Maria's PhD activities. They don't support her financially (e.g., by paying any university-related costs), professionally (e.g., by releasing her from teaching duties to attend academic seminars or workshops), or emotionally (e.g., by encouraging her progress). There will be no reward when she finally graduates. Maria is not particularly distressed by the school's lack of engagement with her academic studies. She knew when she started the PhD that doing so was an independent decision, that it was connected to her personal life and professional goals, and that the school neither required further study by its teachers nor had any responsibility for supporting them while studying. She is aware of all of this, but still feels a little uneasy that there was zero acknowledgement from the school with regard to her PhD work.

A number of universities in the region hold an annual doctoral colloquium. At the three-day colloquium, students present their work-in-progress and receive feedback from fellow students and professors from the participating universities as well as from other invited professors. Students also take part in one-on-one coaching sessions with the professors. It is a great opportunity for the PhD students to (re-)motivate themselves and to plan for the year ahead. Maria applied to attend the colloquium and has been accepted. There are financial costs involved, and Maria is willing to cover those herself. Her school, however, won't allow her to attend the colloquium because it would require one day away from her regular teaching duties (the other colloquium days fall on a weekend). She decides not to appeal their decision because she knows what their answer will be.

6.3.2 Questions

1. How reasonable are Maria's long-term professional career goals? Where does a completed PhD fit into these goals?

6.3 Doing a PhD Part-Time

2. How would you describe Maria's imagined future teacher identity? What are the characteristics and job expectations of this identity?
3. Does Verena Secondary School's attitude toward Maria's PhD studies surprise you?
4. By not participating in the colloquium, what will Maria miss out on that might be useful for: (a) her PhD studies, and (b) her teaching work at the school?
5. Regarding the doctoral colloquium, do you think the school's treatment of Maria is fair? What alternatives might there be?

6.3.3 Research Topics

Understanding Language Teachers' Motives for Doing a PhD While Teaching Full-Time
What motivates language teachers to study toward a PhD part-time while teaching full-time? What is their goal? How does doing a PhD relate to their work?

1. Through a university program that you have access to, contact up to five PhD students who are also full-time language teachers.
2. Meet with them individually to *interview* (M9) them about their motives for doing a PhD while teaching. Present them with the following five possibilities and ask them to comment on each one in relation to their own motivations and experiences: (1) for personal development, (2) for academic development, (3) for research knowledge and skills development, (4) for teaching practice development, and (5) for the benefit of their students.
3. After they comment on each of these, invite the teachers to add any further reasons, and then ask them to share their experiences of studying part-time. How do they cope with work and studying at the same time? Record the five interviews and transcribe them.
4. What are the main reasons the teachers give for studying toward a PhD? How do they explain their motives? Why is further study important to them? What professional development goals do they have for themselves?

Scrutinizing University Doctoral Web Pages for Language Teacher Relevance
How useful is doctoral study for practicing language teachers? What promises do doctoral programs make to language teachers, if any?

1. Search the internet for *web pages* (M6) of university doctoral programs in TESOL or Applied Linguistics. Select programs from a range of geographical contexts. Include those that provide sufficient information about their rationale, goals, and relevance to the language teaching and learning profession.

2. Analyze the web pages for *keywords, phrases, and statements* (M10) that show the programs' commitment and relevance to language teachers. What do they say? Is there any explicit content that applies to in-service language teachers wanting to do a PhD?
3. Do the doctoral programs appear to offer value for practicing teachers? Do programs in different geopolitical contexts vary in what they promise prospective students?

6.3.4 Resources

Cong-Lem, N., Truong, K. D., Zhu, B., & Long, Z. (2025). Identity transitions, experiences, and agency: A collaborative autoethnography of Asian international TESOL doctoral students. *The Language Learning Journal*, *53*(2), 143–158. https://doi.org/10.1080/09571736.2024.2349052

Koay, J. (2023). Self-directed professional development activities: An autoethnography. *Teaching and Teacher Education*, *133*, 104258. https://doi.org/10.1016/j.tate.2023.104258

Ooi, L. H. & Othman, J. (2023). Challenges faced by ESL in-service teachers enrolled in a teacher education programme via open distance learning in Malaysia. *Asian Association of Open Universities Journal*, *18*(2), 121–131. https://doi.org/10.1108/AAOUJ-12-2022-0173

6.4 Going on a Short-Term Study-Abroad Exchange

Keywords
- United Kingdom and Colombia
- University
- BA student of Spanish and education
- Study abroad
- Inequitable educational experiences

6.4.1 Pre-reading Reflection

1. Have you ever studied abroad – either as a language learner or a teacher? If not, why not?
2. What are some of the benefits of studying abroad for language teachers?
3. What could go wrong, professionally, during study abroad?

Margaret, a BA student specializing in Spanish and Education at a British university, was selected to go on a study-abroad sojourn to Colombia for six weeks. She was part of a group of thirty students from four regional universities who were sponsored by an international organization. Their expenses were fully covered during their stay – from airfares to accommodation to living costs. The study-abroad program involved living with a homestay family, Spanish lessons, observing Spanish classroom teaching at a local school, and going on field trips to educational institutions. The overall goal of the program was for the students to improve their Spanish speaking skills, develop intercultural competence, learn about language teaching methods, and become familiar with the educational system of a different country. Although the study-abroad program was short, a further aim was for the students (pre-service teachers) to develop both personally and professionally by experiencing a different culture and living independently away from their familiar home environments. They would receive university credit toward their undergraduate degree.

The group met regularly during the study-abroad sojourn; not only during lessons and when together on field trips, but also for sessions during which they reflected on their observations and experiences. Margaret enjoyed these sessions. She found the facilitators – teacher educators from the participating universities – to be kind and supportive and the conversations stimulating and reassuring. They not only critically deconstructed recent experiences, but they also planned strategies for ensuring productive work in the future. One educational field trip toward the end of their stay in Colombia received special attention, and Margaret was somewhat unsettled as a result of the discussion. Five members of the group, including Margaret, had visited a rural school not far from the city where they were stationed. They were chaperoned by a local tour guide and a lecturer from the host university. Both the guide and the lecturer warned the group that the school was located in a very poor area and that teaching and learning took place in difficult circumstances. They were warmly welcomed at the school, in Spanish, by two of the teachers and escorted into one of the teaching areas (more than one class was taught in the same teaching space).

Simply by the way the students dressed, it was immediately clear to Margaret how poor they were. And looking around the teaching space, there was little evidence of any attractive learning resources. The few minutes of the lesson that Margaret observed consisted mainly of teacher talk with students copying down words from the board into their notebooks. Probably because of her own limited Spanish, it wasn't clear to Margaret what subject was being taught. Other unsupervised students appeared not to be doing anything – perhaps they were in another class level. Margaret left the school feeling very uneasy.

During the next full group session, Margaret reported on the school visit and tried to express the cause of her discomfort. It wasn't only because of the poverty, or the lack of resources, or the teaching methods. She was obviously aware that educational differences existed around the world and was expecting to come across these on her study-abroad trip to Colombia, especially in rural areas, with which she had no personal experience. What disturbed her, instead, was the group's presence at the school in the first place. On the drive home from the school, Margaret felt that she had been to a tourist site – to gaze at the poor and their unfortunate learning conditions. The group of White foreigners had left without offering anything in return. The tour guide had done his job and received his payment. Margaret tried to share these thoughts and associated feelings with the group. She struggled to articulate them clearly, and for once she didn't quite get the support she was looking for.

6.4.2 Questions

1. Whether language learner or language teacher, who are typically participants in study-abroad programs? Think specifically of the following demographics: socioeconomic status, ethnicity, nationality.
2. What are some of the benefits of a homestay during study abroad? What functions could the homestay family perform in achieving the goals of study-abroad sojourners?
3. How might the field trip to the rural school have been better planned and executed by the study-abroad organizers?
4. Why do you think Margaret struggled to articulate her thoughts and feelings about the visit to the school? What prevented her from saying explicitly what was on her mind? Why was she not supported?
5. Should the visit to the rural school have taken place?

6.4.3 Research Topics

Investigating What In-service Language Teachers Learn While Studying Abroad

What is it that language teachers learn when studying abroad? Does learning relate only to professional development? What about learning beyond the classroom?

1. Through a local university in your region, establish contact with in-service teachers from abroad who are studying there for a graduate qualification such as an MA in Applied Linguistics or TESOL.
2. Obtain consent to work with five to ten teachers for four weeks (or longer, if feasible), preferably with the support of one of their teacher educators.
3. At the end of each week, ask the teachers to send you *a photograph* (M12) that depicts something they have learned during the week and that will be useful to them when they return to teach in their home country.
4. Accompanying the photograph, request that they write a 100–200-word description of what it is they have learned.

5. After the four weeks (or longer), collate the visual and written data for each teacher and arrange to meet them virtually on Zoom or a similar platform. *Interview* (M9) them individually for about thirty minutes to ask for clarifications and to probe further into their learning and its usefulness for their post-sojourn teaching.
6. What people and places are in the photographs and how did they influence the teachers' learning? What new knowledge and skills will the teachers take back to their home countries? Did they experience any emotional challenges or learning difficulties?

Questioning Inequities in Opportunities for Pre-service Teachers to Study Abroad
Who gets to study abroad and who doesn't? What are pre-service teachers' perceptions of study-abroad opportunities in their own teacher education program and generally?

1. Design an *anonymous questionnaire* (M17) on Google Forms or Qualtrics (or similar) to be distributed to a closed group of early-stage, pre-service teachers studying language teaching or on education courses.
2. On the questionnaire, ask the teachers if they intend to seek opportunities to study abroad, and to give reasons for their answer. Include questions about: (a) who typically studies abroad as part of their program, (b) who does not, (c) what enables some to study abroad but not others, (d) what the potential benefits are of study abroad, (e) what the benefits are of staying at home, and (f) how study abroad could be made more accessible for all.
3. Include space on the questionnaire for respondents to reflect on their perceptions of opportunities and inequities in study abroad for (non-)participants beyond their own teacher education program.
4. Give the teachers about ten days to respond to the questionnaire. After analyzing the findings, share them with the closed group of pre-service teachers.
5. Do the pre-service teachers have strong desires to study abroad? Are they aware of socioeconomic inequities that enable or prevent opportunities to study abroad? What ideas do they have for increasing study-abroad opportunities for pre-service language teachers?

6.4.4 Resources

Kasun, G. S. & Saavedra, C. M. (2016). Disrupting ELL teacher candidates' identities: Indigenizing teacher education in one study abroad program. *TESOL Quarterly, 50*(3), 684–707. https://doi.org/10.1002/tesq.319

Monari Mwebi, B. & Brigham, S. M. (2009). Preparing North American preservice teachers for global perspectives: An international teaching practicum experience in Africa. *Alberta Journal of Educational Research*, *55*(3), 414–427. https://doi.org/10.11575/ajer.v55i3.55336

Vu, N. T., Ta, T. M. H., & Le, T. T. H. (2024). Teacher returnees from overseas programs in the west: A narrative study in Vietnam. *Frontiers in Communication*, *9*, 1311179. https://doi.org/10.3389/fcomm.2024.1311179

6.5 Developing as a Teacher-Researcher

Keywords
- Singapore
- Secondary school
- English teacher
- Desire to become a teacher-researcher
- Time and workload constraints

6.5.1 Pre-reading Reflection

1. Reflect on your experiences with time management in your university studies. How do or did you allocate time for reading, lectures, assignments, and personal interests?
2. Consider the importance of time management in pursuing research while working as a teacher. How might teachers prioritize their responsibilities and commitments to create space for research activities?
3. How important is engagement in research (i.e., doing research) for the professional development of language teachers?

Ms. Wong is a young English teacher at a secondary school in Singapore. With an MA degree in Applied Linguistics from a good university, she embarked on her teaching journey eager to make a difference in the lives of her students. Before she started university, she struggled to decide between studying to become a teacher or a social worker. Coming from a wealthy family, she has had a desire her whole life to help those less fortunate than herself. Ms. Wong's interest in action research stems particularly from its immediate relevance to classroom life, her aspirations to continuously improve her teaching methods, and the potential to improve her students' language learning. She further believes that doing action research is a stepping stone to learning about other approaches to research.

Teaching in a busy secondary school in Singapore comes with its challenges and demands. Ms. Wong constantly juggles between lesson planning, marking assignments, attending meetings, and organizing extracurricular activities. The full curriculum and high expectations leave her with very little time to spare, let alone planning and conducting the action research projects she has in mind. Despite her hectic schedule, however, Ms. Wong maintains a deep interest in action research. She recognizes the potential benefits it could bring to her students and her teaching colleagues, especially those who are willing to collaborate with her. Through her research, she hopes to identify effective teaching strategies tailored to the diverse needs of her students, ultimately enhancing their learning outcomes. During her MA, Ms. Wong completed a course on teaching strategies and this topic is something she is very interested in. More generally, Ms. Wong sees research as an avenue to staying updated with the latest educational trends and to contributing to the ongoing discussions in the field, perhaps by publishing some of her findings in local teacher journals. She sees herself in the future as being a teacher-researcher.

However, the reality is that time is a luxury she cannot afford. The demands of her teaching job leave her with little to no time for research. Every moment outside of school hours is precious, often allocated to personal responsibilities or much-needed rest. Despite her enthusiasm for research, Ms. Wong finds herself unable to dedicate the necessary time and effort to embark on her research journey. Her desire to engage in action research is further fuelled by the educational landscape in Singapore. With a focus on innovation and continuous improvement, there is a growing emphasis on evidence-based practices in education. Ms. Wong sees action research as a means to align her teaching methodologies with best practice and to contribute to the development of English teaching in her school and the overall improvement of the education system in Singapore more broadly. She has big goals.

The demands of her teaching, however, leave Ms. Wong torn between her passion for research and the constraints of time. She constantly feels a sense of urgency, pressuring her to get going with the action research ideas she has. Yet, the reality of her situation means that time remains a scarce resource. Ms. Wong is faced with the realization that research may require sacrifices, compromises, and creative solutions. Despite these challenges, she remains determined to find a way to balance her desire to develop into a recognized teacher-researcher with the demands of her job at the school she loves.

6.5.2 Questions

1. In what ways can teacher education programs, like Ms. Wong's MA in Applied Linguistics, prepare teachers to balance the demands of teaching with their research aspirations?
2. What strategies or approaches could Ms. Wong explore at school to carve out time for action research within her busy teaching schedule?

3. There appears to be no requirement from Ms. Wong's school for her to do research. Is she putting too much pressure on herself?
4. Because of time constraints at school, do you think Ms. Wong should sacrifice what she enjoys at home and in her leisure time in order to achieve her research ambitions? Why, or why not?
5. Do you predict that Ms. Wong will be a successful teacher-researcher in the future? Give a reason for your answer. What do you think her career trajectory might look like?

6.5.3 Research Topics

Exploring Research Time Possibilities for Language Teachers Using a Time-Tracking App

Do teachers have enough time for action research at school? How do they know? Are they too overloaded with other duties?

1. Engage with a language teacher in a primary or high school who is eager to do action research but struggles to find the time during the school day.
2. Meet with them for a *short interview* (M9) to inquire about their work schedules and workloads, their perceptions of the time available during the day, and their desires for research.
3. Ask them to download a time-tracking app (such as Toggl Track) on their smartphone and to activate it for one working week during school times. Set the app to record time allocated to classes, meetings, preparation time, recess time, grading time, and non-work time (i.e., time wasting).
4. At the end of the week, view the data from the app with the teacher. Focus on two questions: (1) How much free time is available in a day, and over the week, that could be used for research purposes? (2) How could the teacher's time allocations be adjusted to make time for research?
5. Repeat the inquiry with a second teacher, and a third. Are common patterns emerging? How could action research be added to or integrated into the workday?

Comparing Teacher-Researchers' Identities in Two Different Settings

How do language teachers reflexively see themselves as researchers in their workplace? How do they describe their teacher-researcher identities? How engaged are they in research?

1. Connect with two language teachers who work in contrasting educational contexts – one that recognizes its language teachers as researchers and allocates time for them to do research, and the other where teachers must find their own time to do research.

2. The workplace settings should be the same for both teachers – high schools, for example, or university language departments.
3. Design a *semi-structured* (M9), *narrative interview* (M16) that elicits the teachers' experiences and stories of conducting research in their current workplaces.
4. Ask the teachers to tell you stories about their research projects, how doing research makes them feel as professional teachers, how they see themselves as researchers (i.e., their identities), and whether their institutions support their research activity.
5. Record the interviews and transcribe them in detail. Search for stories, and analyze them for significant characters, timelines, and where the action of the stories takes place.
6. Do a comparative analysis of the two teachers' experiences.
7. Which teacher is more engaged in research? How does their research activity relate to their reflexive teacher-researcher identities? Does institutional support (or lack thereof) contribute to their identity construction in some way?

6.5.4   Resources

Pham, C. H., Chau, N. N. T., & Nguyen, K. H. N. (2023). "Follow your research career or choose your family": Female language teachers' agency in their research engagement. *Cogent Education*, *10*(2), 2236456. https://doi.org/10.1080/2331186X.2023.2236456

Rose, H. & McKinley, J. (2022). May I see your credentials, please? Displays of pedagogical expertise by language teaching researchers. *The Modern Language Journal*, *106*(3), 528–546. https://doi.org/10.1111/modl.12794

Uyen, N. T. T. & Vien, T. (2021). Teachers as researchers: The perceptions and practices of Cantho tertiary EFL teachers. *European Journal of Foreign Language Teaching*, *5*(5), 57–83. http://dx.doi.org/10.46827/ejfl.v5i5.3916

6.6   Being Active in a Language Teacher Association

Keywords
- Tunisia
- High school
- Member of a teacher association
- Developing professionally
- Time and work constraints

6.6.1   Pre-reading Reflection

1. Name your top three professional development goals? Would you consider them to be ambitious?

2. What are the benefits of joining a professional language teacher association?
3. Imagine being in a full-time job where your workload is too heavy. How might this affect your professional development?

Dr. Lisa Gharbi is a high school teacher in a small city in Tunisia, North Africa. She is a hard worker and ambitious. Soon after graduating with her undergraduate language teaching qualification, she got her first job teaching English and French at a local school. Within a year she started studying part-time for her MA at one of the city's universities. And three years later, sponsored by her wealthy family, she went to the UK to do her PhD in applied linguistics. She plans to work in a university one day as a teacher educator but feels she needs more experience teaching languages in the public school system. So, when she returned to Tunisia with her PhD, she successfully applied for the position she now holds at an academic high school.

In Dr. Gharbi's professional development plan, with a tenured university job as her goal, she has an ongoing research program. She also has an innovative approach to teaching, which takes into account recent pedagogical developments she encounters in her reading and conference attendance. She further believes that being an active member of a professional language teacher association would help her gain broader insights into both the profession and the language teaching "industry." Her school principal suggested that this might also benefit the school and thus agreed to give her two hours a week if she was appointed to an executive position on a relevant professional body. Dr. Gharbi consequently joined the national English teacher association that is affiliated to an international network of similar associations, and at the following national conference was appointed to the executive committee as a member-at-large. She held this position for one year, and loved it. She regularly met teachers, teacher educators, and researchers from schools and universities across the country at local and national meetings and online, some of whom were very experienced and had served in the field for many years. Dr. Gharbi felt that she was becoming more confident talking about language teaching and learning in Tunisia. She had always felt a little uneasy that she had done her PhD overseas, but now she was feeling much more at home. When the general secretary of the committee became ill, Dr. Gharbi was asked if she would temporarily step into the role, at least until the next Annual General Meeting (AGM) when a new committee would be elected. Without much thought she agreed to do so.

It didn't take long for Dr. Gharbi to realize that she might have taken on more than she probably should have. On the one hand, she was learning an enormous amount. Part of her role was to liaise with her international counterparts, and she loved doing this. She discovered how language teaching and learning took place in other countries, what their priorities and policies were, and she was invited to attend some of their online workshops and meetings. This information helped her make sense of her own work environment and gave her an invaluable overview of language teacher education. On the other hand, this all took up a lot of her time – much more than the two hours her principal had assigned to her at school. She also calculated that being so immersed in international matters meant that she was neglecting her work for her home Tunisian association. Dr. Gharbi started to feel the pressure. Perhaps she was doing too much too quickly. Perhaps she was compromising her own professional development – "spreading myself too thin," she reflected.

6.6.2 Questions

1. What is your opinion of the first few years of Dr. Gharbi's professional teacher journey?
2. Why do you think Dr. Gharbi got elected to the association's executive committee so easily? What counted in her favor?
3. Professional development is personal, but also benefits others. Who probably also benefitted from Dr. Gharbi's work on the professional association? In what ways?
4. Should teachers be able to negotiate some control of their workloads? What could Dr. Gharbi have done to lessen her commitments?
5. Do you agree with Dr. Gharbi that she was "spreading" herself "too thin"? How could she have strategized her professional development better?

6.6.3 Research Topics

Investigating Professional Association Work's Influence on Teacher Professional Development

How does serving as a member on a professional association committee contribute to a teacher's professional development? Is it worth the extra work? What do they gain?

1. Through a local professional language teachers' association, get in touch with a member of the executive committee who is also a language teacher in a local school. Alternatively, work with a teacher you know from your institution who is a committee member.
2. Prepare a *narrative interview* (M16) schedule, and let the teacher know what you are interested in learning about. Send them a list of topics to be covered before the interview.
3. The schedule will inquire about the professional experiences of the teacher, including their training, current work and workload, interest in joining the professional association and serving on the executive committee, and their desires for the future.

4. Set two hours aside for the interview. During the interview, ask the teacher to tell you about their experiences. Invite them to tell you their stories. Share your own stories to contribute to the conversation. Record the narrative interview.
5. Transcribe key moments in the interview, and from these, *construct a story* (M16) of the teacher's professional life and how serving the association influences their work and goals.
6. Share the story with the teacher, and then meet again to discuss it. Ask the teacher if they have anything to add or clarify.
7. How important is the committee work to the teacher? Does it increase their workload significantly? Does it relate in any way to their classroom teaching?

Asking About Primary and High School Teachers' Representation on International TESOL and Applied Linguistics Associations
How well represented are primary and high school language teachers on the committees of international TESOL and applied linguistics organizations? Is there a weighting in favor of university academics? Is the professional development of school teachers disadvantaged in any way through (non-) representation?

1. *Review the web pages* (M6) of four or five large international TESOL, ELT, or applied linguistics associations. Look specifically at the membership of their committees, such as the executive committee, awards committee, research committee, professional development committee, and marketing and publications committee.
2. Do you identify any primary or high school language teachers on those committees? What is the academic and workplace background of the members of the committees?
3. Write to the president of the associations and ask questions about committee representation – specifically, if school-level language teachers are welcome on committees; how they are targeted, recruited and supported; and what contributions they potentially make to the association.
4. Are there reasons why school teachers are or are not represented on the associations' committees? How do they benefit professionally by being on a committee?

6.6.4 Resources

Creagh, S., Thompson, G., Mockler, N., Stacey, M., & Hogan, A. (2025). Workload, work intensification and time poverty for teachers and school leaders: A systematic research synthesis. *Educational Review, 77*(2), 661–680. https://doi.org/10.1080/00131911.2023.2196607

Slaughter, Y., Bonar, G., & Keary, A. (2022). The role of membership viewpoints in shaping language teacher associations: A Q methodology analysis. *TESOL Quarterly, 56*(1), 281–307. https://doi.org/10.1002/tesq.3068

Xing, H., Liu, L., Jiang, A. L., & Hunt, N. (2024). Unpacking a female language teacher's identity transformations: A perspective of multiple I-positions. *Frontiers in Psychology, 15*, 1291940. https://doi.org/10.3389/fpsyg.2024.1291940

6.7 Introducing Translanguaging in the Classroom

Keywords
- Kathmandu, Nepal
- Lower secondary school
- Nepali and English teachers
- Teacher Professional Support (TPS) workshops
- Not understanding translanguaging

6.7.1 Pre-reading Reflection

1. What do you know about translanguaging as a concept and as a pedagogical practice?
2. What is your view about a teacher insisting on "English only" in their English classroom?
3. If you have read any research on translanguaging or attended a conference presentation about translanguaging, what do you remember about what you read or heard? If you haven't, what would you like to read or hear?

Soti Secondary School is located on the outskirts of Kathmandu, Nepal. It is a large school with an innovative principal. She is a respected leader and community member and is often seen at local professional and social events engaging with neighborhoods and organizations. She loves to see her school do well and encourages initiatives that reflect new ideas and promise better outcomes for the students. The school has an active Nepali Language Department, with its teachers involved in local professional associations. The Nepali language teachers collaborate with teachers from nearby schools to organize teacher meetings and other Teacher Professional Support (TPS) activities endorsed by the local education authorities. The Nepali Language Department is a strong department and is popular with the students, who get good results.

The English Language Department, on the other hand, has not been doing as well. The school has struggled to fill all English teaching posts and staff seem to come and go. It is a large department because all students at the school study English as a subject. A handful of English teachers have been at the school for many years and are rather set in their ways, both in terms of classroom practice and their outlook on professional development, which is very narrow, if not altogether non-existent. The English Language Department is not a disaster, though, and produces satisfactory results. It is just not as vibrant and progressive as the Nepali Language Department – in the eyes of the principal and the school community.

One of the newer members of the English Language Department, Mr. Paudel, is currently doing his MA in Applied Linguistics part-time at one of the Kathmandu universities. In his studies, he has recently come across the concept of *translanguaging* and how it can be applied in language learning classrooms. If he were to introduce translanguaging into his classes, he could use some Nepali in his lessons, and he could let students do the same – not only in their speaking and writing, but also when integrating technology for assignments and projects, for example. This intrigued him, and so he decided to explore the possibility of raising awareness of the idea and applications of translanguaging with his colleagues in the English Language Department in one or two professional development (PD) workshops. He proposed this to the school principal, who was immediately excited about the prospect. She said she would contact the regional education authority to have the PD workshops sanctioned as an official TPS activity. She further recommended that the Nepali Language Department become involved. Mr. Paudel was energized and set about making plans for two workshops, which the principal asked him to organize and lead.

Mr. Paudel scheduled a meeting for all Nepali and English teachers to announce the topic and the workshop schedule. The teachers were used to participating in TPS activities and had no objection to workshops, especially since they were scheduled during school time and counted toward their annual PD goals. Teacher Professional Support gave them time off regular teaching, they enjoyed socializing and the catering, and, as they say, they "always learn something." But this first meeting did not go well. Within the first fifteen minutes, a lot of questions were asked. Neither the Nepali teachers nor the English teachers understood the concept of *translanguaging*, and when Mr. Paudel said, "we will learn more about it, but for now, it is like code-switching," there was an uproar. The Nepali teachers said it was not relevant to them; all the students speak Nepali, the teachers speak Nepali, and they are studying Nepali – why would other languages come into the classroom? Some of the English teachers had always insisted on "English only" classrooms and did not allow their students to speak Nepali – how will they learn English if they don't use it? After the meeting Mr. Paudel felt somewhat deflated and decided he would report back to the principal and ask for advice.

6.7.2 Questions

1. The teachers appear amenable to professional development initiatives, especially those embedded in school time. How could the school build on this positive attitude when planning further workshops?
2. Is translanguaging an appropriate topic for a TPS activity in this school context? Why, or why not?
3. Is Mr. Paudel the right person to organize and lead the translanguaging TPS workshops? Give a reason for your answer.
4. Do you think there is a chance the TPS workshops will go ahead? What, in your opinion, is the main barrier? What might save them?
5. What advice should the Soti Secondary School principal give Mr. Paudel? How should she go about doing this?

6.7.3 Research Topics

Evaluating the Effects of Facilitating a Translanguaging Workshop with Busy In-service Language Teachers

What can busy in-service language teachers learn about translanguaging in a one-hour workshop? What are their views about translanguaging after the workshop?

1. Recruit a group of about five to ten language teachers from a local school or university who know little or nothing about translanguaging but are interested and willing to learn about the concept and its applicability to their teaching.
2. As workshop facilitator, inform the teachers that you are not a translanguaging expert but that as a group you will all learn together.
3. Prepare some basic and short pre-workshop reading and distribute it to the teachers. For the workshop, prepare two or three introductory PowerPoint (or similar) slides and relevant group tasks and discussion topics.
4. Facilitate the workshop, working through the slides and activities, keeping the discussion focused and collegial.
5. At the end of the workshop, distribute a pre-prepared *evaluation survey* (M17) which asks participants to reflect on their workshop experience and their learning. Include specific questions, but also allow for reflective freewriting.
6. Do the teachers feel that they learned anything useful about translanguaging? Was it worth the time? Could they take anything about translanguaging back to their classrooms?

Asking Language Teachers What Teaching Techniques or Activities They Will Not Easily Forgo

Which of their classroom teaching techniques or activities do language teachers believe work well? Which of these have they been using for a long time? Which will they not be willing to give up?

1. Contact two (or more) experienced language teachers and ask them to write a one-paragraph description of a language teaching technique or activity that they have used for some time and believe works well in their classrooms. Collect the descriptions and read them carefully.
2. Meet with the teachers and ask them to show you a lesson plan with accompanying teaching materials that include that particular technique or activity.
3. Examine the *plans and materials* (M13) to understand their aims and procedures.
4. *Observe the teachers* (M3) teaching a lesson that includes the specified technique or activity.
5. After the lessons, *interview* (M9) the teachers individually about the effectiveness of the technique or activity, why they continue to use it, and if they would be willing to give it up if new methods are suggested. Make notes of what the teachers say after the interview.
6. Why do teachers hold onto some teaching techniques and activities, and give others up? What about these activities do they believe works well in their classrooms? Do the teachers have a positive outlook in terms of their professional development?

6.7.4 Resources

Cenoz, J. & Gorter, D. (2022). Pedagogical translanguaging and its application to language classes. *RELC Journal, 53*(2), 342–354. https://doi.org/10.1177/00336882221082751

Nyimbili, F. & Mwanza, D. S. (2021). Translanguaging challenges faced by teachers and learners in first grade multilingual literacy classrooms in Zambia. *International Journal on Studies in English Language and Literature, 9*(3), 20–31. https://doi.org/10.20431/2347-3134.0903003

Saud, D. S. (2023). Translanguaging practices in EFL classrooms: Teachers' perspectives from Darchula. *KMC Journal, 5*(2), 59–73. https://doi.org/10.3126/kmcj.v5i2.58230

7 Teacher Research

Cases in this chapter

7.1	Teachers' Conceptions of Research	*page* 187
7.2	Choosing a Dissertation Topic	191
7.3	An Ethical Dilemma on a Teaching Practicum	194
7.4	Developing a Teacher-Researcher Identity	198
7.5	Publishing Research in English	202
7.6	Unsuccessful Research Collaboration	205
7.7	Lack of Research Training	209

7.1 Teachers' Conceptions of Research

Keywords
- Australia
- University
- Teacher educator and PhD student
- Workshop on teacher reflection
- Confusing research and reflective practice

7.1.1 Pre-reading Reflection

1. What's the first word that comes to mind when you think of doing research? What does this word mean?
2. Is it still research if a project has only one participant, who is also the researcher?
3. What type of research would you expect busy language teachers to be doing in their classrooms? What would their research look like?

Daniel Aziz works as a lecturer at a university in Sydney, Australia. He has an MA in Applied Linguistics from the same university, and is almost finished with his PhD, again at the same university. Daniel has worked as an English teacher in the Australian school system for nearly twenty years. When he decided to do his PhD, he felt it was best to leave his teaching position and study full-time. His PhD research is on language teacher reflection and how this relates to teacher learning and professional development. Soon after starting his

PhD, he was appointed to a graduate teaching assistantship and after a year as a student, a two-year, fixed-term lecturer position was advertised at his university. He thought he would take a chance and apply, relying on his experience as a teacher and his knowledge of the institution to get him the job. Daniel's application was successful.

Daniel's lecturer contract requires him to focus on language teacher education – teaching – and he has no research requirement. He is fully involved in working with pre-service language teachers. He teaches courses, observes and mentors student teachers on their practicum, and supervises their action research projects. He also conducts workshops for in-service teachers from city schools who come onto campus, usually on weekends or in the evenings, specifically for professional development purposes. The topic of one such workshop was the same as his PhD, *teacher reflection*. A group of about twenty language teachers gathered on campus one Saturday morning for a three-hour workshop to develop skills appropriate for effective teacher reflection in their high school language classes. Teachers of English, French, Arabic, and Spanish were part of the group.

The workshop introduced teachers to the concept of reflection and then presented several methods that teachers could use to reflect on their classroom practice, such as writing and analyzing a digital reflective journal, being observed and then having a conversation with the observer about the lesson, and giving a questionnaire to learners to ask for their feedback on one's teaching. Daniel hadn't got very far illustrating these methods, when one of the teachers asked how they were different from doing research. This was an interesting question, and initially Daniel didn't know what to say. He decided he would ask the teachers what *they* thought research was. These are some of their comments:

1. "Well, it's obviously what academics do at university, like you. They must do research. It's part of their job – publish or perish!"
2. "Research needs a large population, and statistics, for it to be proper research."
3. "I spend a lot of time attending online webinars and coming to learn at workshops like these. This is research."
4. "Action research is fine for teachers – focusing on our own classrooms. I learn a lot about my work by doing action research."
5. "I think you need a control group, or something. I haven't done research before."
6. "For my master's dissertation I interviewed a group of French learners from my school after they returned from study abroad. I examined their experiences – fascinating."
7. "Telling stories is powerful. We could use stories to discover things."

Daniel was surprised at the wide range of research conceptualizations the teachers exhibited. Listening to these comments and taking part in the discussion that followed during the workshop, he realized that he had always, perhaps naively, assumed that teachers would have similar thoughts about what research is. The workshop was a bit of a wake-up call. He was nearly finished with his PhD, and even though he had surveyed research methods for his project, he said, "I remained in my bubble." If Daniel planned to stay in teacher education at university level in the future, especially if his contract introduced a research component, he would have to start thinking more broadly about research from a practitioner's perspective.

7.1.2 Questions

1. Do you think Daniel made the right decision to apply for the lecturer position? Give a reason for your answer.
2. During the teacher workshop, Daniel was surprised by the range of teachers' research conceptualizations, even though he himself is doing a research PhD. Did this surprise *you*?
3. Of the seven teacher comments, which do you most strongly align with in terms of your ideas about research? Why? Which do you most disagree with?
4. What *are* some similarities and differences between research methods and methods of teacher reflection? Do the different methods reflect their different purposes?
5. What path lies ahead for Daniel as a teacher educator and researcher working in a university?

7.1.3 Research Topics

Discovering Pre-service Language Teachers' Conceptions of Their Future Research

Do pre-service language teachers expect to do research when they start to teach? What kind of research do they imagine they will be doing? What do they understand by research?

1. Engage with a class of pre-service language teachers at a university or in a teacher education program that you have access to.
2. Spend two class sessions with them. In the first session, have an open discussion about the teachers' ideas about language teacher research, who does it, why, when they find the time, if it is required, and what outcomes they would expect.
3. Toward the end of the session, ask the teachers to write a *journal entry* (M14) of about 300 words in which they reflect on their expectations of doing research when they start to teach. What kind of research projects do

they expect to do? What topics will they investigate? What research methods will they use?
4. Read all the journal entries before you meet the class a second time. When analyzing the entries, search for *metaphors* (M11) that describe research and research processes, such as explore, search, probe, and discover.
5. At the second meeting, present the pre-service teachers with the list of metaphors and ask them to write next to each one (a) how it relates to their understanding of what research means to them *as teachers*, and (b) what approach to research the metaphor implies, that is, how they will do research in the future when they are teachers according to the metaphor.
6. Analyze the responses, together with the original journal entries, for teachers' conceptualizations of research, and their expectations of their future research activities.

Rating English Teachers' Level of Engagement with Research Reading
How much research-based reading do practicing English teachers do? What kind of reading do they do? Why don't some teachers engage with research-based reading?

1. Design a *closed-item questionnaire* (M17) for distribution on Google Forms or Qualtrics (or similar) to language teachers working in primary and high school contexts.
2. At the start of the questionnaire ask respondents to specify their workplace context, years of English teaching experience, and highest teaching qualification.
3. Include about fifteen to twenty statements that ask teachers about their research-based reading activity – for example, "I read research journal articles," "I spend between one and two hours per week reading research-based literature," "I search the internet to find literature relevant to my teaching practice," and "My school makes teaching journals available for all teachers."
4. For each statement provide a five-point rating scale from *Strongly Agree* to *Strongly Disagree*. At the end of the questionnaire, leave space for respondents to add any comments about their reading activity – for example, their preferences, their time commitment and enthusiasm for reading, and expected outcomes of their reading activity.
5. Analyze the quantitative data for frequency counts and convert to percentages. Compare these with the respondents' teaching experience and qualifications.
6. How much reading do the English teachers say they do? Where do they get their reading? Do more highly qualified teachers read more?

7.1.4 Resources

Banegas, D. L. (2018). Towards understanding EFL teachers' conceptions of research: Findings from Argentina. *Profile: Issues in Teachers' Professional Development, 20*(1), 57–72. https://doi.org/10.15446/profile.v20n1.61881

Kang, Y. & Yang, L. (2022). Examining EFL teachers' changing conceptions of research: A case study of a continuing professional development program in mainland China. *Frontiers in Psychology, 13*, 933061. https://doi.org/10.3389/fpsyg.2022.933061

Nguyen, M. X. N. C., Dao, P., & Iwashita, N. (2022). Nurturing teachers' research mindset in an inquiry-based language teacher education course. *The Modern Language Journal, 106*(3), 599–616. https://doi.org/10.1111/modl.12795

7.2 Choosing a Dissertation Topic

Keywords
- England, United Kingdom
- University
- MA in TESOL dissertation student
- Choosing a topic
- Topic ideas versus knowledge of methods

7.2.1 Pre-reading Reflection

1. Have you done research before? If yes, what was the topic? If you haven't done research, what topic would you like to explore?
2. What do you think are the main differences between qualitative and quantitative research methods? Which would you prefer?
3. In what ways might teachers' research findings be useful?

Ying is an international student studying at a university in London, UK. She has completed all the coursework for her MA in TESOL and it is now time to begin her 15,000-word dissertation, the final component of her degree. She needs to decide on a topic. Ying comes from China. After finishing her BA degree, she taught English for two years in informal contexts (i.e., short-term, part-time jobs) mainly within her family networks. She did well as an undergraduate student but didn't want to go into full-time employment immediately after graduating. She was supported by her family, who felt she needed more "life experience." Ying enjoyed her part-time teaching, and the reduced workload gave her time to read about language teaching, participate in online webinars and discussions, engage in professionally oriented social media, and explore opportunities for studying abroad. She became very excited about studying further, realizing that she needed a master's degree and then probably a PhD to get a full-time position as a college English teacher in China, which was what she really desired.

Ying applied to several UK universities and was successful in obtaining a place on the MA in TESOL program, where she is now studying. She sailed through the coursework, passing all courses with high grades. It seems she had spent her two years as a part-time teacher well – gaining some teaching experience and knowledge from her reading and online work. Learning about research was new to her, however. Almost all the courses had a research component, such as analyzing extracts of data provided by the lecturer or generating some personal reflections for later thematic analysis. She had also done some interviews with classmates, and in one course, interviewed a language learner from the university's affiliated community language school. When Ying did the compulsory research methods course, she realized that most of the course research activities involved what was called "qualitative" research; for example, working with words, searching for themes, asking what the content was about, and trying to understand the experiences of the participants (including her own when she analyzed her reflections) from their perspectives.

This was all very interesting, but it did not seem to gel with what Ying perceived to be "research." From her undergraduate studies in China, she learned that research involved numbers, with many participants. She had learned about experiments, and surveys, but was quite unfamiliar with trying to interpret themes. This seems like an enormous responsibility for researchers, and then the outcomes only apply to a few people. How can you generalize the findings? What use is the research, then? In her MA studies she had been taught some basic statistics and how to apply the calculations to interpret experimental data one of the lecturers had given the students. She loved manipulating the numbers and felt far more comfortable working with formulas than with words and themes. These "quantitative" methods aligned more with what she had encountered in her undergraduate studies. It felt more like research to Ying.

Ying wants the topic of her dissertation to be relevant to her future college English teaching work back in China. She also wants the findings to be useful in some way. She has a few topics in mind but can't reconcile these topics with the methods she prefers. For example, she did one course on teaching methods and another one on teacher professional development. In both these courses, "identity" was discussed, and this concept seemed interesting to Ying. A course on discourse analysis was also interesting, as was one that examined the educational politics of teaching in multilingual contexts. As far as Ying can figure out, these broad topics appear more suitable to qualitative research methods, rather than the quantitative methods she prefers. She needs to choose a topic soon; after doing so she will meet with

7.2 Choosing a Dissertation Topic

a supervisor assigned to her who specializes in the research methods appropriate for her topic.

7.2.2 Questions

1. In what ways did Ying's two-year experience immediately prior to embarking on her MA studies contribute to her professional development as a teacher and a researcher?
2. Why did Ying lean more toward quantitative research, in terms of both her conceptions of research and her preferences for doing research?
3. Do you think the MA in TESOL program sufficiently prepared Ying to begin her research dissertation? Give reasons for your answer.
4. Why is Ying concerned about her research topic being relevant and her findings being useful to her future work as a college English teacher in China?
5. How would you advise Ying about choosing her topic before meeting with her supervisor?

7.2.3 Research Topics

Investigating Preferences for Qualitative Research Methodologies Among Graduate Students

Why do graduate students in TESOL/Applied Linguistics choose qualitative research methodologies for their dissertations? What do they understand by qualitative research?

1. Contact a university with a graduate teacher education program in TESOL or Applied Linguistics and which requires students to complete a dissertation as a component of their degree.
2. Arrange with the program organizer for you to meet individually with students who are doing a qualitative-oriented dissertation.
3. Prepare a *semi-structured interview schedule* (M9) and interview each student for about an hour. In the schedule ask questions, with appropriate follow-up prompts, about why the students have chosen a qualitative research methodology for their dissertations, whether they have done a research methodology course, what about qualitative research appeals to them, why they did not choose a quantitative or mixed-methods methodological approach, and what they understand by qualitative research.
4. Aim for about eight to ten interviews. Record the interviews.
5. Analyze all interviews for salient and common responses.
6. What do the students mean by qualitative research? Why do they choose to use this approach? Is it a personal choice or is it because of the training they receive?

Inquiring into Topic Choice Among TESOL Dissertation Students
What topics do MA-level TESOL dissertation students tend to choose? How do they go about making their choice? Do they always have a choice?

1. Recruit a *focus group* (M8) of about five dissertation supervisors from a university TESOL teacher education program.
2. Before meeting with the group, ask the supervisors to check their records to recover the topics of the MA-level dissertations they have supervised over the past five or so years.
3. Also ask them to reflect on why their students chose those particular topics, if they had a choice (or did the supervisor or the institution assign them topics), and if they believe the topics were useful to the students after graduation.
4. At the focus group meeting, which could be virtual or preferably face-to-face, facilitate a discussion about these topics. Aim to get the supervisors' opinions about what challenges the students face when deciding on a topic, if they should have topics assigned to them instead, what kind of research they do or should be doing, and if students are always happy with the topics they ultimately choose. Record the focus group discussion.
5. Analyze the recording by searching for themes that relate directly to topic choice.

7.2.4 Resources

Man, J. & Zhan, J. (2023). Ensuring sustainable academic development of L2 postgraduate students and MA programs: Challenges and support in thesis writing for L2 Chinese postgraduate students. *Sustainability*, *15*(19), 14435. https://doi.org/10.3390/su151914435

Paltridge, B. (1997). Thesis and dissertation writing: Preparing ESL students for research. *English for Specific Purposes*, *16*(1), 61–70. https://doi.org/10.1016/S0889-4906(96)00028-2

Tavakoli, P. & Hasrati, M. (2018). MA TESOL dissertations in a changing global landscape: A case from Iran. *Iranian Journal of Language Teaching Research*, *6* (1), 109–128. https://doi.org/10.30466/ijltr.2018.20493

7.3 An Ethical Dilemma on a Teaching Practicum

Keywords
- United States
- University
- MA in TESOL student teacher on practicum

- Project with Spanish-speaking learners
- No institutional approval to present findings

7.3.1 Pre-reading Reflection

1. Have you ever applied for ethics approval for a research project from an institutional ethics committee or review board? What was the experience like if you have? If you haven't, have you heard what it is like?
2. Some institutions in various parts of the world don't require their researchers to obtain ethics approval. What could go wrong?
3. What ethical issues should we be particularly careful about when researching children/young people?

John is a student teacher at a university located in the southern United States. He is in his early twenties and enrolled in the MA in TESOL program. He decided early to pursue a career in English teaching, at least in the medium term because, as he says romantically, "I want to leave this place and see the world." John has an outgoing personality – he loves meeting new people, talking to them, and getting to know them. This is one of the reasons he so much enjoyed his one-semester teaching practicum, which he recently completed in a rural school a few miles away from his university. The school serves a diverse population of students, many of whom are English language learners. During his practicum, John had the opportunity to work closely with a group of ten-year-old language learners from South America, who primarily spoke Spanish at home.

For the first few weeks of the practicum, John was required to observe a lot of teaching, and only later was he able to interact more directly with the learners. One assessment requirement was to develop a portfolio of his practicum experience, including producing a journal of written reflections and a report on a project which he had to develop and carry out. Seeking to engage his students in a meaningful way, John decided to embark on a project where the students would create digital stories about their language learning experiences since moving to the US. He believed this project would not only improve their language skills but also allow them to reflect on their personal journeys and changing identities in a new country.

The students enthusiastically embraced the project, spending many hours crafting their digital stories and eagerly sharing them with their classmates. John was impressed by the depth of their reflections and the creativity they displayed in their presentations. As the project came to a close, John found himself in possession of a collection of informative narratives detailing the challenges and triumphs of his students' language learning journeys. He was reminded of similar narratives he had read in some of the research literature he had come across in his graduate courses.

John was inspired by his learners' stories and began to contemplate the possibility of presenting a report on them at a local language teachers' conference, an annual event that was promoted in all local schools and at which graduate students were encouraged to present. John believed that sharing their narratives could provide valuable insights into the experiences of Spanish-speaking language learners in rural communities. John was excited about this prospect and so approached his students and their families for permission to present on their stories at the conference. To his delight, they agreed, with the condition that the students remain anonymous to protect their privacy.

As John was preparing to submit his proposal to the conference organizers, he realized that he had overlooked a crucial aspect of research ethics – obtaining Institutional Review Board (IRB) approval from his university. While he had obtained consent from the students and their families, he had not followed the proper procedures mandated by his academic institution. John reflected on what to do next. He was eager to share his students' stories and shed light on the experiences of language learners in rural schools. He believed that their narratives could trigger important conversations about educational equity and inclusion. He also thought it would be great to meet with graduate TESOL students from other universities at the conference. But he also recognized the importance of adhering to ethical guidelines and obtaining the necessary approvals before disseminating the students' work. He worried about the potential consequences of proceeding without proper authorization, both for himself and for the school where he had completed his practicum.

7.3.2 Questions

1. What ethical considerations should teacher-researchers keep in mind when engaging in research projects involving their students, particularly when seeking to share their work beyond the classroom?
2. How do you think John's personality influenced his decision-making process regarding presenting the learners' narratives at the conference?
3. How might John have better prepared for this ethical dilemma during his practicum? What steps could he have taken to ensure he was following proper research protocols from the outset?
4. What should John do next? Should he present at the local language teachers' conference?
5. If John decides not to present at the conference, what could he do with the learners' digital stories? He does, after all, have their permission to make use of them.

7.3.3 Research Topics

Identifying Teacher-Researchers' Awareness of Potential Ethical Dilemmas in Classroom Research

How aware are teacher-researchers of ethical issues that might arise in their classroom-based research? Do they always obtain informed consent from participants? Who do they turn to if something goes wrong ethically?

1. At a local language teachers' conference, conduct a workshop for teachers who are also active researchers in their classrooms.
2. Start the workshop with a brief overview of ethics in research and then facilitate a question-and-answer (Q&A) discussion with participants about their ethical practices.
3. Present participants with five 100-word *scenarios* (M14), each of which presents an ethical dilemma, such as not obtaining informed consent, being deceptive as a researcher, sharing data inappropriately, and mis-using participant information.
4. Ask the participants to reflect on each of the five scenarios and respond to them in a few sentences by explaining (a) what the ethical dilemma is, (b) why it is important to avoid the ethical issue, and (c) how the ethical dilemma might be overcome in the research design.
5. Collect the responses to the scenarios and analyze them according to the three (a)–(c) categories.
6. How aware of the dilemmas are the teacher-researchers? Do they consistently pay attention to ethical issues in their own research practices?

Investigating Opportunities for Small-Scale Research Projects While on a Practicum

Is it appropriate for student teachers to conduct research while on their teaching practicum? What research projects are feasible while on a practicum? Is there time and space for research while on a *teaching* practicum?

1. Meet with experienced practicum coordinators of three or four language teacher educator programs at universities or colleges of education. Arrange to interview them individually.
2. Before the interviews, prepare a *semi-structured interview schedule* (M9) that enquires into the policies and practices of their particular program regarding conducting research while on a practicum: Is it allowed? Is it encouraged? Are there guidelines for doing practicum-based research? What ethical approval procedures are followed? What is done with the research findings?

3. Conduct each interview for about one hour, asking the primary questions and probing with follow-up questions. Ask the coordinators if there is any documentation with respect to practicum research, such as policies or guidelines, and if so, request to see it.
4. Record the interviews and transcribe them.
5. Analyze the transcripts together with any documentation. Focus on the weight given to research in the overall teacher education program, and specifically research during the teaching program.
6. If the student teachers do research while on their practicum, are they supervised? What is the scale of their projects? Are their findings useful? What are they used for – an assignment, a teacher conference presentation?

7.3.4 Resources

Briggs, S. (2019). Ethical research in the secondary school classroom. *Teachers and Curriculum*, *19*(1), 61–66. https://doi.org/10.15663/tandc.v19i1.332

Charpentier-Jiménez, W. (2023). Students' perceptions of ethics in applied linguistics research at a Costa Rican public university. *Actualidades Investigativas en Educación*, *23*(1), 1–25. http://dx.doi.org/10.15517/aie.v23i1.51587

Yaw, K., Plonsky, L., Larsson, T., Sterling, S., & Kytö, M. (2023). Research ethics in applied linguistics. *Language Teaching*, *56*(4), 478–494. https://doi.org/10.1017/S0261444823000010

7.4 Developing a Teacher-Researcher Identity

Keywords
- China
- University
- College English teacher
- Developing interest in research
- Teacher and researcher identity tensions

7.4.1 Pre-reading Reflection

1. Think about a time when you were at a crossroads about a potential life-changing decision (e.g., Should I do an MA? Should I change my career?). How did this make you feel?
2. Sometimes very good teachers become leaders or administrators and so do less teaching. Is this a good or a bad thing?
3. How does doing research as a teacher change the identity of the teacher?

7.4 Developing a Teacher-Researcher Identity

Dr. Li Min is a dedicated college English teacher at a large urban university in China. She has a PhD in English Literature and has been teaching English for about ten years at two universities. During this time, she has established herself as a good English teacher. Min is very interested in teaching and learning and enjoys seeing the development of her students' language skills and critical thinking abilities. She is constantly concerned about their motivation to learn English since many students at her current university don't seem particularly enthusiastic about learning English. Over the years, she has become increasingly interested in doing research in the field of language teaching and learning, never having continued any research (or even further reading) in the discipline of her PhD. She is especially drawn to the study of psychology and learner motivation, and how motivation leads to engagement in classroom work. Teachers in Min's department have been encouraged to engage in research activities as much as possible, and their research is now discussed in their annual performance reviews.

Recently, the Dean of Min's department invited her to participate in a departmental research forum. The forum had been established as an informal platform for English teachers in the department to talk about research ideas and any research they might be doing. Not many attended regularly, but participating in the research forum provided Min with some valuable insights and opportunities to collaborate on various projects with those colleagues who did attend. She found herself immersed in discussions about research methodologies, data analysis techniques, and academic publications. While she enjoyed the intellectual stimulation, she experienced a sense of discomfort, not knowing if she was ready to accept a new identity as a teacher-researcher.

Over time she found herself becoming even more interested in research, with new questions emerging every day. She began to think about the possibility of transitioning from being solely an English teacher to becoming a teacher-researcher. The Dean's encouragement and support added to Min's internal conflict. She felt grateful for the opportunity to do some research and expand her academic horizons. She had even received some funding from the department to attend a local conference with an international speaker – she said she "learned a lot!" She would love to present her own research one day. But she feared losing sight of her professional commitment to teaching and the meaningful connections she had made with her students over the years.

As Min struggled with these emotions, she sought guidance from some of her English teacher colleagues, most of whom were not interested in doing research. Some encouraged her to explore research possibilities, while others cautioned her against losing sight of her desire to be an expert classroom teacher. They said that doing research would be adding to her workload, and she was already not spending enough time with her family. Min found herself caught between her love for and dedication to teaching, her family commitments, and her developing fascination with research. She was not sure which path to follow.

While Min is experiencing this identity dilemma, she continues to work hard at teaching and developing more relevant knowledge about research. Deep down she remains torn between two conflicting identities. Min knows that she needs to confront this situation head-on and make a decision that aligns with her values and aspirations. Whether she chooses to grow as a researcher or reaffirm her commitment to teaching only, or somehow both, one thing is certain – her professional development journey is far from over.

7.4.2 Questions

1. There appears to be no contractual requirement for Min to do research. What do you think is motivating her to learn about and do research in language teaching and learning?
2. What is your opinion of the departmental research forum as a place for Min to learn about research and become involved in research activity?
3. What is an "identity dilemma"? Answer in relation to Min's experience.
4. Min consulted her teacher colleagues about what direction her career should go in – they gave her conflicting advice. With which teachers do you agree, and why?
5. Min's "professional development journey is far from over." What does this mean for Min? Where do you see her career heading over, say, the next ten years?

7.4.3 Research Topics

Analyzing CVs of High-Profile TESOL Academics for Displays of Professional Identity

What do the CVs of high-profile TESOL or applied linguistics professors tell us about their researcher and teacher identities? How do the professors project their professional identities publicly?

1. Search *the webpages* (M6) of high-profile TESOL or applied linguistics university professors to find their CVs. Download ten CVs of professors from a range of geographical contexts.
2. Analyze the *contents and format* (M5) of the CVs, focusing on:
    a. emphasis given to teaching and research
    b. service and professional contributions (e.g., membership and roles on professional organizations and associations)
    c. ordering of the content (e.g., research performance before teaching)
    d. sequence and topics of headings and subheadings
    e. use of font size, bold, italics, and visuals.

3. For each CV, write extensive notes under the a–e categories above. In your notes include descriptions and your interpretations of how the professor's identity as a teacher and researcher is made evident, foregrounded or de-emphasized; that is, how they project themselves – who they are – as professionals in their CVs.
4. What do the ten CVs have in common in terms of displaying the professors' teacher and researcher identities? What are their most apparent differences? How do the academics express their researcher identities? What kind of researcher are they?

Exploring Reasons Why Some Language Teachers Refuse to Do Research
Why do some language teachers decide not to do research? Do they see themselves as teachers rather than researchers? Is being a researcher not part of their professional identity?

1. *Consult recent literature* (M6) on language teachers' engagement in research, that is, doing research as part of their professional teaching practice. From the literature, gather information about why some language teachers do not do research – for example, because of time constraints, lack of research methodology knowledge and skills, no research requirements in their job contract, no interest.
2. Draw up a list of about ten to fifteen reasons that would be applicable to primary and high school language teachers.
3. Use your professional networks to distribute the list digitally to local primary and high school language teachers who self-identify as non-researchers. Ask them to respond to each reason on the list, indicating how applicable it is to their experience on a rating scale from *Very applicable* to *Not at all applicable*.
4. Leave them space to comment on each of their responses.
5. Analyze the rating scales using *descriptive statistics* (M4) and analyze the contents of the comments for themes.
6. What are the highest ranked reasons language teachers give for their lack of research engagement? What in their personal and professional experiences are emotional, cognitive, practical or institutional barriers to doing research? Are there differences between primary and high school teachers? Do you note any desire to engage in research?

7.4.4 Resources

Achirri, K. (2020). A dynamic interplay of professional identities: Teacher-researcher's identity (re)construction. *The Qualitative Report*, *25*(6), 1695–1712. https://doi.org/10.46743/2160-3715/2020.4179

Jones, L. (2023). The "Teacher Research Group" as a collaborative model of professional learning. *Educational Action Research*, *31*(3), 409–423. https://doi.org/10.1080/09650792.2021.1960577

Sato, M. & Cárcamo, B. (2024). Be(com)ing an educational researcher in the Global South (and beyond): A focus on the research-practice relationship. *Educational Researcher, 53*(6), 359–369. https://doi.org/10.3102/0013189X241231548

7.5 Publishing Research in English

Keywords
- Mexico
- University
- Spanish and English language teacher educator
- Forced to publish in English
- Inequity in scholarly dissemination

7.5.1 Pre-reading Reflection

1. Should university students be able to submit written assignments in a language other than the medium of instruction?
2. Have you read books or articles in academic journals published in languages other than English? Why or why not?
3. What might the difficulties be in writing a research article in English if English is not one's first language?

Harold Rodríguez is an up-and-coming scholar of both English and Spanish teacher education at a reputable university in central Mexico. Since graduating with his PhD from the same university where he now works, he has been involved in teacher education for nearly ten years. Before he embarked on his PhD studies, he taught both English and Spanish in various high schools and at university level in the region for five years, as well as doing a stint teaching Spanish in the US for about a year. Dr. Rodríguez entered academia with a desire to bridge the gap between theory and practice in language education. Over the past few years he has read widely about and researched the area of language teacher preparation, particularly in the Mexican context, aiming to enhance the quality of language teaching in the country and beyond.

Dr. Rodríguez has conducted some innovative research projects and has reported on the findings in research journal articles and other scholarly publications, such as in book chapters. He has also presented his work at local and international conferences. His work encompasses a wide array of topics, from language teacher identity to innovative pedagogical approaches. His findings have local relevance, but he is confident that some of the implications of his research are important for a much wider audience too. He is excited about his work and wants to share it. However, despite his potential significant contributions to the field, Dr. Rodríguez struggles with what seems to be a necessity to publish his research in English-language journals in order to gain international recognition and to spread his ideas and findings.

This issue is multifaceted. While publishing in English journals grants Dr. Rodríguez access to a global audience and enhances his academic reputation, it also perpetuates an imbalance in scholarly dissemination. As a Spanish-speaking educator based in Mexico, Dr. Rodríguez is not happy about the inequity of a publishing industry dominated by English-language publications. He believes that valuable insights from Spanish-speaking scholars often go unnoticed, as their work remains inaccessible to non-English-speaking audiences. Despite his reservations, Dr. Rodríguez acknowledges the pragmatic necessity of publishing in English. In an increasingly interconnected world, academic visibility is paramount, and English serves as the so-called "lingua franca of academia," as he puts it. But perhaps even more important than this argument is Dr. Rodríguez's belief that some of his ideas are really worth spreading.

Among his colleagues, he constantly questions the fairness of a system that marginalizes non-English-speaking scholars – and wonders about the ethical implications of this situation. He recognizes the importance of advocating for greater inclusivity within the academic community and is committed to fostering dialogue and collaboration across linguistic boundaries, and supporting initiatives that promote the dissemination of research in multiple languages. At the same time, he remains aware of how challenging working toward these goals will be. He knows of an example that illustrates this challenge: An international conference held in the US always had presentations in English, but last year the conference organizers decided to allow researchers to present in languages other than English. Some of his colleagues had gone to the Spanish sessions and noticed that they were very poorly attended. People seemed to want to go mainly to the English presentations.

The publishing predicament that Dr. Rodríguez finds himself in highlights broader issues of linguistic diversity and academic equity. He is aware of this, and continues to address the situation in his reflections, discussions with colleagues, and at professional meetings. However, his main concern is with his own research and getting his findings to the right audience. While he continues to navigate the complexities of publishing in English journals, he remains committed to advancing language teacher education in Mexico and beyond.

7.5.2 Questions

1. What about Dr. Rodríguez's personal and professional background do you think makes him so determined to have his ideas and research findings both disseminated and noticed?

2. What are the potential benefits and drawbacks for Dr. Rodríguez of publishing his research in English-language journals?
3. What are the potential benefits and drawbacks for Dr. Rodríguez of publishing his research in Spanish-language journals in Mexico?
4. What strategies could Dr. Rodríguez employ to ensure that his research reaches both English-speaking and non-English-speaking audiences without compromising academic visibility and impact?
5. What would you suggest Dr. Rodríguez do to advocate for greater inclusivity within the language teacher education community in Mexico regarding the dissemination of research in multiple languages, taking into account the challenges and constraints he faces?

7.5.3 Research Topics

Examining Journal Editors' Opinions About Publishing in English in Their Journals

What are the views of editors of international English-language journals about publishing articles in their journals only in English? What advice do they have for speakers of other languages who want to publish their research in their own language?

1. Contact the editors (or editors-in-chief) of five international TESOL, ELT, or applied linguistics journals that publish in the English language. Their contact details are available on the journals' webpages.
2. Invite the editors to take part in a short *email exchange* (M17) in which you will ask them a few questions about (a) their opinions about publishing their journal in English, (b) their experiences of working with non-native English-speaking researchers who publish in their journal, and (c) any advice they have for researchers who wish to publish their work in other languages.
3. Inform the editors that you will be having email discussions with five editors.
4. Analyze the written email responses from the editors by searching for themes within the three (a)–(c) categories.
5 Are the editors in any way critical of the English-language publishing industry? How do the editors, or their associates, work with non-native English-speaking researchers to get their articles published?

Probing Non-native English-Speaking Presenters' Emotions When Presenting in English at International Conferences

How do non-native English-speaking researchers feel when presenting in English at an international conference? What is their level of confidence? Do they experience feelings of anxiety or vulnerability?

1. When next attending a large international TESOL or ELT conference, arrange to meet about five non-native English-speaking researchers immediately after their presentations. Plan to conduct short, twenty-minute *semi-structured interviews* (M9) with them, preferably over a cup of tea or coffee.
2. Before the interviews, prepare an interview schedule that aims to capture the researchers' emotional experiences both during and immediately after the presentations and that centers on their use of English for the purpose of presenting their research.
3. Add a question that inquires into their opinion about presenting in languages other than English at major TESOL and ELT conferences.
4. Record the brief interviews. Listen to the recordings repeatedly and try to recognize expressions of emotions in the tone of voice used by the researchers. Also pay attention to themes that relate specifically to emotions and presenting in English.
5. Did the researchers feel that their presentation was a success? How did they feel about it? How did they perceive their use of English during the presentation?

7.5.4   Resources

Alsabahi, R. (2022). English medium publications: Opening or closing doors to authors with non-English language backgrounds. *English Language Teaching*, *15*(10), 18–31. https://doi.org/10.5539/elt.v15n10p18

Soler, J. (2019). Academic publishing in English: Exploring linguistic privilege and scholars' trajectories. *Journal of Language, Identity & Education*, *18*(6), 389–399. https://doi.org/10.1080/15348458.2019.1671193

Warren, L. K. & Sato, M. (2024). Multilingualism and native speakerism in academic journals' language policies: Exploring a potential power of applied linguistics journals in promoting equitable publishing practices. *Studies in Second Language Acquisition*, *46*(3), 921–932. https://doi.org/10.1017/S0272263124000068

7.6   Unsuccessful Research Collaboration

Keywords
- Vietnam
- High school
- English teachers doing research
- Collaborating on a research project
- Unequal research contributions

7.6.1 Pre-reading Reflection

1. Have you done group work where some group members do less work than others? If so, how did you resolve the situation?
2. What are the risks and benefits of collaborating with others when conducting research projects?
3. Are you someone who prefers to work alone or with others?

Ms. Anh and Ms. Phung have been dedicated English teachers at an urban high school in Vietnam for over a decade. Their passion for teaching English and commitment to professional development have earned them respect among their colleagues and admiration from their students. As the school emphasizes continuous improvement and values research as a means of enhancing teaching practices, both teachers have attempted small-scale research projects over the years to refine their practice. Engaging in research, particularly action research, is actually a national requirement for teachers, and their performance is evaluated according to the success of their research projects.

Under these circumstances, Ms. Anh and Ms. Phung decide to collaborate on a study aimed at encouraging their students to read more English outside the classroom. Collaboration is encouraged for these projects since working together means that teachers can learn from and motivate each other. Ms. Anh and Ms. Phung understand the importance of fostering independent reading habits, and so they design a project to not only assess the current reading habits of their learners but also to implement strategies to increase their engagement with English texts beyond the school curriculum.

Their project involves several stages, and they decide to divide up the work between them. Together, they first designed a survey to gather data on their students' reading preferences, frequency of reading in English, and the factors influencing their reading habits. They then implemented interventions such as recommending material to read, organizing a book club, and providing resources for online reading platforms. They tracked the progress of their students over a set period, monitoring changes in reading habits and assessing the effectiveness of their interventions. They divided up these research tasks, and both agreed that the distribution was about even.

Initially, both teachers were enthusiastic about the project and worked closely together. However, as time passed by, Ms. Anh found herself shouldering most of the workload. She spent long hours compiling the survey responses, organizing book club meetings, and tracking student progress, while Ms. Phung's contributions become increasingly sporadic. The project was far from over – there was still quite a bit to do. Despite her growing frustration, Ms. Anh didn't confront her partner with this developing issue. She appreciates their collaboration and is hesitant to jeopardize their professional relationship. However, as the deadline for the project approaches, she realizes that things are not fair the way they are. While she has invested significant time and effort into the research, Ms. Phung stands to benefit from the project's outcomes without having contributed proportionately.

Ms. Anh decides to seek advice from a trusted colleague on how to deal with the matter diplomatically. She knows this colleague well and has collaborated with her very successfully on a few action research projects over the years. Ms. Anh expressed her concerns about the unequal distribution of work and the impact it may have on their project's credibility and fairness. With her colleague's advice, she decides to initiate a candid conversation with Ms. Phung. The meeting does not go well. During their discussion, Ms. Anh acknowledged Ms. Phung's busy schedule and offered her support in completing the remaining project tasks. She suggested dividing up the workload more transparently and setting clear deadlines to ensure accountability. Unfortunately, Ms. Phung did not respond positively. She said she had indeed contributed to the project and had "done my bit," outlining the ways that she felt she had. This shocked Ms. Anh because to her it was clear Ms. Phung had not done what she said she had done.

7.6.2 Questions

1. Reflecting on the importance of collaboration in research, what are the potential benefits of teachers working together on projects like the one conducted by Ms. Anh and Ms. Phung?
2. Ms. Phung is described as a dedicated and respected teacher. What do you think went wrong with this particular research project?
3. Drawing on this case of Ms. Anh and Ms. Phung, what strategies could collaborating teacher-researchers employ to establish clear expectations and accountability in their research partnerships?
4. What communication skills and approaches might have facilitated a more constructive dialogue between Ms. Anh and Ms. Phung during their attempt to address the unequal research contributions?
5. What are the implications of the unresolved situation between Ms. Anh and Ms. Phung for their professional relationship and the credibility of their research project? In other words, what's going to happen next?

7.6.3 Research Topics

Investigating Benefits and Challenges of Collaborative Research for Individual Researchers

What are the personal benefits of researching in a team? What problems may arise for individual researchers in collaborative research?

1. Identify a university researcher through their publications (e.g., single-author as well as two or multiple-author publications) or through your professional networks who has evidently done both independent and collaborative/team research.
2. Request the researcher to write a 1,000-word *reflective narrative* (M16) in which they compare their experiences of doing both independent and collaborative research. Allow them to focus on any aspect of the research process, from conceiving the project, data collection and analysis, to writing for publication.
3. Collect the narrative and analyze it for main characters, critical research incidents, tensions, and achievements.
4. Invite the researcher to take part in a one-hour *interview* (M9) in which key findings from your narrative analysis are discussed in depth.
5. Did the researcher prefer doing independent or collaborative research? What were their reasons for their preference? What lessons for novice researchers could be learned from this researcher's experience?

Questioning the Contribution of Language Teachers' Research Activity to Their Performance Evaluations
Should language teachers who are employed as full-time teachers have their performance evaluated according to their research activity? What research activities, if any, are applicable to the quality of a teacher's job performance?

1. Locate a primary or high school that has a reputable ESL teaching and learning program and where English teachers' performance is reviewed periodically according to both their classroom teaching practice and their research activity (e.g., action research, exploratory practice, systematic reflective practice, research reading, conference participation).
2. Design a *formal, structured interview schedule* (M9) with a fixed number of questions in a pre-set order. With permission of school management, briefly interview all English teachers in the school about their opinions of the school's performance review policy and procedures. Ask specifically about the inclusion of research activity in the review. Clarify what counts as research for the purposes of their performance review.
3. Record the brief interactions with teachers. After analyzing the teacher interviews, *interview* (M9) a member of the school's management team to (a) find out more about the review policy from the management's perspective, and (b) critically discuss the teachers' responses.
4. Why is research activity considered in teachers' performance evaluations? Is research a contractual requirement? How do teachers feel about the review policy and practices?

7.6.4 Resources

Becker, A. (2024). Applied linguistics communities of practice: Improving the research practice relationship. *Applied Linguistics*, *45*(2), 272–286. https://doi.org/10.1093/applin/amad010

Nguyen, T. T. P. & Nguyen, C. D. (2024). An evaluation of researcher–teacher collaboration with practitioners engaged in instructing English language with young learners. *Education 3–13: International Journal of Primary, Elementary and Early Years Education*, 2323648. https://doi.org/10.1080/03004279.2024.2323648

Pham, A. H. V., Newton, J., & Macalister, J. (2024). Teacher research for professional development: The tales of two teachers. *RELC Journal*, https://doi.org/10.1177/00336882241245446

7.7 Lack of Research Training

Keywords
- Türkiye
- University education department
- Becoming language teacher educators
- Presenting a conference poster
- Lacking research knowledge and skills

7.7.1 Pre-reading Reflection

1. What are some of the tensions you might experience as you transition from one role to another (e.g., student to teacher, teacher to teacher educator)?
2. Does a teacher writing a reflective journal (i.e., reflecting on their teaching practice) count as research?
3. What does presenting a poster at a conference entail? Have you seen a poster presentation or presented one yourself?

Hakan and Esma are two English teachers working in a Foreign Languages Department at a university in a large city in Türkiye. Hakan is thirty-seven years old and has been teaching English for about fifteen years. Esma, also in her late thirties, has been teaching English for eight years, having first worked as a social worker for a few years after graduating. Both now have master's degrees and are recognized by their institution and their colleagues as excellent teachers. In fact, in the past few years they have been invited to take on more responsibility, providing training for the English teachers in the department as well as for in-service English teachers from schools and other universities who come to campus to do short courses. During the Covid-19 pandemic they even offered some of these training courses online using Zoom.

At first, they enjoyed the challenge of taking on a trainer role, although it did create a bit of tension when they found themselves training some of their English teacher colleagues (i.e., those working with them as teachers in the same department). It felt strange to be teaching their friends! They didn't do much training for the first year or so and continued to focus mainly on their English teaching responsibilities. However, the training part of their job seemed to gradually increase over the past two years. Their head of department asked them more frequently to do training workshops and to run courses for external teachers and institutions. They both felt they were becoming more of a teacher educator (or more particularly, an in-service teacher educator – ISTE) than an English teacher. Hakan and Esma had several discussions about this change in their circumstances, and they agreed that it was probably inevitable in their career trajectories. So, they decided to embrace the opportunity and develop their knowledge about language teacher education and their skills at presenting in-person professional development workshops and online training sessions.

But then their head of department informed Hakan and Esma, as well as other ISTEs in the department, that another university in the city was hosting a teacher research conference, which was being sponsored by an international TEFL organization. At the conference teachers and teacher educators would be presenting posters based on their research. The head of department proposed that Hakan and Esma should attend the conference and present their work. Now, they had not been doing any formal research, besides their usual reflections that they wrote up as entries in their digital journals. They emailed each other about the head's proposal, and this is their exchange:

HAKAN: "What are we supposed to present? I used to do some action research when I first started teaching, but I haven't for many years now. I was also never really sure if it WAS proper action research! Maybe I could summarize my reflective journal entries, but what would I say about them? Should I do some sort of analysis? Remember that workshop we did with school teachers late last year, when we asked them to complete an evaluation form at the end? It was interesting – can we do something with that?"

ESMA: "We didn't ask the teachers if we could use their evaluation responses, so I don't think we can use them, right? I haven't done any research since my master's, and even that was more like a literature review. I didn't actually collect any information from anyone. Doing something with your journal sounds like a great idea; they call it reflective practice, I think. I just don't know how to do research. I'll write to the conference organizers and see what they expect with the posters. It could be good for us."

7.7 Lack of Research Training

Hakan and Esma spoke to their head of department, saying that they are in the process of contacting the conference organizer, adding that they intend going to the conference; in fact, they are already preparing their posters.

7.7.2   Questions

1. Hakan and Esma gradually became in-service teacher educators over time. How did this happen, and what was their reaction to this process?
2. If you were Hakan or Esma, how would you have responded to the head of department's proposal to participate in the conference?
3. Hakan and Esma both declare that they do not have research knowledge and skills. Do you agree with them? Give a reason for your answer.
4. Hakan and Esma had a brief exchange by email. What did this exchange achieve? What did they come to realize as a result of this exchange?
5. How do you feel about Hakan and Esma going to the conference to present a poster? How do you rate their chances of doing a good job? Why?

7.7.3   Research Topics

Evaluating the Quality of Poster Presentations at a TESOL or Applied Linguistics Conference
What makes a good research-based conference poster? Is it the content or the format or the interaction with the poster presenter?

1. *Search the internet* (M6) for advice about presenting research-based conference posters.
2. Gather advice about best practice and compile a checklist, which should include items such as what the poster looks like (i.e., formatting and organization of content), what the poster is about (i.e., the content), and how the researcher interacts with the audience (e.g., answering questions).
3. Take the checklist to your next TESOL or applied linguistics conference and attend the poster presentation sessions. Select several posters of interest and examine each one, working through the checklist. Take *photographs* (M12) of the posters for later in-depth analysis.
4. Interact with the poster presenters. Ask them about the content of the poster and, if appropriate, their development of the poster. Take notes of your conversations.
5. After the conference, analyze the *photographs of the posters* and the conversation notes.
6. Which posters where the most outstanding and why? Was the advice given on the internet, and that informed your checklist, good advice? What did the researchers say about their posters?

Identifying Key Stages in the Process of English Teachers' Transition into a Researcher Role

When in their careers do English teachers become researchers? What happens that turns them toward research activity? What keeps them doing research as part of their professional work?

1. Recruit four or five English-teacher educators who work in a university context and who have research as part of their job contract. They will be experienced researchers with a research track record and a substantial number of publications.
2. Conduct an *informal narrative interview* (M16) with each researcher during which you ask them to reflect on their early English teaching career and how, why, and when they became involved in research.
3. Was there a key moment when research became a part of their professional lives? What happened? Who were the key people involved in that transition? What was going on in the teachers' careers at the time?
4. During the narrative interviews, allow the researchers to tell their story of how they became researchers, but try to focus on the *transition stage* where they shifted from being solely an English teacher to being involved in research, no matter how minimal the engagement.
5. Record the interviews and transcribe the parts of the narratives where the transition stage is described.
6. Do the researchers have anything in common? Did they exhibit agency in their transition? Did the job description or their institutional requirements have an influence on their pathway toward becoming a researcher?

7.7.4 Resources

Cirocki, A., Indrarathne, B., & Alcívar Calderón, V. E. (2024). Effectiveness of professional development training on reflective practice and action research: A case study from Ecuador. *Reflective Practice, 25*(5), 676–694. https://doi.org/10.1080/14623943.2024.2384124

Eryılmaz, R. & Dikilitaş, K. (2023). Identity tensions of in-service teacher educators: A narrative inquiry. *Language Teaching Research*, https://doi.org/10.1177/13621688231216816

Hosseini, M., Bahrami, V., & Dikilitaş, K. (2024). From research reading and doing to research use: Tracking trajectories of becoming research-informed second language teachers. *System, 125*, 103445. https://doi.org/10.1016/j.system.2024.103445

8 Professional Service

Cases in this chapter

8.1	Proofreading for a Faculty Journal Publication	*page* 213
8.2	Teaching at a Community Language School	216
8.3	A Teacher Meets with Dissatisfied Parents	220
8.4	A First-Year Teacher Joins School Committee	224
8.5	Giving a Talk to Pre-service Teachers	228
8.6	Serving as a Cooperating Teacher	232
8.7	On a Department of Education Working Group	235

8.1 Proofreading for a Faculty Journal Publication

Keywords
- Malaysia
- University
- English teacher
- Proofreading Faculty documents
- Feeling exploited

8.1.1 Pre-reading Reflection

1. Teachers sometimes experience tension between different aspects of their work, for example teaching and administration. What tensions do you think exist for university language teachers?
2. Have you ever felt exploited in a workplace before?
3. How good are you at saying "no"?

Kanmani teaches English as a Second Language (ESL) to undergraduate students at a tertiary education institution in Malaysia. She has a Bachelor of Education degree in TESL (Teaching English as a Second Language) from a local university and a master's degree in Applied Linguistics from a university overseas. Kanmani has been employed at this institution for six years and she is very passionate about teaching. In addition to teaching three courses, she is responsible for coordinating one of them.

In the faculty, it is a common practice to seek English language teachers' services to proofread and edit faculty documents, reports, and other publications. Kanmani is not happy about being requested to provide such services. She feels she did not sign up for such work when she joined the university as an English language teacher. Furthermore, she feels that being a language teacher doesn't necessarily make her the most suitable person to edit official documents. However, she has a hard time refusing to do this work and explaining why it is not something she wants to do. This is particularly difficult when requests come from her superiors. Once she politely declined a request from a colleague and he did not take it well. He criticized her in front of others for being unhelpful.

Kanmani was recently asked to proofread an annual peer-reviewed journal published by the faculty. It was a collection of research articles written by her colleagues who work in a number of different departments. For previous publications, the faculty had obtained proofreading services from other English language teachers, but for this publication she was informed that it was her turn. She therefore felt obliged to do the work, even though she was not particularly happy about it. She realized that only proofreading the articles would not be adequate because they all required substantial editing to reach an appropriate publication standard. There were a couple of articles that she simply could not edit; because of language errors, she struggled to understand the content. She spent a lot of time proofreading and editing what she could. For the rest, she gave feedback indicating sections that required rewriting. She was able to keep to the given deadline. After some time passed, these articles were sent back to her for finalizing with a note emphasizing the urgency of the task. However, the issues she had marked were not addressed properly and for some articles it was clear there had been no attempt at correction or revision. She felt she was being pressured to give the green light for publication. When she was told by the colleague who was coordinating the publication that she could not accept the articles as they were, they had a rather heated argument. Ultimately, she ended up sitting down with the relevant authors of the articles and doing the rewriting for them so they could meet the publication's deadline.

Kanmani felt exploited. She had spent a lot of time, energy, and emotional labor on this task. She felt angry for not being able to use that time and energy for work she believes takes priority, such as further enhancing teaching material for the course she coordinates or assigning more essay writing tasks for her students so she can give them detailed feedback.

8.1.2 Questions

1. Do you think Kanmani is qualified to perform the proofreading and editing services requested of her?

2. Is it fair to expect Kanmani to perform these services for the administration of her faculty?
3. Kanmani appears to have a clear understanding of how to prioritize different professional tasks. What appears to be her reasoning for this prioritization?
4. Apart from her unwillingness to do proofreading and editing, what other challenges does Kanmani face during her experience of editing the peer-reviewed journal articles?
5. What could Kanmani have done differently to avoid rewriting sections of the articles herself?

8.1.3 Research Topics

Exploring University English Teachers' Multiple Professional Identities
What do university English teachers perceive their main role to be in their workplace? Teaching, research, professional service – anything else? How does their work affect how they see themselves – their reflexive identities?

1. Gather a group of English language teachers from the English Department of a university you have access to. Ask them to meet as a group for one hour. Aim for no more than ten teachers.
2. When you meet, explain that you are interested in exploring the work they do, including the service roles that form part of their workload, and how their work relates to how they see themselves as professionals.
3. Next, present each teacher with a *blank body outline silhouette* (M2). Instruct them to color in the body outline and to add words, shapes, objects, and emojis to show the work they do in their university jobs and to represent their teacher identities.
4. Let the teachers share and discuss their art both during and after working on the body silhouette. When they have finished, have a *focus-group discussion* (M8) about the service they provide or the professional contributions they make to their institutions. Record the discussion for later careful analysis.
5. How much and what kind of service or administrative work do they do? How do they depict this work in their body silhouettes? Do they resent doing this work, or welcome it? Is it too much or about right? Does the service work in any way enhance their work as English teachers?

Discovering Additional Service or Professional Duties of Indigenous Language Teachers
What additional jobs are Indigenous language teachers often asked to do in institutions? Is it fair that they are asked to do these jobs? Who asks them, and why?

1. Contact a teacher of an Indigenous language at a university. In a brief conversation or email exchange ask them if they are ever asked to do jobs or engage in activities outside of the usual language teaching in the classroom. If so, invite them to take part in a longer *semi-structured interview* (M9) with you to explore this topic further.
2. Design the interview schedule to include questions about (a) the typical classroom teaching load of the teacher, (b) service or administrative work that would be considered normal for all language teachers at the university, (c) additional service or professional work that the teacher is called on to do, (d) whether this additional work is of an Indigenous nature, and (e) the teacher's attitude toward doing and being asked to do this additional work.
3. In the interview schedule, include follow-up prompt questions for each of the main questions to ensure in-depth coverage and a good flow of conversation.
4. Conduct the interview face-to-face, if possible, over refreshments. Record the interview.
5. When analyzing the interview transcript, aim to discover examples of the additional work the language teacher does that relates to Indigenous language and cultural practices.
6. What is the nature of this additional work? Does it add significantly to the teacher's workload? Does the teacher feel that it is fair to be asked to do this work? Does the work enhance their professional career?

8.1.4 Resources

Leach, T. (2022). The hammer and the scalpel: A teacher's experience of workplace bullying. *Studies in Technology Enhanced Learning*, *2*(3), 355–368. https://doi.org/10.21428/8c225f6e.f773a305

Samadi, L., Bagheri, M. S., Sadighi, F., & Yarmohammadi, L. (2020). An investigation into EFL instructors' intention to leave and burnout: Exploring the mediating role of job satisfaction. *Cogent Education*, *7*(1), 1781430. https://doi.org/10.1080/2331186X.2020.1781430.

Thomson, M. (2019). Four ways teachers can manage workload and stress. *Voices Magazine*, British Council. https://www.britishcouncil.org/voices-magazine/teachers-manage-workload-stress (Accessed November 14, 2024).

8.2 Teaching at a Community Language School

Keywords
- Melbourne, Australia
- High school and Sri Lankan temple

- English and Sinhala language teacher
- Promotion offered at high school
- Giving up Sinhala language teaching

8.2.1 Pre-reading Reflection

1. Consider the role that community language schools serve in an immigrant community. Do you know who learns and teaches heritage languages at these schools?
2. What are some of the benefits of being a head of a language department at a high school?
3. How important should a consideration of one's financial situation be when making decisions about one's professional work and contributions?

Mrs. Devika Silva is a second-generation immigrant from Sri Lanka living in Melbourne, Australia. She teaches English at an inner-city high school with a large immigrant population. It also has many international students who seem to come and go; some on short-term study-abroad programs and others for the duration of their high-school years. Mrs. Silva qualified as a teacher at a university in Melbourne – she has a BA and a Postgraduate Teaching Diploma and has been teaching for about ten years. She has no desire to study further, and instead pursues her professional development through workshops and short courses offered by the school, personal reading, some action research, and engagement with professional organizations.

In Melbourne there is a vibrant community temple where Mrs. Silva teaches the Sinhala language to children. The temple teaches both Buddhism and Sinhala and is also involved in many other community projects. Because of her passion for education and a deep connection to her cultural roots, Mrs. Silva has been teaching at the community language school for many years, even before she graduated from university. The work is unpaid, volunteer teaching. She learned Sinhala from her parents and was herself a student at the same temple. She loves to "give back," as she says. Teaching Sinhala also gives her practice speaking and writing the language because she doesn't get much opportunity to do so outside the temple, something she feels a bit guilty about. She is married to an English-speaking Australian and has no children, and so she really only speaks Sinhala at the temple and when she visits her parents.

Recently, Mrs. Silva received an enticing offer – a promotion to head the English Department at her high school. This promotion would not only elevate her professional status but also provide much-needed financial relief. Times have been tough for Mrs. Silva, with her having recently bought a new house. However, accepting the promotion would mean taking on additional responsibilities that might stretch her already limited time and energy. One consequence of this would be the potential resignation from her role as a Sinhala teacher at the community temple.

Mrs. Silva, of course, is not happy about this possibility. She loves the work at the temple, but at the same time finds the promotion professionally very attractive. She values the opportunity to lead and inspire other teachers within the high school English Department. She already has some ideas for what the department could be doing better. Personally, the promotion would not only validate her years of hard work but also open doors for further professional development. And the financial stability it offers would help with the financial burdens she currently faces.

But Mrs. Silva cannot ignore the significance of her role within the Sri Lankan community. Teaching Sinhala at the temple allows her to preserve her cultural heritage and transmit this to the younger generation. The sense of fulfillment she derives from nurturing her students' language skills and cultural identity is very important to her. Resigning from this role would feel like abandoning a crucial aspect of her identity and betraying the trust and expectations of the community.

Accepting the promotion would not only affect her personal life but also the lives of her high school students and colleagues. Resigning from her role at the community temple would leave a void that is not easily filled, disrupting the continuity of cultural education for the younger generation. Mrs. Silva's head is filled with questions. Should she accept the high school offer of promotion to head of department? Should she resign from the community language school? She is absolutely certain that she can't do both jobs. She feels this is a decision she must make herself and not seek advice from friends and mentors.

8.2.2 Questions

1. How do you feel about Mrs. Silva's approach to professional development? Do you support it or not?
2. Do you predict that Mrs. Silva would do a good job as head of the English Department? Give a reason for your answer.
3. Teaching at a community language school is an additional service contribution teachers make outside of their usual place of work. Is this too much of a burden for language teachers?
4. Why do you think Mrs. Silva decides not to consult her friends and mentors about what she should do?
5. What do *you* think Mrs. Silva should do about the dilemma she faces? Should she accept the offer of promotion and leave her Sinhala teaching position at the temple?

8.2.3 Research Topics

Outlining the Characteristics of a Head of a Second Language/Foreign Languages Department at a High School

What characteristics should a head of a second language/foreign languages department at a high school have in order to be effective in meeting the needs of teachers and learners in the department? What characteristics pertain particularly to being a *languages* department in a *high school*?

1. Consult a high school that has a section or department that teaches a language or languages as second or foreign languages.
2. Meet with the head of the department (HOD) for a brief *interview* (M9) to discuss what features a HOD should have that contribute toward meeting the professional and learning needs of the teachers and students respectively in their second language/foreign languages department. Record the interview.
3. Analyze the interview and search for characteristics that are pertinent to a *languages* department and department in a *high school*.
4. Show the list of characteristics to a HOD of a second language/foreign languages department at a different high school that you have access to. In a brief *interview* (M9), ask the HOD there to add any new characteristics to your list. Have a discussion about the growing list of characteristics and record the discussion.
5. Post the list of characteristics on a relevant language teachers' mailing list or Facebook group. Invite a constructive critique of the list of characteristics, asking the respondents to focus on characteristics pertaining to a HOD in a *languages* department in a *high school*.
6. What features of a HOD do language teachers value? Do the teachers believe that the HOD should also be a teacher? In what ways do students benefit from the work of a good HOD?

Inquiring into Support Community-based Heritage Language Schools Could Use from Qualified Language Teachers

Who teaches the heritage language at a community-based heritage language school? Are they qualified language teachers? Does the school need support or assistance from qualified volunteer language teachers?

1. Negotiate access to a local community-based heritage language school, preferably in collaboration with someone you know who is a member of the school community.
2. Using a small-scale *ethnographic research design* (M7), set up short meetings with leaders in the school and as many members of the community as is feasible, such as teachers, parents, and young learners. Aim to observe language classes.

3. Visit the school several times and interact with as many people as possible without intruding. Write *field notes* of school and classroom observations (M3) after each visit.
4. After becoming familiar with the social and physical contexts of the school, arrange an *interview* (M9) with one of the school community leaders. Prepare an interview schedule that focuses on language teaching and teachers in the school. More specifically, ask questions about the quality of teaching in the school, the expected quality of teaching, and any teaching needs the school has. Record the interview.
5. Collate the full dataset, and analyze it for themes that highlight teaching practices, expectations, and needs in the school. Draw on both field notes and interview data.
6. Is the school happy with the way heritage language teaching is going? Does the school need outside teaching assistance? If so, what kind of teaching help does the school need?

8.2.4 Resources

Driver, M. (2024). Realities of comfort and discomfort in the heritage language classroom: Looking to transformative positive psychology for juggling a double-edged sword. *The Modern Language Journal, 108*(S1), 147–167. https://doi.org/10.1111/modl.12899

Escudero, P., Diskin-Holdaway, C., Pino Escobar, G., & Hajek, J. (2025). Needs and demands for heritage language support in Australia: Results from a nationwide survey. *Journal of Multilingual and Multicultural Development, 46*(2), 437–454. https://doi.org/10.1080/01434632.2023.2189261

Sappa, V., Boldrini, E., & Aprea, C. (2015). Combining teaching with another job: A possible resource to face professional challenges. Preliminary findings from a Swiss study in vocational education and training. *Empirical Research in Vocational Education and Training, 7*, 13. https://doi.org/10.1186/s40461-015-0026-4

8.3 A Teacher Meets with Dissatisfied Parents

Keywords
- Singapore
- Public high school
- Chinese mother-tongue teaching and learning
- Post-Covid change of pedagogy
- Meeting with dissatisfied parents

8.3 A Teacher Meets with Dissatisfied Parents

8.3.1 Pre-reading Reflection

1. What do you understand by mother-tongue teaching and learning?
2. Have you ever had to mediate a disagreement between two people or two groups of people? If so, how did it go?
3. When do teachers and parents get to talk to each other? What typically brings them together?

Danmore High School (DHS) is a very successful public school in Singapore. It offers a full curriculum at varying levels to satisfy multiple examination options for its students. Like many public schools in Singapore, the school has an excellent leadership team, is financially sound, and its facilities are plentiful and well maintained. On the whole, teachers at the school have very high professional standards: They hold appropriate qualifications and regularly participate in professional development activities offered by DHS and the wider educational community. They aim to be innovative and keep up with recent trends and developments in their particular school subject. Generally, the teachers work well together in their subject teams and produce excellent results, which make both students and their parents happy.

Danmore High School is well known for its strong languages program. Besides English, which is compulsory for all students, DHS offers a range of mother-tongue languages, including Chinese, Tamil, and Malay. Chinese Mother Tongue is the biggest subject and is popular with students. Traditionally, going back about twenty years, the Chinese teaching methods involved mainly rote memorization, rigorous drills, and an emphasis on written characters. But over time teaching shifted to a more communicative approach to encourage learners to "communicate their ideas with clarity and confidence." The incorporation of culture teaching (i.e., traditional customs, history, and some literature) into the language curriculum also occurred over time. However, the advent of the Covid-19 pandemic generated a huge shift in pedagogical approaches, requiring the teachers to explore more innovative and interactive teaching methods, making use of technology and varied learning resources to engage students in remote and blended learning environments. These methods worked well under the circumstances and teachers were satisfied with students' engagement and overall motivation for learning Chinese. As the world gradually emerged from the pandemic, Chinese teachers at the school made a conscious decision to retain some of the new methods that had proven effective during Covid times.

This move was noticed by the students' parents. Citing concerns about cultural preservation, linguistic authenticity, and the perceived erosion of academic rigor, a vocal group of parents advocated for a return to the methods used pre-Covid. They argued that those teaching practices instilled discipline, ensured language learning, and developed knowledge of Chinese cultural heritage. Ms. Wang, one of the older and more experienced members of the Chinese teaching staff, was asked by senior management to liaise with the parents to "sort the problem out." Ms. Wang agreed to do so but was not impressed with the request. She felt, as a senior staff member, that she had enough on her plate already, with plenty of service roles to keep her busy; jobs that she enjoyed and was good at, like chairing the curriculum and assessment development committee, and leading the Chinese teachers' action research group. She also represents the school's languages program at regular Ministry of Education meetings.

With the help of the school's public relations office, Ms. Wang set up a meeting with a delegation of parents. To prepare for this, she consulted with all the Chinese Mother Tongue teachers, who were adamant that their pedagogical choices were the right ones. They urged Ms. Wang not to compromise. Ms. Wang had not expected this strong position from them, and she was pleased to witness their loyalty and determination to continue with what they felt was the right path forward for the program and for their students. Ms. Wang spent many hours preparing her notes for the meeting. She invited a colleague to join her, and they worked on their meeting strategy together. She knew she had the support of her team and DHS management. The meeting time finally came – she and her colleague entered the venue and were met by a group of twelve parents seated around the seminar table, with their leader sitting at the head. They were ready.

8.3.2 Questions

1. Does DHS sound like the type of school you would like to teach at? Why or why not?
2. Did the Chinese teachers make the right decision to continue with their Covid-era teaching methods once Covid was over? If yes, why? If not, what else could they have done?
3. What makes Ms. Wang the right person to liaise with the parent group? Should she have agreed to do so?
4. Do you believe that communicating with the parents of young learners is an important part of a teacher's work? What might it depend on?
5. How do you think the meeting with the parent group will go? Who will get what they want – the teachers or the parents? Give reasons for your answer.

8.3.3 Research Topics

Investigating Language Teachers' Attitudes Toward Engaging with Learners' Parents
How do language teachers of young learners feel about engaging with their learners' parents? What do they communicate about? Do they believe the engagement is productive and that it benefits the learners?

8.3 A Teacher Meets with Dissatisfied Parents

1. Design a *questionnaire* (M17) with open-ended, short-answer questions that enquires into the experiences and attitudes of language teachers of young learners, preferably at primary school level.
2. On the questionnaire, include questions about (a) the background and teaching experience of the teachers, (b) how often they engage with their learners' parents, (c) how they engage with the parents (e.g., parents' meetings; complaints; school reports; regular, scheduled communications), (d) their attitudes toward dealing with parents, (e) how engaging with parents makes them feel (i.e., their emotional responses to the engagement), and (f) the typical outcomes of the teacher–parent engagement.
3. As a final question on the questionnaire, ask the teachers to *tell you a story* (M16) about one encounter with a parent.
4. Distribute the questionnaire to primary school language teachers in networks that you have access to. Use a platform such as Google Forms, Qualtrics, or Microsoft Forms. Make the form anonymous and give a time limit for responses to be posted.
5. Analyze the data thematically question by question. For the final short-story question, note who the characters are in the story, when and why they meet, if there is an issue or a problem that gets them together, and how the teacher reflects on the engagement.
6. How do teachers feel about interacting with parents? What's the main reason for their engagement? Do teachers believe meeting is worth their time and effort? Do they look forward to or fear meeting with parents?

Monitoring the Lasting Effects of Emergency Remote Teaching (ERT) After the Covid-19 Pandemic
Who in a language department made decisions about shifting away from online ERT after the Covid-19 pandemic? Why was the decision made? How were decisions made?

1. Locate a language teaching department in a high school or university that switched to online ERT during the Covid-19 pandemic. What has happened to their teaching approach since the end of the pandemic?
2. Invite two or three teachers from the department to meet with you to *talk informally* (M9) about their experiences of suddenly moving to ERT, and then to describe any changes to the teaching approach in the department since the end of the pandemic.
3. Focusing on methods, ask them to show you any available *materials or technology* (M13) that they used for ERT and what they are using now.
4. Once you are familiar with the teaching approaches, spend time talking about decision-making: Who made decisions about changing teaching approaches after Covid? What decisions were made? Was there buy-in

from other or all teachers? Was all online ERT abandoned, or were some useful lessons carried over into post-Covid language teaching?
5. Write a brief report with answers to these questions. Include in the report advice for managers who assign decision-making powers to teachers.
6. Distribute the report to an appropriate professional social media group and ask for feedback.

8.3.4 Resources

Baikovich, H. H. & Yemini, M. (2025). Parent–teacher relationships in international schools in Cyprus: Challenges and opportunities. *Globalisation, Societies and Education*, *23*(2), 543–559. https://doi.org/10.1080/14767724.2023.2207121

Gruber, A., Matt, E., & Leier, V. (2023). Transforming foreign language education: Exploring educators' practices and perspectives in the (post-)pandemic era. *Education Sciences*, *13*(6), 601. https://doi.org/10.3390/educsci13060601

Lin, X. & Huang, H. (2023). Novice teachers' identity exploration in their relations with parents in an era of social networking sites: A case study in China. *Social Sciences & Humanities Open*, *8*(1), 100752. https://doi.org/10.1016/j.ssaho.2023.100752

8.4 A First-Year Teacher Joins School Committee

Keywords
- Uzbekistan
- High school
- First-year English teacher
- Teacher joins school's IT committee
- Given tasks beyond level of expertise

8.4.1 Pre-reading Reflection

1. How should service roles be distributed across the teaching staff of a school? How should decisions about these roles be made?
2. What are some of the personal benefits and drawbacks of serving on committees?
3. Some people enjoy doing admin, and others don't. What about you?

Lobar completed her BA degree in Education and immediately began teaching at a high school in Tashkent, the capital of Uzbekistan. In her four-year qualification she specialized in Applied English, which included learning the English language and also learning how to teach English. By the time she graduated she felt ready to enter her first job and to start her career as an English teacher. After a few interviews she was offered a job at her current high school, where she has been for six months. The school is new, with modern buildings and facilities, and is technologically advanced – meaning that it has an abundance of equipment for the use of teachers and students and is globally connected via a stable internet. Although the school was only established ten years ago, it has a good reputation. It is particularly well known for its technological innovations in teaching and its international collaborations. In fact, the school is partly sponsored by a wealthy international organization.

These attributes are what attracted Lobar to the school. She liked its contemporary appearance and the admiration it receives from both the public and the professional community. The school was close to where she lived in Tashkent, and she knew a few of the teachers who worked at the school because they came from the same neighborhood. During the first few weeks at the school these colleagues helped Lobar to settle into her new job; they showed her around the campus, told her about the school and its community, and supported her emotionally at times when she felt a bit overwhelmed by all the new work. Lobar appreciated these colleagues and was pleased to have them in her professional life.

In the classroom, Lobar enjoyed teaching English. She followed the syllabus closely but was pleased to discover that she had some freedom to be flexible with what she taught and how she taught. The administration of her work and the management of her classes were also going well. But as all teachers know, school service extends beyond the classroom. Lobar found this out when the school principal asked her to join the school's Information Technology (IT) committee. She immediately said yes, firstly because she felt she couldn't refuse the principal's request, and secondly because she expected that as she gained experience, she would be required to do more in the school, and she might as well make a start. Her colleagues were impressed with this appointment because the IT committee was an important one in the school and many teachers clamored to be on it. Lobar, unfortunately, knew little about IT, and she was the first to admit this.

At the first IT committee meeting, Lobar noticed that no one else from the English section was there. Nor was there anyone from the other language sections, including Russian, Uzbek, and the growing Chinese program. Within a few minutes, as the chair of the committee was introducing new members, Lobar discovered she was on the committee as a representative of all language programs in the school. She was shocked – this seemed like a major responsibility, not only for someone in a junior position and new to the school but also for someone with a lack of expertise in IT. Her role would be to monitor the technology needs of the language programs and request appropriate orders through the school's IT Department. She wasn't in charge of the budget but had to consult with the head of the IT Department about costs and balances every time she requested equipment. She found this new position daunting, and it wasn't at all what she was expecting, or wanted to spend her time doing. It just seemed too much for her to handle so early on in her time at the school. Straight after the committee meeting, she arranged a meeting with her special group of supportive colleagues to talk about what she should do.

8.4.2 Questions

1. First-year teachers, like Lobar, should be slowly introduced to service roles in a school. Do you agree or disagree, and how should this process be controlled, and by whom?
2. Do you think the school principal made a mistake inviting Lobar to serve on the IT committee? If he wanted her to serve on a committee, how could he have gone about things differently?
3. Should Lobar have accepted the invitation? Did she have any choice?
4. Lobar was shocked to hear of her responsibilities at the first IT committee meeting. How would you have responded if you were Lobar?
5. What do you think Lobar is going to say to her group of friendly colleagues? What do you predict their advice will be?

8.4.3 Research Topics

Examining Teacher Emotions and Self-Efficacy as a New Committee Member

How does a teacher feel when joining an established school committee? What are their expectations? What emotions do they experience at the first meeting?

1. In an institution or language school where you work or that you have access to, identify active committees that hold regular meetings. Contact the chairpersons of these committees and ask them when they expect to welcome a new member to a future meeting.
2. Meet with that new member prior to the meeting for a brief *semi-structured interview* (M9). Prepare a schedule that asks them about (a) how they got onto the committee, (b) what their expectations are of potential committee work, (c) how they feel emotionally about serving on the committee, and (d) what they expect their contribution will be. Record the interview.
3. As soon as possible after the committee meeting, *interview* (M9) the teacher for a second time. Ask them about their experience of the first meeting, focusing especially on their contribution during the meeting and their emotions immediately before, during, and immediately after the meeting. Record the interview.
4. Two to three months later, conduct a third and final *interview* (M9) with the teacher. In this interview, ask the teacher a series of questions that probe how

their participation in meetings is progressing, and how they feel about being a member of the committee. Again, record the interview.
5. Analyze the three interview transcripts in detail, searching for themes that reveal the teacher's expectations, emotions, and perceptions of efficacy as a committee member.
6. Does the teacher find it worthwhile being on the committee? Are they contributing to committee work? How do they feel emotionally about being a committee member?

Investigating Schools' Professional Service Induction Processes for New Language Teachers
Do schools have policies and processes in place for inducting new language teachers into professional service roles? What is the rationale for the schools' decisions about their policies and processes?

1. Engage with up to five language schools or university language departments that regularly welcome new teachers to their institutions.
2. Meet with a manager in each of these institutions who has knowledge about staff workload distribution and human resources policies.
3. Before the meeting, ask the manager if the institution has any written policy statements about new staff induction and workload, and if so, if they would be willing to share a copy of the policy with you. *Review the documents* (M6) before meeting with the manager.
4. At the meeting, discuss the policy document with the manager. *Interview* (M9) them about service role workload distribution for new teachers and about whether an induction period applies to new teachers, that is, whether new teachers have a lighter (or heavier) service load during an induction period.
5. Repeat the same procedures for all five institutional managers. In any case that no induction period applies, enquire into the rationale for such practice.
6. Do new language teachers have a lighter service role workload during an induction period at any of the institutions? Why or why not? Do institutions have written policies about new-teacher service roles and workload? What do the institutions have in common and how do they differ?
7 From the document and interview data collected, are you able to draw up a set of common guidelines for language schools or departments? Can you present these at a conference or write a short article about them?

8.4.4   Resources

Admiraal, W., Røberg, K.-I. K., Wiers-Jenssen, J., & Saab, N. (2023). Mind the gap: Early-career teachers' level of preparedness, professional development, working conditions, and feelings of distress. *Social Psychology of Education, 26*, 1759–1787. https://doi.org/10.1007/s11218-023-09819-6

Colognesi, S., Van Nieuwenhoven, C., & Beausaert, S. (2020). Supporting newly-qualified teachers' professional development and perseverance in secondary education: On the role of informal learning. *European Journal of Teacher Education, 43*(2), 258–276. https://doi.org/10.1080/02619768.2019.1681963

Gray, P. L. & Seiki, S. (2020). Institutional performativity pressure and first-year teachers. *Frontiers in Education, 5*, 71. https://doi.org/10.3389/feduc.2020.00071

8.5 Giving a Talk to Pre-service Teachers

Keywords
- New Zealand
- Primary school and university
- English teacher and PhD student
- Doing a guest lecture for pre-service teachers
- Students not interested and lecturer absent

8.5.1 Pre-reading Reflection

1. Have you worked full-time as a teacher and studied part-time? Or vice versa? What are some of the challenges of doing so?
2. Teachers are busy enough; should they also be doing community outreach work?
3. What do you think are legitimate service and administrative jobs school teachers should be doing?

Kendall Bryan teaches English at a suburban primary school in the city of Christchurch in New Zealand. He describes the school, which is attended by middle-class students, as "pretty ordinary." By this he means that it does not have a prestigious reputation, but it is also not a "bad" school. Kendall likes his job – he is happy with the school leadership, he gets on well with his colleagues and students, and he feels he has freedom to teach the way he wants to, within the constraints of the curriculum. Kendall has been at the school for five years. He is very enthusiastic about his own professional development and sees himself as a language teacher educator in future years. He is enrolled at the local university as a part-time PhD student.

Kendall's PhD research focuses on language teacher identity, particularly how identity is manipulated by neoliberal educational policies at institutional levels. He worries about how language teachers and their learners fit into the complex machinations of curriculum development, educational funding, and Ministry of Education decision-making. In doing all of this, he wants to focus on the classroom – that is, how his topic is relevant to what goes on with teaching and learning language at the classroom level. Kendall is now in his third year and has collected some fascinating data. He did his research in the school where he teaches, and so it has local relevance. One of the lecturers at his university recently asked Kendall if he would talk to his undergraduate pre-service teachers about his research.

The plan was for Kendall to present at one of the late-afternoon lectures when he was not teaching at school. The class was part of a course on developing learning communities and was compulsory for all students majoring in Education. Kendall thought this would be an excellent opportunity to share his research and to gauge the level of interest and motivation of teachers preparing to become teachers in the New Zealand school system. Doing community outreach was also one of his service requirements at his primary school, and this lecture would certainly qualify as a contribution in this regard.

Kendall prepared well for his lecture; it took up a lot of his spare time, but he felt that the preparation helped him consolidate some of his ideas about his developing research project. The lecture went quite well. It lasted an hour. He gave some input about his research findings after framing the research questions and indicating how they may be applicable to the pre-service teachers who would soon be embarking on a teaching career in New Zealand schools. He tried to make connections with the students' learning and with their lives, and he desperately tried to engage them in discussion. The students didn't seem very enthusiastic about talking about the topic or about education generally. They didn't seem interested in what was happening in class. This surprised Kendall – they were after all going to become teachers and were investing a lot of time and money preparing for that profession. Kendall also noticed that the course lecturer, after introducing him at the beginning of the class, left the lecture room. He was left alone with the students.

After the lecture, as Kendall reflected on the experience over a cup of coffee in the university cafeteria, he found himself feeling rather depressed. He wondered if he had wasted his time preparing for and presenting his talk. Had the lecturer used him to get a free period? What was wrong with the students? Were they not interested in education – interested in what was happening with education in their own country? On the one hand, this motivated Kendall to work even harder on his PhD, to try to find answers to these questions; but on the other, he did feel somewhat despondent about undertaking any further community outreach work when this was the kind of reception he might expect.

8.5.2 Questions

1. What is your opinion of Kendall's PhD topic? Will it have useful implications for the real world of language teaching and learning?

2. Do you think Kendall will be a good language teacher educator one day, preparing future teachers for the teaching profession? Give a reason for your answer.
3. Summarize why Kendall felt despondent after his guest lecture? What do you think was the main reason?
4. Kendall identified one benefit from doing the lecture – feeling more motivated to work on his PhD. How confident do you feel about his research making a difference?
5. Was Kendall's outreach contribution worth it, or should he have focused on doing something else, considering his teaching and research experience? What might that be?

8.5.3 Research Topics

Analyzing Teachers' Stories of Their Community Outreach Experiences

What kind of community outreach work do language teachers engage in? Do they find it emotionally and professionally worthwhile? How do they balance their school teaching work and outreach work?

1. The next time you attend a teacher conference, arrange to present a workshop on community outreach for language teachers. Write the abstract so that the workshop will be inviting for teachers who wish to reflect on their outreach work – the benefits and challenges, and the role it plays in their professional lives.
2. Arrange workshop activities so that the workshop is teacher-led, with you acting as a facilitator.
3. During the workshop, ask the teacher participants to construct a personal pen-and-paper narrative about their experiences of doing community outreach work.
4. Give them clear guidelines for how to construct the narrative, for example writing only one page, including significant characters and communities or institutions in the story, the nature of the work done, the time and place of the work, and the outcomes of their outreach work.
5. Invite the participants to include multimodal features in their narratives, such as drawings, colours and shapes, and emojis.
6. When they have completed their narrative, ask them to take a photo of their one-page narrative and upload it to a Google (or similar) document via a QR code you make available to them.
7. Invite all the teachers to access the Google document after the conference and to continue adding comments to their own and each other's stories, giving them a deadline.

8. Analyze the stories after the deadline. What is the main type of community outreach work language teachers do? How is their community work associated with their school language teaching? Do they enjoy community outreach work? Is it a worthwhile endeavor for them?

Measuring Undergraduate Pre-service Language Teachers' Investment in Their Teacher Education

How much do undergraduate pre-service language teachers desire to become language teachers? How invested are they in their teacher education? What is their long-term commitment to language teaching as a career?

1. Secure agreement to participate from a class or group of undergraduate pre-service language teachers at a university that prepares teachers to teach in the local school system. Aim for as many teacher participants as possible.
2. Design an anonymous *quantitative questionnaire* (M17) that includes closed-ended questions such as *Agree-Disagree* Likert-type scales, checkboxes, rating or ranking options, and multiple-choice items.
3. Include questions about (a) the teachers' biographical details, (b) their reasons for choosing language teaching as a study option, (c) their desire to become a teacher, (d) contributions they wish to make as language teachers, (e) their commitment to the local school system, and (f) the teachers' medium- to long-term professional goals.
4. Distribute the anonymous questionnaire on a platform that the teachers have easy access to, such as Google Forms or Qualtrics. Give them a suitable amount of time to complete and submit the questionnaire.
5. Use both *descriptive statistics* (doing frequency counts and calculating percentages) and *inferential statistics* (making comparisons and predictions across and beyond the data) to analyze the data (M4).
6. What is the state of pre-service teacher investment in their teacher education? What significant trends emerge from the statistical analysis? Do the questionnaire respondents want to become teachers? How much so?

8.5.4 Resources

Havia, J., Lutovac, S., Komulainen, T., & Kaasila, R. (2023). Preservice subject teachers' lack of interest in their minor subject: Is it a problem? *International Journal of Science and Mathematics Education, 21*, 923–941. https://doi.org/10.1007/s10763-022-10277-3

Monica Assante, G. & Momanu, M. (2021). Community engagement in schools: A grounded theory to understand in-service teachers' practices. *Proceedings of CBU in Social Sciences, 2*, 16–21. https://doi.org/10.12955/pss.v2.196

Thurlings, M. & den Brok, P. (2018). Student teachers' and in-service teachers' peer learning: A realist synthesis. *Educational Research and Evaluation, 24* (1–2), 13–50. https://doi.org/10.1080/13803611.2018.1509719

8.6 Serving as a Cooperating Teacher

Keywords
- Wisconsin, USA
- High school
- Cooperating teacher and university student
- Working with a student teacher
- Potential mental health issues

8.6.1 Pre-reading Reflection

1. What type of work does a mentor do? What is their role?
2. Do you think you are a good judge of people's personalities? Are you easily able to tell what kind of person they are?
3. What challenges might a pre-service student teacher face when starting a teaching practicum?

Maddy Johnson is an experienced Spanish teacher in the bilingual program at a high school in a mid-sized city in the state of Wisconsin, United States. She has been teaching at this school for five years and has previously taught at various other high schools in the state for about ten years. Maddy has an MA in Bilingual Education and has participated in many professional development workshops and teacher conferences over the years. She is a very good, well-respected teacher. She enjoys her teaching and does a good job, but she is not overly ambitious. She relies on her considerable experience to "produce the goods," as she says. She gets on very well with people and is a keen observer of their behavior, often figuring out their identities and personalities long before anyone else. She can "smell trouble a mile off," as she likes to put it. This certainly counts in her favor in the school environment.

Maddy is registered with several universities in the district as a cooperating teacher to work with pre-service teachers who embark on their teaching practicums in local schools. Her appointments have always been approved by administrators at her high school when requests for student placements come in from universities. And Maddy always does a good job. She is known as a popular cooperating teacher who works closely with her paired student teachers; she develops a good relationship with them, clearly communicates the needs of the

8.6 Serving as a Cooperating Teacher

school and the students, allows them freedom to observe and then slowly take on some teaching responsibilities, demands respect for the teaching profession, and demonstrates a love of languages. Maddy has probably worked with more than ten student teachers in the bilingual program in the school.

Her most recent student teacher was a young, local woman, Veronica, studying at one of the city's universities. She was a graduate student in the TESOL program, with no teaching experience, but was interested in learning more about bilingual education. The teaching practicum was not required in her program and Veronica was doing it as an elective. Maddy welcomed her to the school and together they worked out an appropriate semester-long program. Basically, it followed Maddy's normal pattern: starting off with some classroom observations, slowly increasing the interaction with students in group work, then designing some lessons, and finally doing some teaching in short periods of ten to twenty minutes while Maddy was in the classroom observing.

Very early on, Maddy noticed that Veronica's behavior seemed odd and that she didn't always follow the program they had planned. For example, during a lesson observation in the first week Veronica didn't sit quietly at the back of the room observing Maddy's teaching as agreed. Instead, she started talking to students near to her, interrupting their work. Maddy noticed that the students looked a little annoyed. After class, Maddy reminded Veronica to observe only during these early weeks, and was shocked when Veronica snapped back saying, "You can't stop me talking to the students." On a later occasion, when Maddy asked Veronica to prepare some materials for a short lesson they were going to teach together, Veronica simply refused, saying it wasn't her job. Veronica never looked relaxed in class but was always fidgeting in her backpack or scrolling on her phone. She almost never seemed to be paying attention to what was happening in class.

Maddy didn't feel she needed to report this conduct but did wonder if Veronica perhaps had some sort of mental health issue. Or was she just a "strange person," as Maddy described her to a colleague? At times, they got on well and Veronica seemed engaged and interested, but at other times, her behavior was erratic and somewhat disturbing. Maddy worked through the semester as Veronica's cooperating teacher, but for the first time it did make her reflect on her long-term commitment to this important service role in the future.

8.6.2 Questions

1. Maddy's high school service as a cooperating teacher is important. What makes the role challenging, and what makes Maddy a particularly good cooperating teacher?
2. What do you think about Maddy's teaching practicum plan for Veronica? Does it sound acceptable?

3. When Veronica spoke to the students near to her during the lesson observation, should Maddy have ignored it and not said anything? Was Maddy right to confront Veronica after the lesson about talking to the students?
4. Should Maddy have reported Veronica's "strange" behavior to the school administrators or to the university? Why, or why not?
5. Do you believe that Maddy needs further training if she wishes to continue to serve as a cooperating teacher at her school? What might that training look like?

8.6.3 Research Topics

Examining Student Teachers' Expectations of Their Cooperating Teacher

What do student teachers expect to learn from their cooperating teacher while on their teaching practicum? What kind of relationship do student teachers expect to develop with their cooperating teacher?

1. Engage with a university language teacher education program that includes primary or high school teaching practicum experience in its qualification.
2. Prior to the first teaching practicum, arrange to meet face-to-face with a *focus group* (M8) of up to five pre-service language teachers.
3. Record the discussion about what their expectations of their assigned cooperating teacher are, particularly, how much they will engage with each other, the nature of the relationship they will develop, and life-long professional lessons they might learn from them.
4. Request each of the students to maintain a weekly *student teacher journal* (M14) during their practicum. Collect them weekly and analyze them for developing themes related to the research topic.
5. After the practicum, *construct a narrative* (M16) of about 2,000 words for each student participant, showing the development of expectations from prior to the practicum to the end of the practicum. Then do a cross-case analysis of all the narratives.
6. What would an ideal cooperating teacher be for a student teacher? How important is a good mentor relationship for a student teacher? What key lessons would the students hope to learn from their cooperating teacher?

Assessing Teachers' Readiness to Identify and Manage Colleagues' Mental Health Issues

Do teachers feel able to identify mental health issues their colleagues may be experiencing? Do they know how to report potential mental health issues? Are school leaders qualified to manage these?

1. Engage a group of four or five primary and high school language teachers from schools in your local community.
2. Prepare a short (one-page) document that outlines the increasing prevalence of mental health issues among teachers in schools. Send the document to the teachers by email.
3. Request a reply, asking the teachers to comment on their awareness of the prevalence of mental health issues in the language teaching profession.
4. Continue the email exchanges with the teachers, asking up to ten questions about (a) any experiences they may have had encountering colleagues' mental health problems, (b) how they dealt with them, (c) their knowledge about mental health in the language teaching profession, generally, and in their school particularly, (d) their awareness of procedures to report mental health issues, and (e) their confidence in their managers dealing effectively with mental health issues in the workplace.
5. For each teacher, collate the email messages into one data file. Analyze the data files for salient themes related to topics (a)–(e) above, and then conduct a cross-case analysis of the teachers' data files.
6. What do the teachers know about mental health in the language teaching profession? Do they feel comfortable knowing that their colleagues will be taken care of in their workplace? Do they desire to increase their awareness about mental health issues?

8.6.4   Resources

Bonilla Medina, S. X. & Samacá Bohórquez, Y. (2020). Modern and postmodern views of education that shape EFL mentoring in the teaching practicum. *Colombian Applied Linguistics Journal*, *22*(1), 55–68. https://doi.org/10.14483/22487085.14576

Houdyshell, M., Kratt, D., & Greene, J. (2021). Student teachers with mental health conditions share barriers to success: A case study. *The Qualitative Report*, *26*(1), 1–26. https://doi.org/10.46743/2160-3715/2021.4266

Mutlu-Gülbak, G. (2023). Expectations for training mentors: Insights from a preservice language teacher education program. *Educational Process: International Journal*, *12*(2): 76–92. https://dx.doi.org/10.22521/edupij.2023.122.5

8.7   On a Department of Education Working Group

Keywords
- England, UK
- Secondary school

- ESL and French teacher
- Local authority curriculum meeting
- No relevance to classrooms and schools

8.7.1 Pre-reading Reflection

1. What specific language needs do immigrant children typically have? How can schools help?
2. Everyone has sat in meetings where the discussion appears to be irrelevant. How does this make you feel?
3. Think of some examples where the working relationship between local authorities or Departments of Education and schools is evident?

Timothy Malton works in a state-funded secondary school in Southwest England. He joined the school fifteen years ago after returning from five years abroad teaching EFL in the Middle East. When he returned, he completed his MA in Applied Linguistics part-time while starting his career as a secondary school ESL and French teacher. Timothy always wanted to teach at the secondary school level. He loves the energy of the age group, and he loves working with students who will soon be finishing school and heading out into the wide world to get on with their adult lives. Timothy is a dedicated teacher – he knows his subjects and he knows how to teach. He constantly takes part in professional development seminars and does a lot of reading. But he believes that the best learning takes place in the classroom, interacting with learners, reflecting on practice, constantly being innovative. He gets excellent teaching evaluations, and his colleagues, his students, and their parents admire his professionalism.

So, when the local education authority asked the school for a language teacher representative to attend a meeting to discuss new secondary school language curriculum developments, the school turned to Timothy Malton. The multilingual immigrant population has been increasing in the region for many years, especially recently, and schools have been adapting their language teaching practices to accommodate the needs of this changing student demographic. But the way they have been doing this has been rather haphazard, says the local authority. They therefore believe it is time to evaluate "where things are at" and to coordinate plans "going forward." Various working groups have been set up – for primary schools, secondary schools, community schools, and higher education.

When Timothy joined the first secondary schools meeting, which took place in person at the local authority offices, he very soon realized that he was the only practicing teacher among the fifteen attendees. Leading the meeting was Ms. Braythorne, invited by the local authority to "kick off" the secondary school discussions. Ms. Braythorne had been a school teacher many years ago and had been working in the Department of Education – in various roles – since leaving teaching. After welcoming everyone to the meeting, she asked them all to introduce themselves and briefly say what it is that they do. Of the fifteen, it turned out that about half worked in Ms. Braythorne's office, and were there to observe, learn, and take notes. Among the remaining participants were Mr. Ahmed, a local community leader, who had never taught a language class in his life; a language assessor, Sarah Roberts, who worked for an international language testing organization; Dr. Jim Reynolds, who owned an English language school in the city; and two student teachers from the local university, who were supposedly representing the student body.

Ms. Braythorne decided that the first item on the agenda, after the introductions, would be an open forum where all could talk informally about their perceptions of the multilingual immigrant population in the area, what their language educational needs are, and how they might be met by secondary schools. Participants were invited to draw on their experience and consider their work contexts. Most people were very eager to chip in, even the notetakers. The student teachers didn't say anything at all, however. The conversation flowed freely and plenty of information was shared. Timothy Malton, secondary school ESL and French teacher, sat back and listened closely to the discussion. After half an hour, he hadn't heard a single thing that had any relevance to his work or to the lives of the many immigrant students who pass through his classes every year. He suspected that language teachers working in secondary schools across the region would feel the same. He questioned the value of the current discussion and wondered what the outcome of the meeting would be. He also wondered if it was worth attending future meetings, if there were to be any.

8.7.2 Questions

1. Timothy Malton appears to be an excellent secondary school language teacher. Considering the whole case, what makes him so?
2. The local authority says that the approach of the schools in the region to accommodating the needs of the multilingual immigrants "has been rather haphazard." Can you think of examples of what they might mean? Is their strategy to set up working groups a good one?
3. With plenty of teaching and administrative roles, Timothy probably has enough on his plate. Do you think it is fair that the school nominated him to serve on the working group?
4. What is your opinion of the working group? How does your opinion compare with that of Timothy's? How would you change the composition of the working group if you had the power to do so?
5. If you were Timothy, would you attend further local authority secondary school working group meetings, if there were to be any? Give a reason for your answer.

8.7.3 Research Topics

Reviewing the Minutes of a Meeting to Assess Equitable Participation and Effectiveness

Do committee meeting minutes reflect equitable participation of all committee members? Are committee meetings always successful in achieving the goals of the agenda?

1. In a language teaching institution that you have access to, perhaps your own, meet the chairperson of an important committee and request to see the minutes of the most recent meeting (if the minutes are a public document).
2. In a variation of *stimulated recall* (M15), work through the *minutes of the meeting* (M6), agenda item by agenda item, asking the chairperson to talk you through their perceptions of the meeting at that time. Who facilitated the discussion? Who contributed? Did all participants feel able and comfortable enough to contribute? Were the agenda goals achieved? Was the meeting effective? Record the discussion.
3. Then meet with another member of the committee, one not in an executive position. Follow the same procedure and ask the same questions to this member to gain a different perspective on the meeting. Record this discussion.
4. Transcribe both recorded discussions. Compare and contrast the answers provided by the chairperson and the non-executive member.
5. Do the chairperson and the committee member agree on the way the meeting was run? What went right and what went wrong in the meeting? Did committee members find it a successful meeting?

Measuring Teachers' Awareness of Ministry-Level Decision-Making in Their Language Classrooms

What evidence do language teachers see of Ministry or Department of Education decision-making in their classrooms? What do they most obviously notice? Do they know how the outcomes of those decisions trickle down into their classrooms?

1. Recruit a group of language teachers from the same program in the same primary or high school.
2. Design a short, ten-item *questionnaire* (M17) with open-ended questions that each require a 100-word written answer.
3. Include questions about the language teachers' knowledge of the types of decisions the Ministry or Department of Education makes about language teaching and learning, how the decisions relate to the work of language teachers in schools and in their classrooms, and about whether they see actual evidence of these decisions in their day-to-day classroom practice.

4. Distribute the questionnaire to the group of teachers digitally and ask them to return it to you within a week.
5. Analyze the questionnaire responses by summarizing the answers for each teacher and then comparing their responses.
6. Invite the group of teachers to meet virtually on Zoom (or similar) to engage in a discussion about your findings. Record the discussion.
7. Do teachers know what kinds of decisions Ministries or Departments of Education make about language teaching and learning? Are they aware of the influence of the decisions in their classrooms? How (dis)empowered does this influence make the teachers feel?

8.7.4 Resources

de Jong, L., Meirink, J., & Admiraal, W. (2019). School-based teacher collaboration: Different learning opportunities across various contexts. *Teaching and Teacher Education, 86*, 102925. https://doi.org/10.1016/j.tate.2019.102925

Simpson, J. & Hunter, A.-M. (2023). Policy formation for adult migrant language education in England: National neglect and its implications. *Language Policy, 22*, 155–178. https://doi.org/10.1007/s10993-023-09655-6

Skerritt, C. (2023). Towards a mechanism for expert policy advice in education. *British Educational Research Journal, 49*(4), 749–765. https://doi.org/10.1002/berj.3867

9 Leadership

Cases in this chapter

9.1	Decolonizing the Curriculum	*page* 240
9.2	Mentoring an Ambitious Novice Language Teacher	244
9.3	Transgender Teacher Writing an Inclusive Language Policy	248
9.4	Electing a New President of a Teacher Association	252
9.5	Establishing a Collaborative Teacher Research Group	255
9.6	Planning a Study-Abroad Sojourn	259
9.7	Coordinating a Refugee Settlement Program in a School	262

9.1 Decolonizing the Curriculum

Keywords
- Colombia
- University Spanish education department
- A head of department and a researcher
- Decolonizing Spanish teacher education
- Figuring out where to begin

9.1.1 Pre-reading Reflection

1. What do the following concepts mean to you: *colonialism*, *decolonization*, and *post-colonial*?
2. Name three languages that are often associated with colonial power. What countries are these languages connected to?
3. What effects did colonization have on language education in a context you are familiar with?

Mariana and Carlos teach Spanish pedagogy to undergraduate pre-service teachers at a public university in a large city in Colombia, South America. Both also have part-time jobs as English teachers at the same private institute in the city, but the university job is what they refer to as their main work. They are both experienced teachers and teacher educators, with post-graduate qualifications in language education. Mariana is the head of the Spanish pedagogy department, and although she is interested in research, she doesn't have much time to do any. Carlos, on the other hand, is heavily involved in research activity; he collaborates productively with colleagues in the department and has published several articles in national teacher journals.

Recently, Mariana and Carlos attended a conference organized by a national association for university language teachers. They decided to go because the keynote speaker was a high-profile scholar they'd come across in their reading. She is of Mexican origin and based at a university in the US. More importantly, the topic of her presentation was decolonizing the language curriculum in schools and universities. Carlos had done some exploratory action research on this topic using his Spanish teaching materials, and Mariana was keen to see if the speaker's ideas could be applied to curriculum development across programs in her department. She was concerned that the Spanish pedagogy textbooks they had been using for many years were published in the US and presented a Western perspective on teacher education and language teaching. In conversation with Carlos and other teacher educators, it was clear that they struggled to adapt the texts to their local conditions. Their students were bored with the materials and couldn't always see their relevance, despite the teacher educators' attempts to re-shape and localize the content.

After attending the conference and listening to the keynote address, Mariana and Carlos sat down together to pool their reflections and understandings regarding what they had heard. They listed some key concepts they both noticed in the talk: *decolonial, glocal, coloniality, writing back,* and *Indigeneity*. They felt they had probably heard of these concepts before but struggled to articulate clearly what they meant – in their professional lives, in their work contexts, for their student teachers. Both, despite this, still felt that changes needed to be made in the department. Mariana was head of department and Carlos had useful research skills. They believed that together they could lead the department and its members in their approach to Spanish language teacher education toward a more relevant and just approach to preparing their teachers for teaching Spanish in Colombian schools. They were a little unsure exactly where to start this process, however. They felt that the first step should probably be to become familiar with the goals of a decolonizing program suitable for their department, and then to gather other teacher educator colleagues who had a similar interest in decolonizing their workplace in order to plan a strategy for implementing the process.

While this was happening, they planned the next step, which was to look beyond the university Spanish education department to their other teaching job: their part-time English teaching in the private institute. Mariana and Carlos felt that here, too, colonial approaches to English teaching were the norm and the materials that were available for use in that setting, like the Spanish teacher education materials, reflected these perspectives. In those English teaching jobs, however, they had much more freedom to innovate in their practices and to generate new or adapt old materials. They decided, therefore, that initially their English teaching would be their decolonial experimental ground. They would collaborate to make decisions about introducing some form of teaching that represented decolonial practice, and then, after the teaching event, would confer to consider the outcomes. If they believed them to be successful, they would transfer the approach to the university department for discussion with the colleagues who came forward as willing to participate in the decolonial agenda.

9.1.2 Questions

1. How will the Spanish language pre-service student teachers benefit from a decolonized curriculum?
2. Why do Mariana and Carlos have the potential to be an effective leadership team to implement the decolonization project? What roles and skills do they bring to the relationship?
3. Was their strategy to try out their ideas in the English language institute a good one? What are the pros and cons of doing so?
4. What do you predict the "buy in" for the Spanish pedagogy curriculum decolonizing project might be from other teacher educators in the department? What might their reasons be for joining or not joining the project?
5. Mariana and Carlos's plans are in the early stages and are somewhat underdeveloped. What would you suggest they do, as leaders, to implement a successful medium- to long-term plan to decolonize the teaching and materials in their department?

9.1.3 Research Topics

Understanding What Teacher Characteristics Make for an Effective Leadership Team

What *teacher* characteristics contribute to effective leadership qualities? What characteristics make for a successful leadership *team*?

1. Identity two teachers who have worked together as a leadership team – for example, two teachers who have led and managed a particular project, or a head and deputy head of a department.
2. Interview the two teachers together. Design a *semi-structured interview schedule* (M9) that is divided into two parts. In the first part, ask the leaders in turn to identify their partner's *teacher* characteristics that make them an effective leader – for example, knowledge of the subject area, empathy, relevant classroom experience.

9.1 Decolonizing the Curriculum

3. In the second part, ask questions to both leaders about what makes a good, productive leadership *team* – for example, willingness to compromise, being a good listener, motivation to succeed.
4. Record the interview. Analyze the transcript for leadership keywords and themes that explicitly relate to the research topic.
5. The same interview procedures and questions could be repeated with another pair of leaders in a different institution, if feasible.
6. Do teachers make good leaders? What is it about teachers that makes them good leaders? How do effective leadership teams work best together?

Exploring Language Teachers' Understanding of Terms Associated with Decolonizing Methodologies
What do language teachers know about decolonizing methodologies? Are they familiar with terminology associated with decolonizing methodologies? Are they interested in knowing this terminology?

1. Design an anonymous *survey* (M17) on Google Forms, Qualtrics, or Microsoft Forms (or similar) to be distributed on your professional social media to as many language teachers as possible in diverse geopolitical regions.
2. Divide the survey into three parts: In Part A ask for demographic information about the respondents, such as language(s) they teach, the country or region where they teach, the level they teach (e.g., primary school, high school, university), and years of teaching experience.
3. In Part B include a list of terms such as decolonizing, colonialism, decolonization, intersectionality, imperialism, colonial ideology, and Indigeneity. Ask respondents to indicate whether they *know*, *don't know*, or are *unsure* about the meaning of these terms.
4. In Part C ask respondents to indicate how important they believe these concepts are to their teaching situation, if they know what the concepts mean, and if they don't, whether they are interested in finding out their meaning.
5. Distribute the survey on your social media and throughout your professional networks. Ask respondents to share the survey link to their social media networks. Set a deadline for submission.
6. Use the digital survey tool to analyze data into *frequencies and percentages* (M4). Then correlate those numbers with the respondents' demographic data.
7. Does teachers' awareness of terms associated with decolonizing methodologies relate to the geopolitical regions they come from? To the age of the students they teach? To their years of teaching experience? Are teachers interested in learning about decolonizing language teaching methodologies?

9.1.4 Resources

García, O. (2023). Decolonizing US Latinx students' language: El Sur in the schools of El Norte. *Applied Linguistics*, *44*(5), 848–864. https://doi.org/10.1093/applin/amad017

Gutierrez, C. P. & Aguirre Ortega, M. (2022). English instructors navigating decoloniality with Afro Colombian and Indigenous university students. *Íkala, Revista de Lenguaje y Cultura*, *27*(3), 783–802. https://doi.org/10.17533/udea.ikala.v27n3a11

Tezgiden-Cakcak, Y. & Ataş, U. (2024). Becoming and being a critical language teacher educator: A duoethnography. *TESOL Journal*, *15*(4), e855. https://doi.org/10.1002/tesj.855

9.2 Mentoring an Ambitious Novice Language Teacher

Keywords
- Iran
- Private language institute
- Administrator and a new teacher
- Mentoring a novice teacher
- Managing an overly ambitions teacher

9.2.1 Pre-reading Reflection

1. Can you imagine yourself in a leadership role where you give advice to junior colleagues? Do you think you would be good at it?
2. It is probably a good idea to be ambitious as a professional teacher. But are there dangers in "running before you can walk"?
3. What do you think is the most important attribute of a good mentor–mentee relationship? Trust is one, for example.

Mr. Ghorbani is a senior administrator at a private language institute (PLI) in Isfahan, Iran. It is a large institute catering for young, public school-going learners who aim to improve their English and, more typically, to work toward achieving good results on standardized international tests. Mr. Ghorbani has worked at the institute for ten years. He started off as an English teacher at the institute but over time gave up his teaching to focus on helping the management team to govern the place. He is particularly good at dealing with human resources issues and overseeing staff recruitment and the induction of new teachers. Mr. Ghorbani is an experienced educator, having worked in the public school system for over twenty years. In fact, he still works as an English teacher in a secondary school.

9.2 Mentoring an Ambitious Novice Teacher

Mr. Ghorbani has worked with many new English teachers at the institute. At first, he worked in an informal mentor role, settling new recruits into their positions. Over time, this mentorship role became more formalized in the institute. New teachers were matched with established senior teachers or administrators when they arrived. The aim was for them to work together over a few months following guidelines formulated by a team of professional developers at the institute led by Mr. Ghorbani. When Arash Abed, a novice English teacher fresh out of university, arrived at the institute, Mr. Ghorbani assigned himself as Arash's mentor. He had a positive impression of Arash – when they first met, he could see himself in Arash as a young teacher; ambitious, motivated, and willing to learn. Mr. Ghorbani believed they would be a good match.

Arash settled quickly into his new English teaching role. In the first weeks of the school year, he turned up to class well prepared, fully engaging his students with interesting material (rumors quickly spread that he was a good-looking, popular teacher), and by all accounts was doing a good job in the classroom. During this time Mr. Ghorbani met regularly with Arash. Although they carefully followed the institute's mentoring guidelines, Mr. Ghorbani drew on his experience as a teacher leader and mentor to deal with the few issues that Arash raised. These were small issues and easily managed. Mr. Ghorbani was enjoying this mentoring experience and expected that now after six months he would be able to let Arash get on with things himself.

However, suddenly, Arash started talking to Mr. Ghorbani about doing his MA degree. Mr. Ghorbani thought this was a bit too soon, and mentioned this to Arash, who didn't seem to take notice. Mr. Ghorbani wondered who Arash had been talking to – why was there a sudden rush to study further? He had hardly started his teaching career. Within a few weeks, quite bizarrely, Arash became consumed by his aspirations, not only to study toward his MA but to pursue even more lofty academic pursuits in the future. He said that in a few years he wanted to work as a teacher educator at a university. He looked forward to doing research so that he could be published; in fact, he had already started working on projects while at the institute. He was even thinking of a PhD research topic!

Recently, at one of their regular meetings, Mr. Ghorbani has tried to advise Arash to slow down, to attend to his teaching and focus on gaining more experience. But it appears Arash doesn't want to hear this. He has stopped consulting with Mr. Ghorbani altogether. And, unfortunately, it has become evident that he has started neglecting his English teaching duties at the institute. His dedication to research and publication and a future university career in teacher education seems somehow to overshadow his obligations to his students and the institute, leading to a growing sense of frustration and disappointment among his colleagues and particularly Mr. Ghorbani, and even his students who, at first, loved him.

9.2.2 Questions

1. Mr. Ghorbani is a senior administrator at the institute. He is also an active mentor and a secondary school English teacher in the city. Do you think he is spreading himself a bit thin? If so, what are the dangers of taking on too much, especially leadership positions?
2. Do you think Mr. Ghorbani is an appropriate mentor for Arash? Could the process of matching Mr. Ghorbani and Arash have been handled in a different way?
3. What do you think might have led Arash to suddenly change his attitude to his work at the institute and his vision for the future? Did Mr. Ghorbani have anything to do with it?
4. As Arash's mentor, what steps could Mr. Ghorbani next take to guide Arash "back on track"?
5. What measures would you suggest leaders at the institute implement to ensure teachers like Arash achieve their longer-term goals while simultaneously fulfilling their duties as English teachers? Give some examples.

9.2.3 Research Topics

Discovering the Top Five Strategies for Ensuring an Effective New Teacher Mentoring Relationship

What good mentoring practices do first-year teachers notice in their mentors? What are the top five effective mentoring strategies they perceive in their mentors?

1. Contact three or four language teachers who have recently started to teach, preferably those in their first year of teaching. They could be language teachers in any type of institution (e.g., high school, university, or a private institute).
2. Arrange to meet them individually, face-to-face or virtually, to have a conversation about their mentoring experience. Before the meeting confirm that they had (or have) a mentor, "buddy," or more senior colleague who served as a mentor or support person during their early months as a teacher. Also ask them to reflect on their mentoring relationship before you meet with them.
3. At the meeting with each teacher, aim to have an *informal conversation* (M9) about mentorship, what makes a good mentor, and the teacher's perceptions of their mentor.
4. During the conversation, ask the teacher explicitly to list five effective mentoring strategies that they experienced or witnessed in their relationship with their mentor. Encourage the generation of these five strategies by engaging actively in the conversation as an interested partner. Record the conversations.

5. After the meetings, construct separate lists of the five strategies for each of the teachers, and then compare the lists. Create a composite list of strategies. Interpret this list in light of the topics and themes discussed with the teachers in the conversations.
6. Which mentoring strategies are considered most effective by the early-career language teachers? What would the characteristics of an ideal first-year teacher mentor be?

Asking Experienced Language Teachers About Their Views on Young, Newly Graduated Teachers

How do very experienced language teachers perceive newly appointed language teachers? What do they notice about them and their work? How do they compare the new teachers' goals, desires, and ambitions with their own when they were a young graduate?

1. Meet individually with three or four experienced language teachers. These teachers should have been teaching for many years, preferably over twenty. They can work in different schools and at different levels (e.g., primary or high school). Ensure that the teachers regularly encounter new, recently graduated language teachers who join their schools.
2. Conduct *semi-structured interviews* (M9) with each experienced teacher. Keep the interviews informal and ask the teachers to reflect on the new teachers they remember during their careers. Invite them to tell stories about those teachers – what they were like, what their interests and goals were, what they ended up doing or becoming professionally.
3. Ask the teachers also to tell you what they were like as young teachers just starting their careers, and if they see new teachers now as being different. Record and transcribe the interviews.
4. Read through the transcriptions closely and search for *metaphors* (M11) that refer to the young, new teachers. Compile a list of these metaphors and describe their meaning by referring to the content of the interview discussion.
5. How do experienced language teachers compare themselves to newly graduated teachers joining their schools? What characteristics of new teachers stand out for experienced teachers?

9.2.4 Resources

Mansouri, B. (2021). Understanding EFL teachers' identity construction in a private language school: A positioning analysis. *Teaching English as a Second Language Electronic Journal (TESL-EJ)*, *25*(2). https://tesl-ej.org/pdf/ej98/a3.pdf

Rizi, A. R. B., Barati, H., & Moinzade, A. (2019). A closer look at EFL teacher education and the role of mentoring in Iran: Teachers' attitudes in focus. *Iranian Journal of English for Academic Purposes, 8*(4), 34–48. https://journalscmu.sinaweb.net/article_95959.html

Ruan, X. & Toom, A. (2022). Exploring female EFL teachers' professional agency for their sustainable career development in China: A self-discrepancy theory perspective. *Frontiers in Psychology, 13*, 906727. https://doi.org/10.3389/fpsyg.2022.906727

9.3 Transgender Teacher Writing an Inclusive Language Policy

Keywords
- Canada
- High school
- French teacher
- Transgender teacher writing a language policy
- Teacher lacks confidence and expertise

9.3.1 Pre-reading Reflection

1. Are you someone who likes to keep a low profile in the work environment, or someone who prefers to be visible?
2. Do you know what *inclusive language* is?
3. Sometimes teachers are asked to take on leadership roles that they don't want to do. How might this affect them negatively?

Sarah Riel was born in a medium-sized city in the province of Quebec, Canada. She went to school there and graduated from a local university, majoring in French Language and Literature. Not knowing what to do with her degree after graduation, she decided to qualify as a teacher. She immediately got a position at a middle school (or junior high school), again in the same town, teaching French. She has been at the school for four years and is developing into a good language teacher, although she is not fully committed to staying in teaching in the long term. Sarah likes the school, and she is happy enough with the job, but "to be honest," as she constantly says, "I see myself doing something else in ten years." Sarah transitioned into her transgender identity before starting her job. Everyone at the school knows and accepts her as Sarah (she/her).

The principal of the school, Dr. Coventry, recently called Sarah in for a meeting, where they discussed the use of inclusive language at the school. He had become aware of some non-inclusive language use among students

9.3 Transgender Teacher Writing a Language Policy

while on the school campus, and he suspected that their language out of school and on social media wasn't much better. Some teachers had also recently spoken to him about feeling increasingly uncertain about using language in their professional contexts, especially when referencing gender and ethnicity. He therefore believed it was time that the school drafted a language policy that included a set of guidelines for the use of inclusive language. He hoped that such a policy, if implemented thoroughly and with sensitivity, would encourage students and teachers to learn about appropriate language use associated with the diverse groups within the school community. Dr. Coventry asked Sarah to start working on a draft, and to let him know if she had any questions. Later that day, she bumped into her friend and colleague, Rodney, as they were walking out the school gate after school and they shared a quick conversation.

SARAH: Yes, I sure do have questions. How about these two, Dr. Coventry? Are you asking me to draft a policy because I'm trans? There are plenty of other teachers who are far more qualified than I am.

RODNEY: Could be. But you're also a language teacher, with a language degree, and you know a lot about how people learn languages. Didn't you just go to that workshop or conference in Montreal on new developments in language education, or something? The school paid for it; maybe they want some payback, hahaha.

SARAH: Yes, but that was on French language teaching methods, not diversity and inclusion, about which I know little. That's kind of specialist knowledge.

RODNEY: But still.

SARAH: You know I'm not an activist; I try to keep a low profile at school and get on with my job. And that relates to my second question. Does he expect me to promote the policy when I've drafted it? I'd hate to have to do that. I'm not good at meetings and working with a lot of people.

RODNEY: Well, I was just thinking, you don't really have a big service role in the school, and you have been here four, five years already. Isn't it time you stepped up a bit and took on some leadership in the school?

SARAH: Not sure what you mean. I've got plenty of admin to keep me busy.

RODNEY: We all do. But I mean something more than regular admin. I think you'd be really good at it.

SARAH: At what?

RODNEY: At admin and management generally, but specifically promoting the language policy, which I know you'll do well. You can get one or two people to help you. Check with Coventry – he may have some ideas about who you can work with.

SARAH: You're too kind, Rod. Thanks for increasing my workload!

9.3.2 Questions

1. Sarah immediately assumed she was asked by Dr. Coventry to draft the language policy because she is transgender. Why do you think she made this quick assumption?

2. What might some of the personal and professional challenges be for Sarah, as a transgender teacher, when she takes on this highly visible leadership role in her school?
3. Sarah shows quite a bit of resistance to taking on the job of writing a draft policy and promoting it. What are her main objections? Do you support her?
4. What is your response to Rodney's contributions to the conversation? Does he raise valid points? Or is he being facetious? Give reasons for your answer.
5. Schools typically give new teachers lighter service or leadership workloads for some time after their appointment. Do you think Sarah is ready for more service or leadership? Why or why not?

9.3.3 Research Topics

Exploring New Teacher-Leaders' Experiences of Learning to Lead
How do new teacher-leaders go about learning the skills of leadership when they take on a new leadership role? What emotions do they experience while learning to lead?

1. Engage with a teacher-leader who has recently taken on (or is about to take on) a new leadership role in their school, such as a (deputy) head of a section or department, a chairperson of a committee, or a leader of a research or curriculum development project.
2. Meet them to establish what the official role expectations are. Ask the teacher-leader how they feel about taking on the new leadership role, if they feel prepared, what their expectations are about the work they will be doing, how it will benefit them professionally, and how long the role will last.
3. Then meet regularly for brief *semi-structured interviews* (M9) for the duration of their leadership work in that role. Ask for updates on the work they are doing and how they feel emotionally about their leadership – if their skills are developing, for example, and whether they are experiencing stress or a sense of self-efficacy. Record the meetings.
4. In between meetings, ask the teacher-leader to maintain a *leadership journal* (M14) with short written entries in which they reflect on their leadership work, their development, and related emotions. Collect the journal entries as they are constructed.
5. At the end of the leader's project, or after a few months, stop the meetings and journal writing. Analyze the data to record the new teacher-leader's experiences and note any leadership skills development. Search for themes to do with learning and leadership strategies that appear relevant to new leaders.
6. What did the new teacher-leader learn about leadership? Did they regret taking on the role, or did they thrive in that position?

Discovering How Teachers Say "No" to Unwanted Leadership Roles
How do experienced language teachers learn to refuse requests for more leadership work? How do they say "no"? Why do they say "no"?

1. Engage with two or three busy language teachers who have been teaching for many years and have also served in leadership roles. It is preferable that they work in different schools.
2. Meet with the teachers in a face-to-face situation for a *focus group discussion* (M8). Before the meeting, ask the teachers to prepare by reflecting on the leadership roles they have had in their careers, both large and small.
3. Prepare for the meeting by designing a schedule of discussion points that cover, briefly, the recent leadership work the teachers have done, and then focus in more depth on the requests they have received to lead projects or teams of people that they have turned down.
4. Ask them why they turn requests down, how they do so, and how they benefit by saying "no." Give all teachers equal opportunity to talk about their experiences. Facilitate an open discussion with them. Record the focus group discussion.
5. Analyze the recording for themes related to the topics discussed in the group. Write a brief, one- to two-page report on the findings and send it to the participant teachers for their comments.
6. How and why do they refuse requests to take on a leadership role? Is it always a good idea to say "no" to requests? Do those who refuse a role later regret their decision?

9.3.4 Resources

Forbes, K. & Morea, N. (2024). Mapping school-level language policies across multilingual secondary schools in England: An ecology of English, modern languages and community languages policies. *British Educational Research Journal, 50*(3), 1189–1207. https://doi.org/10.1002/berj.3959

Martino, W., Omercajic, K., & Kassen, J. (2022). "We have no 'visibly' trans students in our school": Educators' perspectives on transgender-affirmative policies in schools. *Teachers College Record, 124*(8), 66–97. https://doi.org/10.1177/01614681221121522

Whitley, J. & Hollweck, T. (2020). Inclusion and equity in education: Current policy reform in Nova Scotia, Canada. *Prospects, 49*, 297–312. https://doi.org/10.1007/s11125-020-09503-z

9.4 Electing a New President of a Teacher Association

Keywords
- Thailand
- Professional language teacher association
- Teacher professional development
- Election of a new president
- Contrasting manifestos of candidates

9.4.1 Pre-reading Reflection

1. What is the role of professional language teacher associations? What do they achieve for teachers?
2. What work does the committee of a teacher association do? Have you served on such a committee?
3. What attributes should the president of a professional teacher association have?

A regional branch of a national English teacher association in Thailand is holding an election to elect a new president. The National Association has its head office in Bangkok, the capital city of Thailand, and has several active branches located in regions across the country. All branches run independently but follow the mission, principles, and values established by the National Association, which itself is affiliated to a large international foreign language teacher association based in the UK. In order to retain this affiliation, the National Association has to demonstrate to the UK office in its annual report productive activity of all its branches, including election processes and outcomes. It therefore keeps a close eye on what is going on at all its branches.

Election time for a new executive committee is normally uneventful. The process happens at the AGM and branches typically struggle to find volunteers to fill leadership positions – for example, President, Vice-President, Secretary, Treasurer, and two or three committee members. The National Association executive committee has heard, however, that a power struggle is brewing at the Chiang Rai regional branch of the Association. The branch has a relatively large membership and is very active. It organizes regular workshops and local conferences for teachers and has successfully won a bid to host an international conference in two years' time. This current election is thus particularly important – it needs leaders in place who have the necessary organizational skills and who can portray to a wide audience an Association that is forward-looking, academically up to date, and professional. The only position up for election at the Chiang Rai branch is President; other members still have a year or two of their terms to complete. And there are two new candidates.

Dr. Siriwong is a local and has worked in the region since graduation. She took leave from her job to complete a PhD at a university in Malaysia and has just recently returned to Chiang Rai. Inspired by new ideas about language teaching and the need for teachers to be active in research, she firmly believes the Association needs a "shake up," as she puts it. Still in her thirties, she is energetic and ambitious. Her election manifesto includes the following:

Furthermore, I believe it is time for a woman to be President. Men have led our Association with distinction over the years, but for the sake of equity, we need to hear a woman's perspective on language education. Most English teachers in Chiang Rai are women, and we can see this reflected in the membership of our Association. It is time for change.

Mr. Wattana is also a local, staunchly so. He is in his fifties and is a well-respected teacher in the region. He has a long history of "being involved" – working on the committee on and off over the years and successfully organizing many regional events. He is very loyal to the Chiang Rai branch of the Association and actively promotes its work on social media every chance he gets. Mr. Wattana also holds a senior leadership position in his school and is highly regarded within the school community. His manifesto concludes as follows:

As you all know, I have been involved with this very successful Association for many years. You know who I am, and you know my work. I am a safe pair of hands. And I am here for YOU!

With the election looming, the Association's members have a difficult choice to make. Not only do they have to consider the work of the Association over the next few years, but they also need to take into account the planning and organization of the upcoming international conference. Where do their priorities lie, and who can lead them along the road to success?

9.4.2 Questions

1. Why do you think association branches "typically struggle to find volunteers to fill leadership positions"?
2. The Chiang Rai regional branch appears to be particularly active. What activities make it so, and how do they compare to those of associations with which you are familiar?
3. Compare the brief extracts from the manifestos of Dr. Siriwong and Mr. Wattana. Which do you think is the most powerful? Why?
4. Who would you vote for in the presidential election? What is your reason?
5. Which president, Dr. Siriwong or Mr. Wattana, would appeal more to the UK head office? Why?

9.4.3 Research Topics

Reviewing Leadership Criteria Required of Executive Committee Members of International Language Teacher Associations

What leadership criteria are considered when electing committee members of international language teacher associations? How do the criteria differ for the various committee roles?

1. *Browse the web pages* (M6) of three or four international language teacher associations.
2. Search the sites for information about the associations' leadership structures – what roles the leaders play, what leadership qualities they need to be elected, and how they are elected. Is teaching, teacher education, or research experience required?
3. Who are the current leaders of the associations (e.g., President and Vice-President, Secretary, Treasurer, Marketing Officer, other committee members)? What can you find out about their leadership qualities from the information provided about them?
4. Collate the findings of your digital document analysis for each association, highlighting its leaders' attributes. Then combine the findings to produce a composite description of the leadership criteria evident across all the associations.
5. What makes a good association president? What *keywords* (M10) are used to describe the leadership qualities of the committee members?

Examining the Leadership Skills Needed to Organize a Local Teacher Conference

What do conference organizers believe are necessary leadership skills to organize a successful teachers' conference? How do they know the skills are effective?

1. At the next two or three local teacher conferences in your region, arrange to meet with the conference organizers, that is, non-professional organizers who may be teachers or teacher educators. If feasible, attend and participate in the conference to observe proceedings.
2. Prepare a similar set of *interview questions* (M9) for the different conference organizers. Ask them why they were invited to or why they volunteered to organize the conference, what makes them the right person to do the job, and what skills are needed to oversee the planning and running of the event.
3. Try not to focus too much on what they did to organize the conference (e.g., arranging the venue and catering, organizing the program of presentations), but rather focus on their leadership qualities (e.g., managing a team and a budget, planning and decision-making, monitoring progress and outcomes, developing good working relationships, being ethical and equitable).

4. Keep the interviews short so as not to detain the busy organizers but allow them to talk freely if they have the time. Prepare a set of primary questions with follow-up prompts, including some that draw on your observations of the conference in progress. Record the interviews.
5. What special leadership skills did the conference organizers explicitly name? Do these skills relate to being a teacher or teacher educator in any way? Did their leadership make for a successful conference?

9.4.4 Resources

Malcolm, W. (2024). Conference planning and management: Challenges, opportunities, and the future. In B. Lacy, P. Lege, & P. Ferguson (Eds.), *Growth mindset in language education*. JALT. https://doi.org/10.37546/JALTPCP2023-01

Shah, S. R. A. & Eusafzai, H. A. K. (2024). Exploring teacher leadership: A study of leadership practices among TESOL professionals in the Arab world. *Forum for Education Studies*, 2(1), 395. https://doi.org/10.59400/fes.v2i1.395

Thumvichit, A., Tangkiengsirisin, S., & Vathanalaoha, K. (2024). Making sense of collective leadership in English teacher associations: Insights from Thailand TESOL's committees. *English in Education*, 58(4), 346–362. https://doi.org/10.1080/04250494.2024.2358752

9.5 Establishing a Collaborative Teacher Research Group

Keywords
- Botswana
- Urban high school
- Setswana language teacher leader
- Establishing a research forum
- Senior administrator's support and conditions

9.5.1 Pre-reading Reflection

1. Think about an innovative school-wide project you would like to lead.
2. Who would potentially support you? What would make it difficult for you?
3. What leadership qualities would you require specifically for this project to be successful?

Mr. Nnana Mabula is a senior Setswana language teacher at a large urban high school in Botswana, Southern Africa. He has a master's degree in Applied Linguistics from the local university and has been teaching for nearly ten years. He decided to complete a part-time MA after teaching for three years because he felt that he was in a bit of a rut at school and needed something to inspire him in his professional development. Even before he embarked on the MA, he had been conducting small-scale action research projects in his classrooms. He had tried to collaborate with language teacher colleagues in the Setswana, English, and French departments, but with no luck. During his MA, he completed a research methodology course and wrote a short dissertation based on a research project that used qualitative methods. He was especially motivated to continue with school-based research after graduation.

The school principal, Ms. Mmabatho, had noticed Nnana's drive and developing research expertise and encouraged him to present at a national teachers' conference in a neighboring city. The school would fund his travel and accommodation expenses if his paper was accepted. It was! His presentation reported on an exploratory action research project on student writing, particularly students' use of AI and plagiarism off the internet. The presentation was a great success. His colleagues back at school heard about it – they also heard that his conference participation had been funded, and that besides learning a lot, he had plenty of fun. Their interest in doing research too was now sparked.

Nnana seized upon their change of heart and proposed to Ms. Mmabatho the establishment of an informal research forum for interested language teachers. He submitted to her a detailed ten-page document outlining the aims of the forum, the work it would do, his role as convenor, and the resources required. In short, the forum would consist of volunteer language teachers who wanted to learn about research, and actually do research in their classrooms, independently or in collaboration with other teachers. Dissemination of any useful or interesting findings was not to be a required goal of the forum members. However, if opportunities arose to publish short articles in local teacher journals or to present at conferences these would be taken up.

On reading the proposal, Ms. Mmabatho enthusiastically supported it. In recent years there had been policy initiatives to increase the research activity of primary and high school teachers in Botswana, and she saw this initiative as a great chance to get research going in her school. She was particularly confident in Nnana's ability as a developing leader to make a success of the forum and to increase the visibility of research activity in the school.

When Nnana received her email reply confirming acceptance of the proposal, he was shocked to see the accompanying conditions:

1. Nnana would be given one free teaching period a week to organize the forum.
2. Other forum members would be given no free time to participate in forum or related research activities.

3. Funding for forum activities would not be forthcoming; not even the small catering funds (e.g., biscuits, coffee) that Nnana had asked for in the proposal.
4. Nnana's funding to attend the conference was a one-off; it would not be repeated. If forum members were to attend conferences, they would need to pay their own way or seek external funding.
5. Any social media posts describing teachers' research activity, or any publications or conference presentations, would have to acknowledge the school.

Nnana felt absolutely deflated when he read the email. How would he be able to get teachers on board now? As a leader he found himself stuck somewhere between the interested teachers and the most senior administrator in the school. He earnestly believed the principal's reply was a challenge – a call to begin negotiating. And he decided he most certainly would.

9.5.2 Questions

1. Initially, the language teachers in the school were not interested in collaborating in research with Nnana. Why do you think this was the case?
2. Nnana independently wrote a proposal to establish a research forum and then submitted it to the principal, Ms. Mmabatho. What could he have done differently to propose the forum to Ms. Mmabatho?
3. List FIVE words from the case that suggest features of Nnana's leadership qualities. Explain why you chose each of these words.
4. Nnana's goals to establish the forum and an active research community were thwarted. What leadership strategies did Ms. Mmabatho use to do so? Why do you think she acted in this way?
5. How would you respond to Ms. Mmabatho's email if you were Nnana? What would you do next – step by step – in your endeavor to establish the research forum?

9.5.3 Research Topics

Reviewing the Coordination of Research Support Offered by University Language Departments or Schools

What kind of support does a university language department or school offer its research staff? Who coordinates the support? What do they do that makes the support offered effective?

1. Work with a university department that includes language teachers who do research, either as a requirement of their contract or as ongoing professional activity.
2. Compose an email message to be sent to individual members of the department. They should be language teachers who are also involved in research and should be the beneficiary of research support provided by the department.
3. In the email message, include a series of open-ended *survey questions* (M17) that ask the teacher-researchers to describe the kinds of research support they receive (e.g., workshops), who coordinates the support, who makes decisions about what support is needed, what relevant qualifications the coordinator has, and what makes them effective (or not).
4. Aim to receive responses from all researchers in the department. Assure respondents that their email messages will remain confidential.
5. Download the messages and analyze the collated data for themes that focus on the work and leadership characteristics of the coordinator.
6. What does the research support coordinator do well? Are they qualified to be a research coordinator? Did the email respondents point out any flaws in the coordination skills of the coordinator?

Exploring the Characteristics of School Principals with Poor Leadership Skills
How do principals of schools with language programs display poor leadership skills? What makes them ineffectual leaders?

1. Meet with a class of pre-service language teachers in an undergraduate teacher education program. Explain to them that you are interested in finding out about the characteristics of school principals with poor leadership skills. Ask them to imagine such a principal, emphasizing that the principal leads a school which includes language programs.
2. Give each student teacher a *blank piece of paper and ask them to draw* (M12) a school principal with poor leadership skills. Invite them to use colors, words, objects, and emojis.
3. Ask the pre-service teachers to write an explanation of their drawing in 100–200 words. Collect the drawings and accompanying written explanations.
4. Conduct a content analysis of the drawings. What does the principal look like? What are they doing or saying? Are there other people in the drawings? What do colors and objects add to the meaning of the drawings?
5. Do the written explanations align with the drawings? Perform a cross-case analysis of all the drawings and written explanations.
6. What characteristics do school principals with poor leadership skills exhibit? Do they adequately consider the language programs in their schools?

9.5.4 Resources

Aharonian, N. & Oppenheimer, O. S. (2024). "If you do not write, you dry up": Tensions in teacher educator research and academic writing. *Education Sciences*, *14*(9), 972. https://doi.org/10.3390/educsci14090972

Shrestha, S., Laudari, S., & Gnawali, L. (2023). Exploratory action research: Experiences of Nepalese EFL teachers. *ELT Journal*, *77*(4), 407–415. https://doi.org/10.1093/elt/ccac029

Weston, K. & Roostalu, J. (2018). A career in research: Tips for running your own research group. *Wellcome*. https://cms.wellcome.org/sites/default/files/research-careers-tips-running-research-group-2018-05-17.pdf

---

9.6 Planning a Study-Abroad Sojourn

Keywords
- Germany and Canada
- University, Teacher Education Center
- German language teacher educators
- Planning a sojourn to a Canadian university
- Teachers disagree on program in meetings

9.6.1 Pre-reading Reflection

1. Have you studied abroad? What were the best and worst parts of the experience? If you haven't studied abroad, would you like to?
2. There's often someone who talks too much during meetings. How should they be controlled?
3. What are the risks of leaders working alone instead of collaborating with other leaders?

Elke Bauer is the coordinator of the study-abroad (SA) program in the German section of the Teacher Education Center at a large city university in central Germany. The Center prepares teachers to teach in the primary and secondary school system in Germany. Elke Bauer prepares pre-service teachers of German language and literature as well as German as a Second Language. Teacher education is her primary academic focus – she is a very experienced German teacher, both at the school level and at university. She slowly transitioned into teacher education about ten years ago when she served as a mentor for teachers from the university doing their practicum in her school. She enjoyed the experience so much that she applied, after completing her PhD, for a job at the university where she now works.

As coordinator of the SA program, Dr. Bauer works closely with the head of the German section and other team leaders. She does the SA work by herself with little support from the other leaders, and she likes it that way. This gives her the freedom to make decisions in collaboration with those studying abroad and their teachers. Numerous SA sojourns take place each academic year. Some of these are easy to organize, such as those for students to neighboring countries in Europe. Students often plan these sojourns themselves, with limited input from the Center, besides the necessary approvals for time spent away and credit toward their qualifications.

One trip that takes place annually is a little trickier to organize because it involves staff members. It is a sojourn to a university on the west coast of Canada and is specifically for the German teacher educators. The sojourn takes place during the summer and lasts two weeks. Since its inception five years ago, the aim of the visit to the Canadian university has been to work with language teacher educators there – German and other European languages – to share teacher education practices, consult with education students, and organize a two-day symposium on a topic to be decided with the Canadian partners. The SA initiative started when a professor from the Canadian university spent a sabbatical at the German university, and while there, proposed an exchange program between the language departments of the two universities. Up to now, the sojourns have been only one way: Germany to Canada.

Dr. Bauer set up a schedule of planning meetings for those going on the SA sojourn to Canada. From the very first meeting things did not go well. Dr. Bauer is usually very good at convening and chairing meetings. She is conscious of having a pre-announced agenda, keeping to the scheduled time, and giving everyone a chance to contribute. When the group of nine educators gathered for the first time, a new staff member, who had not participated in this sojourn before, had many questions. This was to be expected, and Dr. Bauer patiently answered them, often with the help of those experienced participants who had done the visit before. Unfortunately, the staff member, Mr. Knoch, did not stick to the agenda and he became somewhat disruptive, disturbing the flow of the meeting.

The second meeting wasn't much better; in fact, it was worse. This time, other participants also became disruptive, and Dr. Bauer found it hard to control them. They asked questions not only about planning the current SA sojourn but broader questions about the lack of *exchange* visits between the two universities, and perhaps contradictorily, about overseas travel and its effect on sustainability and climate change, and even about what they might achieve by visiting the Canadian university in the first place! Dr. Bauer was at a loss. These teachers had agreed, and actually applied, to participate in the SA program, and now it appeared as though they were undermining it, questioning its viability. Dr. Bauer wondered what on earth had happened – where it had all gone wrong.

9.6.2 Questions

1. Why would language teacher educators in Germany want to study abroad in Canada, and vice versa? What would the benefits be?
2. Dr. Bauer prefers to work alone as a leader, managing the study-abroad program by herself. Is this a wise approach? What might an alternative approach be?
3. After five years, the study-abroad "exchange" is currently only one way – teacher educators from Germany going to Canada. Why might the visits not be going the other way?
4. Where did it all go wrong? Why did the meetings turn out to be such a disaster?
5. Do you think the study abroad sojourn will go ahead? Give specific reasons for your answer.

9.6.3 Research Topics

Understanding What Kind of Leader Organizes Language Program Study-Abroad Sojourns

Who would be interested in organizing study-abroad sojourns for language learners or teachers? What kind of person would they have to be to do a good job?

1. Recruit up to five study-abroad (SA) coordinators for language learners or language teachers in local schools or universities. First, arrange to meet them one-on-one for a short *semi-structured interview* (M9).
2. Design an interview schedule that includes questions about (a) their interest in the SA coordinator's role, (b) what they enjoy about doing the coordination, (c) what they think they do well and where they struggle, and (d) what makes an ideal SA coordinator for language learners or teachers.
3. Record all the interviews and collate the answers for (a)–(d), and any other common questions you ask the coordinators.
4. Send the summarized answers to each of the coordinators and then arrange to meet them online for a *focus group meeting* (M8) to discuss the findings. Facilitate open discussion and encourage the coordinators to talk about further experiences and ideas about SA coordination.
5. Is there a particular type of person who takes on a SA coordinator role? What leadership attributes do they possess? What educational interests do they have?

Researching the Cause of Disruptive Committee Meetings

Why are committee meetings sometimes a shambles? Why is the agenda not adhered to? Is it because they are badly chaired?

1. Send out a call within an organization (e.g., a language school or department) that you have access to, asking for teachers to volunteer to talk about committee meetings they have (regularly) attended that were disruptive and disorganized.
2. Recruit as many teachers as possible in the organization. Design a *simple anonymous survey* (M17) on Google Forms (or Microsoft Forms) with one task that requires respondents to describe the meeting in up to 500 words. Ask them to describe why the meeting was not effective, what or who caused it to be disrupted, what the chairperson did in the meeting, and how the meeting could have been better managed.
3. Distribute the survey link to the volunteer teachers and request that it be completed in two weeks.
4. Download all the 500-word descriptions and analyze them for common themes.
5. Why were the meetings disrupted? Was it because of the chairperson's skills? Were issues of power among committee members at play?

9.6.4 Resources

Brennan, S. & Holliday, E. (2019). Preparing globally competent teachers to address P-12 students' needs: One university's story. *Global Education Review, 6*(3), 49–64. https://ger.mercy.edu/index.php/ger/article/view/525

Calderon, F. (2024). Becoming a language teacher educator: An outsider perspective. *Journal of Curriculum and Pedagogy, 21*(3), 310–317. https://doi.org/10.1080/15505170.2024.2373134

Hendy, N. (2022). *How to chair a meeting effectively*. High Speed Training. https://www.highspeedtraining.co.uk/hub/how-to-chair-a-meeting/

9.7 Coordinating a Refugee Settlement Program in a School

Keywords
- Connecticut, USA
- Elementary school
- Part-time English teacher
- Coordinating refugee student settlement
- Cooperative colleagues but heavy workload

9.7.1 Pre-reading Reflection

1. How familiar are you with the needs of recent refugees and immigrants in a school setting? What might the most urgent of these needs be?

9.7 Coordinating a Refugee Settlement Program

2. Why would an ESL teacher's position in a school be only part-time?
3. Is it possible for a leader to be too successful? What might the consequences of such success be?

Jan Crosby is a part-time ESL teacher at a public elementary school in a city in Connecticut, USA. She has been at the school for two years and loves the job. When she applied, she knew upfront that it would be only two to three days a week, but that suited her well at the time because she had a young family and needed to spend time with them. She was also studying for an MA in TESOL at the same time, and has now completed that qualification. Before settling down as a teacher in the USA, Jan worked for a US agency abroad teaching English in both South America (Ecuador) and the Middle East (Jordan). During the two years at the elementary school, Jan has developed a reputation as a reliable teacher who engages her students in their learning and who networks productively among her colleagues in the ESL program and beyond in related school subjects. Although there is no official head of the ESL program, teachers and administrators in the school turn to Jan when they need advice or want something done related to ESL pedagogy or policy. With the increasing number of refugee students arriving in the district, all of whom will end up in the ESL program, the school principal has invited Jan to coordinate the recent "new wave of arrivals," as the principal calls it. This increase has been signalled for some time in the school community, and is made up of both refugees (e.g., from Ukraine and Palestine) and recent immigrants entering the US across the southern border.

The principal believes Jan would be suitable for taking on this coordinator role not only because of the leadership skills she has already demonstrated in the school, but also because she is familiar with the geopolitical regions from which the refugees are now coming. Jan and the principal negotiated a new contract for her, which would take her to a nearly full-time position. She would continue to teach ESL but would now also be leading the new wave refugee/immigrant settlement program (as it is now being called). Jan planned to get a team together as a first step, not in a formal sense, but merely to bring together willing teachers to operate within the guidelines for accepting students into the school community and then looking after them when they get there. She thought there may be some reluctance to contribute from teachers, but after putting out a call for expressions of interest to receive information and to attend regular meetings, Jan was overwhelmed by the response. She would be working closely with school counselors, and religious leaders if necessary. And they too would be joining the meetings.

It didn't take long for Jan's refugee/immigrant-related leadership work to become all-consuming. She never expected that the level of interest and commitment from her colleagues would be so high. They constantly contacted her with questions about what they could do, or what they should do next. Were they following the guidelines correctly? Could they design some materials for the refugee/immigrant students in their classes – and would Jan check these? Can they speak to their students' parents, and how should the conversations go? Jan began to feel totally overwhelmed – and felt that her ESL teaching was being neglected. In fact, she longed for the days when she was "merely" an ESL teacher. She also missed the one or two days each week that she spent at home with her young children. But she had to put these thoughts aside for now. Her work at school was developing into a great success. She was managing a very effective program for the new refugee and immigrant students, and despite what she thought about her ESL classes, her considerable experience meant that she was still doing a good job in the classroom.

9.7.2 Questions

1. If you were Jan, would you have accepted the principal's invitation to take on the role of coordinator of the refugee/immigrant settlement program? Consider her qualifications, personal background, teaching experience, and leadership skills.
2. Do you think Jan is going to burn herself out trying to balance her coordinator role and her ESL teaching? What evidence do you have for your answer?
3. Who should Jan consult to seek advice about coordinating this program? How would they be able to help?
4. Who else might suffer if Jan's challenging workload situation continues?
5. What are your views about Jan's ongoing ESL teaching? Do you think she will experience problems in the future?

9.7.3 Research Topics

Identifying the Influence of Life Experiences on Effective Leadership Skills
How does life experience, such as teacher training, previous countries of work, teaching jobs, and family life, contribute to leadership qualities? What specific past life incidents do leaders believe make them good leaders now?

1. Arrange to meet one experienced leader in the field of language teaching and learning who is acknowledged by their peers to be an outstanding leader. The leader's major role could be a head of a department or institution, the president of a professional association, or the principal investigator in a team of researchers, for example.
2. Conduct a *life-history narrative interview* (M16) with the leader. Ask them to tell you the story of their professional life experience and to include any other non-professional life experiences that they are willing to share. Allow

up to two hours for the interview and encourage open, free-flowing storytelling.
3. During the interview, direct the leader to focus on specific incidents or experiences that have influenced their development as a leader. Are there past life or professional experiences that have made them good leaders today?
4. Record the lengthy interview, transcribe it, and then construct (or re-story) the interview transcript into a chronological narrative of the leader's professional life, as revealed in the life-history interview. In the narrative, focus specifically on their leadership skills, how they became good leaders, and how their life experiences influenced the development of their leadership qualities.
5. Did something happen in their life that made them a good leader? Does the leader draw on previous teaching experience? Are relationships with any colleagues, students, or mentors significant?

Considering the Special Leadership Qualities Needed When Working with Refugees

What special qualities should those coordinating refugee programs have? How are they different from the leadership skills necessary for other types of leadership roles?

1. Consult easily accessible *literature on the internet* (M6) that addresses working with refugees in community centers, community language schools, and non-governmental organizations. The literature could be open-access academic articles or embedded in websites of relevant organizations.
2. Search the literature for keywords and phrases that indicate qualities appropriate for working with refugees or recently arrived immigrants. Examples may include *empathy, resilience, sensitivity to different cultures, language awareness, patience, being a good listener, compassion.*
3. Compile a list of appropriate words and phrases with a brief glossary. Then present the list by email to coordinators of refugee programs in your region. Ask them to comment on the relevance of each word and phrase in relation to their experience. How do the words and phrases relate to who they are and the work they do?
4. Ask them to add any other words and phrases that apply to them as coordinators.
5. Collect the responses and collate them into a composite list, with glossary, and illustrative stories of the respondents' experiences.
6. Could the findings be presented at a relevant conference? Perhaps a short report could be written that could be distributed to appropriate centers and schools that work with refugees.

9.7.4   Resources

Hlado, P. & Harvankova, K. (2024). Teachers' perceived work ability: A qualitative exploration using the Job Demands-Resources model. *Humanities and Social Sciences Communications*, *11*, 304. https://doi.org/10.1057/s41599-024-02811-1

Li, G. & Qin, K. (2024). Supporting and advocating for immigrant and refugee students and families in America's urban schools: Educators' agency and practices in everyday instruction. *Urban Education*, *59*(2), 600–628. https://doi.org/10.1177/00420859221082671

Ridley, J. & King, N. (2024). "I have meaningful work:" Crafting teaching and advocacy at an ESL after-school program. *TESOL Journal*, *15*(1), e729. https://doi.org/10.1002/tesj.729

10 Teacher Wellbeing

Cases in this chapter

10.1	English Teacher Educator and ASD Experience	*page* 267
10.2	A Teacher on Maternity Leave and FOMO	271
10.3	Coping with Post–Study-Abroad Workload	274
10.4	Native-Speakerism and Teacher Anxiety	278
10.5	Dealing with Students' Complaints	281
10.6	Language Teacher Status and Teacher Commitment	285
10.7	A Teacher Educator Under Pressure to Retire	288

10.1 English Teacher Educator and ASD Experience

Keywords
- Chile
- "Happy schools"
- EFL teacher and language teacher educator
- ASD (Autism Spectrum Disorder)
- Supervising a student teacher at university

10.1.1 Pre-reading Reflection

1. Would you describe a *mentor* as a coach, manager, friend, or supporter?
2. Language teacher educators and teachers need to be familiar with Autism Spectrum Disorder in their work. Would you agree?
3. Do you believe that language teachers should meet specified professional standards before they can practice?

Schools known as "happy schools" in Chile follow the methodology of Lefebre Lever (1902–1972). In these schools, students learn the same curriculum as in formal schools; they follow the Ministry of Education guidelines and the national curriculum. However, they are not officially recognized as formal schools, and since they use different learning methodologies students are required to sit an official examination administered by the Ministry of Education at the end of each year (i.e., so that the courses are officially recognized). The aim of these schools is to maintain an environment of respect and equity, to be free from discrimination, and to promote a culture of inclusion and integration. For this reason, many parents of students with special educational needs enroll their children in these schools.

These "happy schools" also cater for many students with ASD (Autism Spectrum Disorder). In 2017, Cristina was a teacher of English as a foreign language in such a school. She had more than thirty years' teaching experience. She holds a master's degree in TESOL from a university in the USA and another in Spanish as a foreign language from a university in Spain. Besides her role as an EFL teacher she has also worked as a mentor teacher/associate teacher in schools guiding and supporting student teachers in their practicums. Cristina has experience working with students with ASD. She knows that they can have interpersonal communication problems and difficulty in understanding and perceiving other people's feelings and thoughts.

In 2020 she started working at a mid-sized university in the north of Chile as an English language teacher educator. Because of the Covid-19 pandemic, some of the practicums were initially suspended and then eventually conducted via Zoom video call. She realized that one of the student teachers under her supervision had shown difficulty establishing relationships with other student teachers in the practicum. Cristina suspected her student teacher might have had some degree of ASD, but she did not know for sure. The student teacher had never previously disclosed any medical condition to anyone in the program. For Cristina, the student teacher's lack of empathy for her students in school, her difficulty socializing with her peers, her lack of self-criticism toward her own performance, and her self-centeredness made her unsuitable for the role as a classroom teacher. In her lessons via Zoom, for example, she would open a meeting and admit some students a few minutes before the class started and then ignore them – she would not greet them. At the start of the class, she would deliver the lesson as if it was a presentation without making any connections with her students. Cristina gave her feedback and suggested she should try to establish a pedagogical relationship with students by greeting them and by asking them how they were, for example, or by talking about the weather or making other small talk before the lesson started. Despite the student teacher agreeing to such a strategy, she did not later take up any of Cristina's feedback or suggestions and continued to do as she had been doing, lesson after lesson.

Drawing on her vast school teaching and more recent university teacher education experience, Cristina believes her student teacher should not be in the ELT program. However, she dares not say this to the student for fear of being accused of discrimination. The current Anti-Discrimination Act in Chile forbids any form of arbitrary discrimination against students. Cristina truly believes that her student teacher should not graduate from the program.

10.1.2 Questions

1. Do you think teachers in schools should have the responsibility of identifying students with ASD? How qualified was Cristina to do so?
2. What could an English language teacher educator do when student teachers do not act on their feedback?
3. Do you agree with Cristina's assessment that her student teacher should not be in the ELT program? Why or why not?
4. Is Cristina right to think that she might be accused of discrimination if she raises her concerns with the student? What might the consequences be?
5. Who else could Cristina talk to? What procedures could be put in place in the university to manage the situation Cristina finds herself in?

10.1.3 Research Topics

Assessing Teacher Educators' Predictions About Who Will Make a Good Language Teacher

Can teacher educators predict who will become good (or not so good) language teachers? What do they base their predictions on? What are the characteristics of good pre-service language teachers?

1. Engage an experienced language teacher educator who prepares pre-service language teachers for teaching in schools.
2. Ask them to *reflect on* (M14) the following questions over the next few weeks while they are working with their student teachers, and ask them to write brief notes on their reflections: Drawing on your experience, can you predict who will become good (or not so good) language teachers? What are the attributes of a good pre-service language teacher? Do you feel you make a difference as a teacher educator?
3. After the weeks have passed, collect the reflective notes from the teacher educator and meet with them to review their ideas and their notes. In a *semi-structured interview* (M9) examine their predictions and what they base them on.
4. Include questions about the teacher educator's perceptions of their power to make a difference in the professional lives of their student teachers. Record the interview and analyze it, focusing on the topic of predictions about good teaching.
5. Does the teacher educator believe they can make pre-service teachers into better language teachers? Can or should they ever dissuade them from teaching? And how do they feel (what emotions do they have) about their ongoing predictions and influence?

Reviewing Teacher Education Program Policies Concerning Excluding Unsuitable Teacher Candidates

Do policies exist in language teacher education programs for excluding pre-service teachers from entering the teaching profession? If so, what are the exclusion criteria? How are the excluded teachers supported?

1. Compose a formal email letter to heads of pre-service language teacher education programs in multiple institutions. Distribute the letter to as many heads as possible, preferably within the same geographical region.
2. In the letter, ask the recipients if their program has formal policies for excluding pre-service teachers or for preventing them from going on to later teach in schools. If they do, request them to send you relevant sections of the *policy documents* (M6) or to paraphrase them for you.
3. Inquire as to what the specific exclusion criteria are, how the policies are implemented, and how excluded pre-service teachers are supported during the decision-making process.
4. Collate the email replies and any policy documentation sent to you. Analyze both, first to establish if there are indeed exclusion policies in teacher education programs, and second, to understand how these policies are implemented, that is, what exclusion criteria are applied and how.
5. Why are some pre-service language teachers excluded from their teacher education programs? If they are excluded, are they supported with counseling and career advice? Are all student teachers allowed to graduate and go on to teach in schools?

10.1.4 Resources

Arancibia, H., Leihy, P., & Saldaña, P. (2022). The Free and Happy School: An outsider alternative in Chile. *Educação & Sociedade, 43*, e245073. https://doi.org/10.1590/ES.245073

Petersson-Bloom, L. & Holmqvist, M. (2022). Strategies in supporting inclusive education for autistic students: A systematic review of qualitative research results. *Autism & Developmental Language Impairments, 7*, 1–15. https://doi.org/10.1177/23969415221123429

Scarlota, N. & Knipp, R. (2022). Experiencing emergency remote teaching as an EFL educator in Chile at the onset of the Covid-19 pandemic. *Issues in Educational Research, 32*(4), 1606–1622. http://www.iier.org.au/iier32/scarlota.pdf

10.2 A Teacher on Maternity Leave and FOMO

Keywords
- Japan
- University language teacher education center
- English teacher
- Maternity leave during new development
- Fear of missing out (FOMO)

10.2.1 Pre-reading Reflection

1. Does pregnancy disadvantage women in the teaching profession? If so, in what ways?
2. What emotions accompany a fear of missing out (FOMO)?
3. What do you feel when you go on leave from work? Are you always happy? Do you feel you may be missing out on something? Are you anxious?

Dr. Kobayashi has worked as an English teacher at a highly ranked university in Tokyo for two years. She started her job at the university's Teacher Education Center after graduating with her PhD in Applied Linguistics from another prestigious university in Japan. She studied part-time while working as an English teacher in various universities and high schools for about five years. Now in her mid-thirties she believes she has done well to progress so quickly in the English teaching field. Dr. Kobayashi is ambitious and desires to become a teacher educator. She loves the idea of university life – the research, the teaching, the committee work, the collegiality among academics. As an English teacher in the Center, however, she does not have the same opportunities that the teacher educators have for conducting research, especially in terms of research time allocation and funding. Her classroom contact hours are also higher, and she doesn't get asked to serve on committees that sound interesting and relevant to her work.

An opportunity finally came up that would give Dr. Kobayashi a chance to work with faculty members across the Center. This two-year initiative, she believed, would allow her to show off her knowledge of the English teaching field and demonstrate her experience of teaching in Japanese high schools. It was exactly this latter experience that was needed for the project that the Center was getting involved in. A large government grant had been awarded to senior researchers in the Center to investigate the motivation of high school students for entering the language teaching profession in Japan. This was the general aim, and there were many sub-research questions, but it was something Dr. Kobayashi felt she could definitely contribute to. "This is my chance," she said. There was much planning to be done. Working groups were set up, tasks were distributed, and there was much excitement in the Center. It had been some time since such a significant project had been undertaken by the Center.

Within no time at all Dr. Kobayashi was immersed in the activities of the project. She was also teaching her usual full load of classes, so overall she was very busy. But she was loving it all. It was exactly what she expected of academic life. Amid this activity and excitement, Dr. Kobayashi discovered she was pregnant with her first child. This was not planned – at all – and at first, she was shocked. She and her husband had thought about children in the future but for now they wanted to focus on their careers. She knew she obviously had to tell her manager, and she was advised to withdraw from the new project. The research team needed someone who would be with them for the duration.

The plan was for Dr. Kobayashi to continue working for a few months and then take maternity leave five weeks before the expected birth. A further eight weeks' maternity leave would follow the birth. In the hope of staying involved in the project, she tried to negotiate a shorter maternity leave period, both with her husband and the Center, but was not successful. Of course, Dr. Kobayashi was happy about the pregnancy and the new family life that lay ahead, but she was also aware that she was exhibiting symptoms of FOMO regarding the project and her professional career!

A further complication arose when it was announced that a recent PhD graduate had been hired as a substitute for Dr. Kobayashi while she was on leave. Dr. Kobayashi had heard about him – he was a "highflier" who had already published several articles and had a book in the pipeline. He was also looking for a permanent job, and this unsettled Dr. Kobayashi somewhat. What if he proved to be a good researcher and they invited him to be on the research team? Dr. Kobayashi wondered if her own job was secure.

10.2.2 Questions

1. Why would English teachers and teacher educators have varying research opportunities in the Teacher Educator Center at Dr. Kobayashi's university? Is this a problem?
2. How do you think Dr. Kobayashi felt when she was asked to be on the research team for the new research project? Why would she feel this way?
3. Dr. Kobayashi was advised by her manager to withdraw from the research project. If you were her manager, could you see another way forward for Dr. Kobayashi regarding her involvement in the project?
4. Is Dr. Kobayashi's FOMO justified?
5. What chance does the replacement teacher have of taking Dr. Kobayashi's job? Should she be worried?

10.2.3 Research Topics

Analyzing Stories of Language Teacher Mothers Who Have Taken Parental Leave

How did language teachers experience parental leave when they became mothers? How did they feel about taking leave?

1. Recruit two or three language teachers who are also mothers. They can be teachers at any level – primary or high school, or university.
2. Arrange to interview them individually for an *informal narrative interview* (M9). Prepare an interview schedule that encourages free and open storytelling about their experiences of taking parental leave from their teaching jobs.
3. Instead of asking formal questions, invite the teachers to talk about their leave experiences by saying, "Tell me about . . ., " for example: requesting leave or being required to take leave, the length of leave, whether they missed work or were they happy to be away from work, whether they kept up with work in any way, whether they considered resigning. Include discussion about returning to work after the leave period.
4. Record the narrative interviews. Analyze each interview by configuring the data into a story that tells of the parental leave experience of each teacher. Compare the teachers' stories.
5. How long was the language teachers' parental leave? Was it their choice to take leave? Do the teachers have suggestions for early-career language teachers who plan to become mothers?

Investigating Tensions in the Professional Lives of Ambitious Early-Career Language Teacher Educators

What tensions do early-career university-based language teacher educators experience? Are the tensions teaching or research related? Do they experience institutional pressure?

1. Engage with four or five early-career language teacher educators who you or others clearly identify as ambitious. They could be working in universities in various parts of the world. Arrange to meet them virtually one-on-one via Zoom or similar.
2. Before the virtual meetings, prepare a dilemma-based case like the one above which narrates the experiences of a young, early-career language teacher educator who works in a university and finds themself struggling to make their way in a competitive professional environment. Include details in the case of the teacher educator's professional background and working context, making them appear familiar to each of the participants you have recruited. The cases should be no more than 500 words long.

3. Send the case to each teacher educator to *read and reflect on* (M16) before your meeting. When you meet, *ask the participants questions* (M9) such as: How does this case relate to your experience as an early-career university-based teacher educator? How does this case make you feel? Ask further questions based on specific details of the case.
4. Record the five case-based discussions, and analyze them for themes related to career ambition, emotional tensions, competition, and professional goals.
5. What professional circumstances make early-career teacher educators so ambitious? Do they feel the need to compete with colleagues? What are their professional concerns?

10.2.4 Resources

Earle, A., Raub, A., Sprague, A., & Heymann, J. (2025). *Progress towards gender equality in paid parental leave: An analysis of legislation in 193 countries from 1995–2022. Community, Work & Family, 28*(2), 172–192. https://doi.org/10.1080/13668803.2023.2226809

Habibie, P. (2022). Early-career scholars and scholarship: A social justice perspective. *Annual Review of Applied Linguistics, 42*, 55–63. https://doi.org/10.1017/S0267190521000192

Koné, K., Kéita, F., & Koita, B. (2024). Raising awareness among the TESOL community about the professional identity tensions of women EFL teachers in Africa. *ELT Journal, 78*(3), 255–263. https://doi.org/10.1093/elt/ccae008

10.3 Coping with Post–Study-Abroad Workload

Keywords
- Cambodia
- University undergraduate program
- English teacher and new roles
- Updating and consolidating online teaching
- Post-study-abroad workload increase

10.3.1 Pre-reading Reflection

1. How do you feel when you're overworked, with just too much to do? What emotions do you experience?
2. What is your typical strategy for managing multiple, competing tasks?
3. Think of your current work or study experience. List the top three jobs or tasks that take up most of your time and energy. Which one would you like to get rid of?

10.3 Coping with Post–Study-Abroad Workload

Dara Chan spent a year studying for her MTESOL (Master of Teaching English to Speakers of Other Languages) qualification in Australia. Before that she taught English at a university in Phnom Penh, Cambodia. She was one of many teachers that taught undergraduate students in the large English language program. She was a product of the program, and a "shining star" according to her head of department, Dr. Seng. He asked her to stay on after graduating, which is common practice for recruiting good quality teachers in the department. Dara, however, never really felt certain about her own abilities as an English teacher. Very soon after starting to teach at the university, she wondered if she shouldn't rather have begun her career at a high school to experience a different workplace and challenge her professional development. But then, after a couple years in the university job, a study-abroad opportunity came up, one sponsored by the government. Dara applied for it and was successful, and the university was happy to give her study leave for the year on condition that she return to her position after completing her studies in Australia.

The year sailed by quickly and before Dara knew it, she was back in Phnom Penh in her same office in the same department. But she now felt like a very different person. She had learned a lot, not only about English teaching and learning, but also about herself as a professional. Dr. Seng and Dara's colleagues agreed. In fact, they unreasonably assumed she had transformed into an expert on everything! Two new roles were immediately piled onto her. One was to coordinate the mentoring of new English teachers who joined the department each year. Dara believed she was a little under-qualified and too inexperienced for this type of work, but it sounded interesting, and she loved the idea of meeting and talking to the young teachers. The other role was to "consolidate and update" (to quote Dr. Seng) online English teaching in the department. A forced start to online pedagogy was made during the Covid years, but the department's approach had been haphazard and not particularly effective. Dr. Seng wanted to continue the development of online teaching and to establish a blended teaching and learning approach across the English program. He thought Dara, with her new qualification and overseas experience, would be just the person to oversee these developments.

Dara realized that these new roles, in addition to her teaching, would be a lot of work, but she was up for the challenge, full of enthusiasm after returning to Cambodia. She also felt she owed the department after they had given her study leave for the year. At first the workload was manageable; Dara set aside periods of time for when the new teachers could contact her, and mentoring meetings were held during office hours. Her first step regarding online teaching was to do some reading and research. She persuaded one of her colleagues, also a study-abroad returnee, to work with her on this initiative. Dr. Seng approved of this collaboration and granted the colleague workload credit. Progress was slow, but her work soon became visible to teachers in the program. Dara conducted one seminar for all English teachers, reporting on her literature research and asking for suggestions about the way forward; it was well attended. She also invited an education technology researcher from the university's education department to talk to a group of English teachers interested in developing their online courses. These initiatives proved popular. Demand from colleagues for more help – with ideas and tech support – increased, well beyond what Dara could provide in terms of her skills and time. She sought ways to manage these requests, on top of the calls for frequent mentoring sessions from new teachers, which she did well and enjoyed, but were now gradually creeping into her personal time. Dara wasn't so sure anymore if she was coping.

10.3.2 Questions

1. Was Dara wise to take on the two new roles assigned to her? Do you think she had a choice?
2. Dr. Seng perhaps had an inflated opinion of Dara's professional development during her year abroad. Why do you think this was the case?
3. Dara asked her study-abroad returnee colleague to help her with the online teaching initiative. What was the purpose of her doing this? What would she hope to achieve?
4. Dara seemed to be coping quite well when she first took on the two new roles. Why did her workload gradually increase?
5. If you were Dr. Seng, and Dara came to tell you about her workload issues, what would your advice to her be?

10.3.3 Research Topics

Exploring Study-Abroad Language Teachers' Feelings About Returning to Their Home Countries
How do language teachers who are studying abroad for a further qualification feel about returning to the workplace in their home countries? How do they expect their work to change when they return? How do they expect to change? What do they feel about these changes?

1. Review *relevant scholarly literature* (M6) on the experiences of teachers (not necessarily language teachers) who study abroad and then return to their home countries, either to the same job or to a new teaching position.
2. Extract from this literature key ideas about the post-sojourn experiences and emotions of language teachers who have obtained an additional qualification.
3. From these ideas compile a representative list of (a) keywords, (b) phrases, and (c) short sentences. Some examples might have to do with workload issues, being promoted, being presented with new opportunities, relationship problems, and feelings of not belonging or fitting in.
4. List about twenty items in a logical sequence in one digital document and distribute it to study-abroad teachers currently studying for a graduate qualification (MA, MTESOL) at a university you have access to.

5. Clearly instruct the teachers to write brief notes alongside each item on the list, stating how they believe it applies to their imagined or expected post-sojourn experiences, including what their emotional response is to each item.
6. In analyzing the responses, pay attention to the educational contexts that the teachers will return to, their future workplaces, their work, and their emotions.
7. Are the teachers looking forward to returning to their home countries? What are they excited about? What do they fear?

Examining Teachers' Strategies for Dealing with Stress Associated with Heavy Workloads
How do teachers with heavy workloads identify feelings of stress? What are their signs of stress? How do they manage these feelings of stress?

1. Recruit a language teacher who is experiencing signs of stress due to a heavy workload in their place of work (e.g., a high school, a private language institute, or a university). Do this in a sensitive manner, cautiously inquiring among your colleagues or professional networks.
2. Prepare to spend time working with the teacher, perhaps over a few weeks or even a semester.
3. During this period, spend time with the teacher when convenient for both of you, *ethnographically* (M7) observing them at work and *informally interviewing* (M9) them at regular intervals. Talk about and try to observe the reasons for their heavy workload, how they regulate it over time, and how they manage stress levels in the workplace and beyond in their personal life.
4. Keep field notes of your observations and record any conversations, if feasible. Constantly analyze the data throughout the period of contact with the teacher.
5. How does the teacher express feeling of stress? What words or phrases are specifically used? Is the teacher coping in the workplace? Does the teacher have access to any support? If so, is it being utilized?

10.3.4 Resources

Alkubaidi, M. & Alzhrani, N. (2020). "We are back": Reverse culture shock among Saudi scholars after doctoral study abroad. SAGE Open, *10*(4), 1–9. https://doi.org/10.1177/2158244020970555

Lemon, N. & Turner, K. (2024). Unravelling the wellbeing needs of Australian teachers: A qualitative inquiry. *The Australian Educational Researcher*, *51*, 2161–2181. https://doi.org/10.1007/s13384-023-00687-9

Wahab, N. Y. A., et al. (2024). Impacts of workload on teachers' well-being: A systematic literature review. *TEM Journal*, *13*(3), 2544–2556. https://doi.org/10.18421/TEM133-80

10.4 Native-Speakerism and Teacher Anxiety

Keywords
- Kazakhstan
- Secondary school
- English teacher from Myanmar
- Learner perceptions of NNEST
- Native-speakerism and teacher wellbeing

10.4.1 Pre-reading Reflection

1. Have you considered teaching in a country different from the one you are most familiar with? What would some of the challenges be?
2. How would you feel if someone said they didn't like your accent? Why would they say that?
3. Like language learners, language teachers also sometimes feel anxious. Think of some examples of what might make teachers anxious – in the classroom, in a school.

Tin Tun has a Bachelor of Education degree from an institute of education in Myanmar. He had taught English in secondary schools for "too many years" in Yangon when he decided he wanted to leave the country and teach English overseas. Tin Tun was thirty-four years old at the time and felt he was still young enough to explore other parts of the world. His English is good, he believes, and so he thought he shouldn't have too much trouble finding a job. He had spent several months searching for opportunities when he came across a website recruiting teachers to teach English in secondary schools in the city of Almaty, Kazakhstan.

The country is trying to develop the teaching of English in schools. All students learn English as a foreign language, but they are not doing too well. One of many reasons is that teachers lack proficiency in English and their methods are traditional and grammar focused. Tin Tun had experimented with some of the newer trends in second language teaching methods in his own classes over the years, and his English proficiency level is good. He thought he would have a chance of success. He didn't know much about Kazakhstan, but Almaty looked interesting.

Tin Tun soon received a positive response from Kazakhstan. There was plenty of paperwork to do to secure the appropriate work visa – and travel and accommodation plans to be made. Surprisingly, this all went relatively smoothly, and before he knew it, he was deep into the first few months of his new secondary English teaching job in Almaty. This, unfortunately, was not altogether smooth. When he first started at the school, he got the impression that his new colleagues were surprised with what they saw – and heard! He wasn't one hundred percent

10.4 Native-Speakerism and Teacher Anxiety

sure about his perceptions, but he believed that maybe they had been impressed with the level of written English in his job application, but when they saw him, and heard him speak, they were disappointed with what turned up at the school. Since English is not Tin Tun's mother tongue, he is what is often labelled a non-native English-speaking teacher, or NNEST. Tin Tun was aware of the debates surrounding NNESTs and NESTs (native English-speaking teachers), and who of these is regarded as better English teachers. And he had also read about the concept of *native-speakerism*, i.e., favoring native English-speaking teachers, but he did not feel this would be a problem because of how easily he got the job in Almaty. And indeed, he hadn't experienced any direct discrimination or disadvantage by his colleagues or those who hired him. Although one other English teacher did suggest that his students might find it hard to understand him because of his "thick accent," and another casually commented with a laugh on how short he was, "shorter than the students."

It soon emerged, however, that some of the students were not as accommodating as the teachers in the school. A group of highly motivated English learners found themselves in one of Tin Tun's English classes. They were not happy. They complained to another English teacher, who had taught them the previous year, saying that Tin Tun "couldn't speak English properly" and therefore could obviously not teach English. The teacher felt obliged to report this matter to the principal, who called Tin Tun into her office to have a conversation. The discussion was polite and constructive, and the principal said she would not be recommending any changes. She was happy with Tin Tun's qualifications and performance; other English learners appeared satisfied with his teaching. Nevertheless, Tin Tun felt anxious about teaching that class. Every time he entered the classroom, he felt uneasy, and he could hardly look at the students who complained about him. He knew this was unfair because they were highly motivated to learn and had genuine concerns about their studies. But this didn't make him feel any better.

10.4.2 Questions

1. Do you think Tin Tun was naïve not to anticipate native-speakerism in his new workplace? Give reasons for your answer.
2. How do you think Tin Tun felt when one of his colleagues described him as being "shorter than the students"? What did the colleague mean by this comment?
3. Did the motivated English learners have a case for complaint against Tin Tun? Did their level of motivation have anything to do with their complaint?

4. Do you agree with the principal's decision not to recommend any changes after discussing the complaint with Tin Tun? Could the principal have done more to support Tin Tun's emotional wellbeing?
5. What could Tin Tun do to "feel better" about working with the complaining learners in the future?

10.4.3 Research Topics

Investigating English Teachers' Accents and Their Perceptions of Learner Attitudes

What do English teachers think about their own English accents? Are they concerned about their students' attitudes toward their accents? Do they believe a teacher's accent is important in English language classes?

1. Design a *narrative frame* (M16) in a digital format that can be distributed to a variety of English language teachers in one or two institutions, including multilingual teachers who originate from different geopolitical contexts.
2. Include in the frame sentence starters that elicit the respondents' opinions about their own accents, any experiences of accent issues in their classes, their perceptions of what their students think about their accent, and the significance and relevance of accent in English language classes. Try also to insert starters about both the teachers' and learners' English accent preferences (e.g., British or American).
3. Ensure that the design of the frame is in story form, that is, the frame tells the story of the teachers' experiences and reflections.
4. Distribute the link to the narrative frame via an institutional mailing list or closed social media account and give a deadline for its return.
5. Analyze the responses thematically, sentence starter by sentence starter (see M16).
6. Are English teachers aware of their accent identity? Do they adjust their accent during lessons? Why or why not? Do they know what their students think of their accent?

Seeking Out Native-Speakerism and Its Consequences for Teacher Wellbeing

How have English language teachers in an institution experienced native-speakerism? How does this experience make them feel? How does it affect their work?

1. With permission, spend some time in an institution (e.g., a private language institute, a university department) that you can easily access.
2. In this context, conduct a series of *rapid interviews* (M9), that is, interviews that last only a few minutes, usually when you encounter people in

non-scheduled circumstances, and possibly with people you don't know very well or at all.
3. When you meet, ask the teachers (non-native English speakers) if they know what native-speakerism means. Explain the concept to them if they don't, and then ask them if they have experienced native-speakerism in their current or another workplace. If so, ask them to describe an example and ask them to tell you (a) how it made them feel and (b) if it affected their work in any way. Make notes after the rapid interviews to record the content.
4. Invite the teachers to participate in a longer *semi-structured interview* (M9) to explore these questions further.
5. In what ways do English teachers experience native-speakerism – from colleagues, from their learners, from institutions? Does native-speakerism affect their daily professional lives?

10.4.4   Resources

Deng, L., Zhang, L. J., & Mohamed, N. (2024). Teacher well-being matters: The case of students' motivation on their own perceptions of native and non-native English speaker teachers. *Porta Linguarum, IX*, 113–133. https://doi.org/10.30827/portalin.viIX.29885

Ershadi, F., Nazari, M., & Chegenie, M. S. (2024). Native speakerism as a source of agency-related critical incidents: Implications for non-native English teachers' professional identity construction. *System, 120*, 103182. https://doi.org/10.1016/j.system.2023.103182

The British Council (2022). Secondary English language teaching in Kazakhstan. Secondary English Language Teaching in Kazakhstan.pdf

10.5   Dealing with Students' Complaints

Keywords
- Australia
- Private language school
- English teacher for study-abroad students
- Student complaints about teaching
- "Non-native" English teacher

10.5.1   Pre-reading Reflection

1. Language teachers sometimes make grammatical mistakes in class in front of their students. Is there a problem with this?

2. How would you feel if one of your students complained to your manager about the quality of your teaching?
3. What would your response be if the manager called you in to their office to talk about the complaint?

Ravi is an experienced English teacher in his late forties. He studied English at university in his homeland, India. When he arrived to live in Melbourne, Australia, he decided to obtain a CELTA (Certificate in English Language Teaching to Adults) qualification and pursue a career in English teaching. He has worked at one of Melbourne's English language schools for a number of years. The international school offers English language courses mainly to students on study-abroad sojourns from various parts of the world. The school's promise, displayed on its web page, is that it offers high-quality English language courses taught by experienced professionals that students can rely on. Given the expensive course fees and the promise of a high standard of education, some of the students naturally have very high expectations, especially since their progress in learning English is tied to important life and career goals. This at times affects the classroom dynamics during lessons, as some students perceive themselves to be paying customers who have the right to implicitly or explicitly express criticism if they don't think the lesson is particularly useful or enjoyable. Ravi finds this type of teaching environment intimidating and feels that it sometimes makes him more nervous in class. He believes it is unfair that some students' failure to satisfy their unrealistic expectations of the courses all too easily leads to questions being raised about his teaching or the quality of the lessons.

On one occasion, Ravi was assigned a group of students for a ten-week course. One student in the class – a woman in her thirties – proved to be particularly challenging for Ravi. She repeatedly sought lengthy explanations and at times explicitly asked why they were engaging in certain activities. At all times, Ravi tried to remain composed and answer all her questions, but he felt that she was attempting to undermine his credibility as a teacher with the other students. He was aware that the woman had plans to pursue postgraduate study in her home country, which required a particularly high IELTS score as a prerequisite. It appeared that she was under a lot of pressure and expected the lessons to align closely with her own learner needs.

Things escalated one day while the student was recording part of a lesson on her smartphone. Ravi happened to make a grammatical mistake when writing a sample English sentence on the whiteboard. The student interrupted Ravi to point out his mistake, which made him feel somewhat embarrassed in front of the class. She was not satisfied with Ravi's correction, and apology, and took matters further by complaining to the course coordinator, questioning Ravi's competence to run the lessons to the high standard promised by the school,

10.5 Dealing with Students' Complaints

especially considering their expensive course fees. The issue was dealt with by the coordinator, who reassured the student that Ravi is an experienced professional who has the full confidence and backing of the school, and that occasional mistakes are a normal part of any teaching and learning environment.

However, Ravi's confidence was shaken. He worried to what extent his career as an English teacher was negatively affected by students' perceptions of him as a "non-native speaker." Specifically, he feared how this incident might affect his job security, especially given the school's heavy reliance on student fees. He struggled to reconcile the students' often unrealistic expectations (supported by the school's pressure on teachers to make the students happy customers) and the provision of good quality language-learning experiences.

10.5.2 Questions

1. What teacher characteristics does Ravi have that open him up to learner dissatisfaction and potential complaints? How can language teachers who possess similar characteristics protect themselves against discrimination in the classroom?
2. What steps could schools take to support these teachers and protect them from discrimination?
3. To what extent should the happiness of students as paying customers influence classroom dynamics? Do you agree with the response of the complaining student in Ravi's class?
4. Ravi's reaction to the student's complaint in the classroom was constrained. What realistic options does Ravi have to challenge the student's actions?
5. What are some useful coping mechanisms available to him if pressure becomes too great and starts negatively affecting his teaching?

10.5.3 Research Topics

Measuring Teachers' Attitudes Toward Meeting Standards in the Workplace
How much pressure do teachers feel when being measured against institutional teaching standards? Do they support having these standards in their workplace? Do the standards directly affect what they do in the classroom?

1. Locate one or two language teaching institutions (e.g., universities) that have codified teaching standards or similar accountability criteria to measure the performance of its language teachers.
2. Design an *anonymous questionnaire* (M17) that has three sections: (a) brief demographic information about the respondents, including details of language classes taught and years of teaching experience, (b) the teachers' knowledge of

the standards, what they measure, and how they are implemented in the institution, and (c) their attitudes toward the standards and their use, including how they affect their teaching and how much pressure the standards put on the teachers' professional and emotional lives.

3. Include in the questionnaire both closed-ended items (e.g., rating scales, multiple choice questions) and open-ended items so that respondents have space to write freely about their ideas and attitudes.
4. Distribute the Google Forms or Qualtrics (or similar) questionnaire link through a contact at the institutions and give a deadline for its completion.
5. Make use of the online forms' software to analyze and categorize the data.
6. Are teachers anxious about working to institutional teaching standards? Do they think about the standards constantly? Are they even aware of the standards?

Exploring the Effects Students' Complaints Have on Teachers
How do teachers react when they receive complaints from their students? What emotions do they feel? Do the complaints affect them in the longer term?

1. Recruit teachers – novice and experienced – who have received complaints in the past from their students, either directly or via their managers. This should be easy to do since all teachers receive some sort of negative feedback from time to time. Aim for four to five teachers.
2. Meet with the teachers one-on-one over a cup of tea or coffee for an *informal conversation* (M9) about their experience of reacting to and dealing with students' complaints, either casual complaints in the classroom or more formal complaints via school management.
3. Discuss the complaint processes and emotional outcomes sensitively when talking with the teachers but try to probe as deeply as possible into how the students' complaints affect the teachers' teaching practices, their relationship with their students, and their wellbeing over time. Record the conversations and later analyze them for common themes most salient to the topic.
4. What is the immediate effect of a serious complaint on a teacher? How do they feel? What do they do next? Do teachers experience regular complaints?

10.5.4 Resources

Cornes, S., Torre, D., Fulton, T. B., Oza, S., Teherani, A., & Chen, H. C. (2023). When students' words hurt: 12 tips for helping faculty receive and respond constructively to student evaluations of teaching. *Medical Education Online*, *28*(1), 2154768, https://doi.org/10.1080/10872981.2022.2154768

De Costa, P. I. & Nazari, M. (2024). Emotion as pedagogy: Why the emotion labor of L2 educators matters. *International Review of Applied Linguistics in Language Teaching*, *62*(3), 1159–1168. https://doi.org/10.1515/iral-2024-0218

El-Dakhs, D. A. S. & Ahmed, M. M. (2023). A pragmatic analysis of students' complaints and professors' responses to complaints: A case study of an Egyptian private university. *Cogent Arts & Humanities*, *10*(1), 2252634. https://doi.org/10.1080/23311983.2023.2252634

10.6   Language Teacher Status and Teacher Commitment

Keywords
- Wales
- Adult ESOL classes for refugees
- ESOL teacher
- Questioning language teacher status
- Doubts about career

10.6.1   Pre-reading Reflection

1. Have you always been certain that language teaching is the career for you? What other options have you considered?
2. Is language teaching more suitable for a particular gender?
3. Which would you prefer: being in a secure but lousy job, or being happy in an insecure job?

When Rhys Williams was in primary school, he already knew he wanted to become a teacher one day. For some reason, he loved school. All the way through his school years, he liked the sense of community that school offered, and the learning that took place, and the extracurricular activities. All of this was something he wanted to continue being a part of. His parents were not very supportive, however, and weren't too pleased when he decided to pursue teacher education at university. And although they didn't stop him from becoming a teacher, they did sow some seeds of doubt in his mind about the teaching profession. Soon after Rhys graduated as an English teacher, he got a job with an organization that provides ESOL classes, among other services, for refugees and asylum seekers in Wales. The organization had a center in his hometown, and so the transition into work was easy. Rhys, who is now twenty-seven years old, has been at the local center for five years. He enjoys the teaching; in fact, he is passionate about it. His students come from various parts of the world, mostly from Africa and the Middle East. They share many stories during class and breaks, and Rhys is learning a lot about their histories and the politics of their countries. One day after class, Gulwan, a seventeen-year-old ESOL student from Afghanistan, stayed a few minutes after class and had a brief conversation with Rhys. He attends a local secondary school but is taking additional ESOL classes with Rhys at the center.

GULWAN: Can I ask you a question, sir?
RHYS: Yes, sure, what's on your mind?
GULWAN: Why did you become a teacher?
RHYS: What do you mean?
GULWAN: I mean, you are a man, you are clever, you could become anything. And you chose teaching.
RHYS: Personally, I love teaching. I enjoy interacting with my students and learning from them.
GULWAN: But you're the teacher, you should be teaching not learning.
RHYS: You know what I mean, right? And of course, I like to know that I am making a difference. It is important to know English. Look how well you are doing with your English. You'll get a job when you finish school.
GULWAN: But isn't English teaching for women? If you want to teach, why not teach science, like Mr. Donald at my school? He is good.
RHYS: I don't think some subjects are for men and others for women. Who teaches you English at school?
GULWAN: Miss Brightman. She is also good. I must go, sir. See you tomorrow.

This brief conversation stayed with Rhys for some time afterward. Yes, of course he was committed to teaching – he had always wanted to be a teacher. His parents' objections had worn off a long time ago. They didn't much bother him anymore. He had done well in his university studies, and the ESOL job at the center felt right. It was the type of place where he wanted to teach, and his learners there were so appreciative. He could clearly see their need – and their learning! High school didn't really seem attractive at the time, although recently he had been thinking about the school system as a more stable option. Gulwan also got him thinking about some overseas experience. He hadn't taught overseas before. Rhys knew of some university classmates who had immediately left Wales after graduation to teach English abroad. Facebook tells him they are loving it. And what about the male-female thing that Gulwan had brought up? Surely this isn't what his parents meant. Or was it about the status of teaching generally? A few weeks after his conversation with Gulwan, Rhys was still feeling somewhat unsettled, in fact more than ever. And for the first time in his short career.

10.6.2 Questions

1. Rhys's parents don't seem to have had any influence on his career. Or have they?
2. In their conversation, Gulwan asks some difficult questions about (a) the status of teaching, (b) English teaching specifically, and (c) teaching and gender. What do you think of Rhys's answers? What would you have said to Gulwan?

3. After his conversation with Gulwan, Rhys was "feeling somewhat unsettled" for some time. What was he feeling specifically? What were his emotions?
4. What might the outcomes of this unsettled state be for Rhys's emotional wellbeing? Do you think it could affect his teaching practice and his relationship with his learners, for example?
5. In the medium to long term, what should Rhys do? If he came to you for advice about his career, what would you say to him?

10.6.3 Research Topics

Discovering Imagined Language-Teacher Identities
How do pre-service language teachers imagine their future teacher identities? How does their imagined identity affect how they feel about themselves now as teachers?

1. Work with a class of final-year pre-service language teachers in a teacher education program at a university or college you have access to. Explain to the teachers that you are interested in discovering their imagined teacher identities – how they see themselves as practicing teachers in the near future, and how they feel now about who they are as developing teachers.
2. Ask them to *draw a picture* (M12) of their imagined future teacher identity, that is, a picture of themselves as a teacher in the next few years. Tell the pre-service teachers to integrate into their drawings information about *where* they will be teaching, *who* they will be teaching, and any other details about their expected work, colleagues, and imagined institutional contexts.
3. Ask them to write a *brief reflective note* (M14) of about 100 words below their drawing, describing how their imagined identity makes them feel now as developing language teachers.
4. Collect the drawings and analyze them for their content. Focus on, for example, facial expressions, objects and other people in the drawings, furniture or buildings, positions of people and objects vis-à-vis each other, and any indications of time.
5. Analyze the written notes for teachers' feelings, emotions, and expectations.
6. How do pre-service language teachers imagine their identities in the years post-graduation? What emotions are associated with these identities?

Measuring Gender Bias in the Language Teacher Profession
Is language teaching really perceived to be "a woman's job"? Why or why not? Why does it matter?

1. Design a *short anonymous survey* (M17) of five questions that asks closed-ended questions (with the option to comment on each answer) about gender bias in the language teaching profession – questions such as: Do you believe that language teaching is a female oriented profession? In your working

context, are there more female or male language teachers? Are women better language teachers than men? Men do not want to become language teachers: Agree or disagree?
2. Include an open question that asks how men and women feel about their relative status in the field.
3. Use Google Forms or Microsoft Forms (or similar) to distribute the survey as widely as possible in your professional networks and ask colleagues to help you distribute it further internationally through their networks.
4. Use the online forms' software to analyze the quantitative data to produce frequency counts of answers to the five questions. Analyze the comments for common themes.
5. Collate the data into a brief one- to two-page report. Meet with two female and two male language teachers to discuss the findings in a virtual *focus group* (M8). Send them the report to read and reflect on before the meeting. Go through the report question by question and encourage free-flowing conversation.
6. Is there gender equality in the language teaching profession? Do teachers believe there should be? Do you think it matters whether there is equality or not?

10.6.4 Resources

de Ruiter, J. A., Poorthuis, A. M. G., Aldrup, K., & Koomen, H. M. Y. (2020). Teachers' emotional experiences in response to daily events with individual students varying in perceived past disruptive behavior. *Journal of School Psychology, 82*, 85–102. https://doi.org/10.1016/j.jsp.2020.08.005

Mombaers, T., Van Gasse, R., Vanlommel, K., & Van Petegem, P. (2023). "To teach or not to teach?" An exploration of the career choices of educational professionals. *Teachers and Teaching: Theory and Practice, 29*(7–8), 788–820. https://doi.org/10.1080/13540602.2023.2201425

Nigar, N., Kostogriz, A., & Gurney, L. (2023). Becoming an English language teacher over lines of desire: Stories of lived experiences. The Australian Educational Researcher, *51*, 1749–1770. https://doi.org/10.1007/s13384-023-00662-4

10.7   A Teacher Educator Under Pressure to Retire

Keywords
- New Zealand
- University
- Teacher educator and researcher
- Nearing retirement age
- Pressure from head of school to retire

10.7 A Teacher Educator Under Pressure to Retire

10.7.1 Pre-reading Reflection

1. Do you think there should be a retirement age for teachers or teacher educators? If so, what should it be?
2. Have you thought about retiring – is it too soon?
3. What emotions do those nearing retirement probably feel? What causes those emotions?

Martin Halstead is sixty-four years old. He has worked at the same university in a large New Zealand city for twenty-five years. Before he joined the university, he taught English in Japan for ten years, gaining much EFL teaching experience in both primary and high schools. At that stage he had a BA degree, so when he returned to New Zealand, he decided to study for an MA in Language Teaching, convinced that he wanted to continue working in the field of second and foreign language education. Just as he was finishing off his studies, a teacher educator position opened up at a local college of education. The college was responsible for training and accrediting school teachers in the country. He applied and easily got the job. Martin had considerable experience as a language teacher and was a fluent speaker of Japanese – a language that was gaining popularity in the school system. His MA grades were also impressive.

Martin never desired to do a PhD, which was not required of teacher educators in colleges of education at the time, and he did little research. He focused on his work as a language teacher educator, and he was good at it. He read constantly and attended any relevant conference that he could get funding for. He was fully up to date with recent trends in the field. The students at the college loved him, not because he was particularly inspiring as a teacher, but because he was steady and reliable, and they felt they could trust him. He seemed to have time for all of them. He gave excellent feedback on their written assignments and was patient and understanding when having conversations about their teaching practice. Martin did seem to motivate them in his quiet, unassuming way.

When the college of education amalgamated with the local university's School of Education fifteen years ago, Martin was almost fifty years old. The university put pressure on all college staff to obtain their PhDs and to become more active in research. Martin declined the PhD offer ("thank you very much," he said) but was happy to do more research. He had always done small-scale action research projects that focused on his own classroom and found the process and the outcomes very useful – it really did "improve my practice." Over the years, Martin has become known as the action research expert in the school, supervising many undergraduate and graduate projects and publishing a few of his own. He is a regular and popular presenter at conferences.

There is no retirement age at Martin's university, and he feels he still has a few good years in him. Of course, at sixty-four years old, he has recently been thinking about retirement, but hasn't made any decisions yet. He is loving his teaching and feels fulfilled in his job, with large numbers of international students coming back to campus post-Covid and recent development in AI technology, which he has already begun to embed in his teaching and assessment practices. "These are exciting times," he commented to his head of school during his most recent annual performance review. It was at this same review meeting that the head surprisingly asked Martin when he was planning on retiring. Martin was shocked. Such questions are not normally asked at the university; in fact, they are not allowed to be asked – except in performance reviews, as Martin later discovered. The head's question, which came without warning, unsettled Martin for the next few weeks. It really shouldn't have, he felt, but it did! He wondered if he was contributing enough. Had there been student complaints? What brought on the question now and not the year before? Was pressure coming from above the head of school? Martin knows his career is in its final stages, but he firmly believes he still has a lot to offer.

10.7.2 Questions

1. What are Martin's strengths as a language teacher educator? And his shortcomings?
2. Before the performance review meeting, Martin appeared to be doing well in his job – emotionally and performance-wise. Why was the head's question about retirement such a shock to him, given that he was already thinking about retirement?
3. Martin "firmly believes he still has a lot to offer." Looking to the future, do you agree?
4. Has Martin's emotional wellbeing been irreparably harmed by his encounter with the head of school? In the short term it appears it has – will he recover?
5. Would a younger teacher educator with a PhD and an active research program not be a better option for the school than Martin? Give a reason for your answer.

10.7.3 Research Topics

Inquiring into Teacher Educators' Post-retirement Anticipated Work Commitments

Do university-based language teacher educators anticipate being connected to their work in some way after retiring? Will they do some research or writing? Will they continue to supervise student research?

1. Consult three or four university-based language teacher educators who are in the latter stages of their careers. These educators should have both teaching and research as part of their job responsibilities.
2. With sensitivity, invite them to talk to you about their post-retirement work goals, if any. Will they continue doing research? Will they do any writing? Do they plan to attend and present at conferences? Will they mentor junior colleagues or supervise graduate student research?
3. Arrange one-on-one, face-to-face interviews for about one hour with each participant. Design a *semi-structured interview schedule* (M9) with detailed questions ordered logically. Keep the discussion future-oriented, focusing on goals and anticipated work. Try not to dwell on the past. Aim to explore reasons for why the teacher educators plan to continue working, or not. Record the interviews.
4. When analyzing the interviews, categorize the themes to produce findings that reveal why senior teacher educators see themselves continuing to be connected to work after retiring, or not, and what their reasons are for their decision.
5. Why would teacher educators want to keep working? Would some want to cut themselves off entirely from their former careers? How do they feel emotionally now about their anticipated post-retirement work life?

Learning from a Recently Retired Language Teacher Educator
What professional lessons can we learn from a retired language teacher educator?

1. Engage with a recently retired language teacher educator. Arrange to meet for a *life-history narrative interview* (M16).
2. Prepare a guide with a list of topics to be covered in the interview. Try not to ask too many direct questions. Instead, say to the teacher educator "Tell me about ...," asking them about their life experiences as a language teacher and teacher educator. Focus on highlights of their career, major transitions from place to place or job to job, and critical career incidents that shaped their professional identity.
3. Ask them to reflect on (a) significant emotional highs and lows over their career, and (b) lessons they have for new teachers just entering the language teaching profession.
4. Aim for a two-hour interview. Record and then transcribe the interview.
5. Analyze the interview by focusing on themes that relate to the topics suggested above. Construct a life story of the teacher educator.
6. What can language teachers and teacher educators learn from the record of the participant's professional life? How can they apply these lessons to their own work? How did the teacher educator participant get through the tough times and celebrate the good times?

10.7.4 Resources

Babic, S., Mairitsch, A., Mercer, S., Sulis, G., Jin, J., King, J., Lanvers, U., & Shin, S. (2022). Late-career language teachers in Austria and the UK: Pathways to retirement. *Teaching and Teacher Education, 113*, 103686. https://doi.org/10.1016/j.tate.2022.103686

Haukås, Å. (2024). Understanding the factors supporting language teachers' sustained motivation until retirement. *The Modern Language Journal, 108* (2), 430–445. https://doi.org/10.1111/modl.12920

Sulis, G., Mairitsch, A., Babic, S., Mercer, S., & Resnik, P. (2024). ELT teachers' agency for wellbeing. *ELT Journal, 78*(2), 198–206. https://doi.org/10.1093/elt/ccad050

Bibliography

Research Topics

References below relate to the *Research Topics* connected to each of the seventy cases. The references are divided into two sections.

1. The first section includes general research methodology texts in applied linguistics or language teaching and learning.
2. The second section includes references to specific methods of data collection and analysis. The labels M1–M17 are cross-referenced in the research topics associated with each case.

General Research Methodology Texts in Applied Linguistics or Language Teaching and Learning

Barkhuizen, G. (Ed.) (2019). *Qualitative research topics in language teacher education*. Routledge.
Barkhuizen, G., Benson, P., & Chik, A. (2025). *Narrative inquiry in language teaching and learning research* (2nd ed.). Routledge.
Dörnyei, Z. (2007). *Research methods in applied linguistics*. Oxford University Press.
Mackey, A. & Gass, S. M. (2022). *Second language research: Methodology and design* (2nd ed.). Routledge.
McKinley, J. & Rose, H. (Eds.) (2020). *The Routledge handbook of research methods in applied linguistics*. Routledge.
Nassaji, H. (2026). *Applied linguistics research: A comprehensive guide to methodology, design, analysis, and evaluation*. Cambridge University Press.
Paltridge, B. & Phakiti, A. (2015). *Research methods in applied linguistics: A practical resource* (2nd ed.). Bloomsbury.
Phakiti, A., De Costa, P., Plonsky, L., & Starfield, S. (2018). *The Palgrave handbook of applied linguistics research methodology*. Palgrave Macmillan.
Rose, H., McKinley, J., & Briggs Baffoe-Djan, J. (2020). *Data collection research methods in applied linguistics*. Bloomsbury.

Research Methods Cross-Referenced in the Research Topics

M1: Action Research

Burns, A. (2009). *Doing action research in English language teaching: A guide for practitioners*. Routledge.

Ceylan, E. & Comoglu, I. (2024). Action research in initial EFL teacher education: Emerging insights from a CAR project. *Educational Action Research*, *32*(3), 438–453.

Edwards, E. & Burns, A. (2016). Language teacher action research: Achieving sustainability. *ELT Journal*, *70*(1), 6–15.

M2: Body Outline Silhouettes

Busch, B. (2021). The body image: Taking an evaluative stance towards semiotic resources. *International Journal of Multilingualism*, *18*(2), 190–205.

Kasap, S. (2021). *The language portraits and multilingualism research*. Proceedings of the XI Eurasian Conference on Language & Social Sciences (February 2–3, 2021), Gjakova, Kosovo. https://www.researchgate.net/publication/350515917. (Accessed August 23, 2024.)

Ollerhead, S., Melo-Pfeifer, S., & Chik, A. (2024). Building a virtual transnational space for initial teacher education with Australian and German students. *Journal of Multilingual and Multicultural Development*, *45*(3), 708–724.

M3: Classroom Observation

Alshehri, E. (2019). Classroom observation for professional development: Views of EFL teachers and observers. *Arab World English Journal*. Special Issue 1, 57–71.

O'Leary, M. (2020). *Classroom observation: A guide to the effective observation of teaching and learning* (2nd ed.). Routledge.

Spada, N. (2019). Classroom observation research. In J. W. Schweiter & A. Benati (Eds.), *The Cambridge handbook of language learning* (pp. 186–207). Cambridge University Press.

M4: Descriptive Statistics

Briggs Baffoe-Djan, J. & Smith, S.A. (2020). Descriptive statistics in quantitative data analysis. In J. McKinley & H. Rose (Eds.), *The Routledge handbook of research methods in applied linguistics* (pp. 398–414). Routledge.

Koval, N. G. (2024). 'The effect is/isn't significant!': Statistical evidence and ELT. *ELT Journal*, *78*(1), 11–19.

Woodrow, L. (2014). *Writing about quantitative research in applied linguistics*. Palgrave Macmillan.

M5: Discourse Analysis

Paltridge, B. (2022). *Discourse analysis: An introduction* (3rd ed.). Bloomsbury.

Prior, M. T. (2015). *Emotion and discourse in L2 narrative research*. Multilingual Matters.

Zajda, J. (2020). Discourse analysis as a qualitative methodology. *Educational Practice and Theory*, *42*(2), 5–21.

M6: Document Analysis, Archival Research, and Internet Research

Morgan, H. (2022). Conducting a qualitative document analysis. *The Qualitative Report*, *27*(1), 64–77.

Roulston, K. & deMarrais, K. (2021). *Exploring the archives: A beginner's guide for qualitative researchers*. Myers Education Press.

Tight, M. (2019). *Documentary research in the social sciences*. Sage.

M7: Ethnographic, Duoethnographic, and Autoethnographic Methods

Blommaert, J. & Jie, D. (2020). *Ethnographic fieldwork: A beginner's guide*. Multilingual Matters.

Burleigh, D. & Burm, S. (2022). Doing duoethnography: Addressing essential methodological questions. *International Journal of Qualitative Methods*, *21*, 1–8.

Yazan, B., Canagarajah, S., & Jain, R. (Eds.) (2020). *Autoethnographies in ELT: Transnational identities, pedagogies, and practices*. Routledge.

M8: Focus Group Interviews

Galloway, N. (2020). Focus groups: Capturing the dynamics of group interaction. In J. McKinley & H. Rose (Eds.), *The Routledge handbook of research methods in applied linguistics* (pp. 290–301). Routledge.

Krueger, R. A. & Casey, M. A. (2009). *Focus groups: A practical guide for applied research* (4th ed.). Sage.

Ortega, Y. (2024). Charlas y Comidas: Humanising focus groups and interviews. *Qualitative Research*, *24*(4), 773–792.

M9: Interviews

Guo, D., Ramos, R. L. M., & Wang, F. (2024). Qualitative online interviews: Voices of applied linguistics researchers. *Research Methods in Applied Linguistics*, *3*(3), 100130.

Talmy, S. (2011). The interview as collaborative achievement: Interaction, identity, and ideology in a speech event. *Applied Linguistics*, *32*(1), 25–42.

Thunberg, S. & Arnell, L. (2022). Pioneering the use of technologies in qualitative research: A research review of the use of digital interviews. *International Journal of Social Research Methodology*, *25*(6), 757–768.

M10: Keyword Analysis

Naeem, M., Ozuem, W., Howell, K., & Ranfagni, S. (2023). A step-by-step process of thematic analysis to develop a conceptual model in qualitative research. *International Journal of Qualitative Methods*, *22*, 1–18.

Pojanapunya, P. & Todd, R. W. (2021). The influence of the benchmark corpus on keyword analysis. *Register Studies*, *3*(1), 88–114.

Seale, C. & Charteris-Black, S. (2010). Keyword analysis: A new tool for qualitative research. In I. Bourgeault, R. Dingwall, & R. De Vries (Eds.), *The SAGE handbook of qualitative methods in health research* (pp. 536–556). Sage.

M11: Metaphor Analysis

Arlius, Y. (2023). *An EFL teacher's metaphor as a window into teacher's professional identity*. Proceedings of the Conference on English Language Teaching, 709–720.

https://proceedings.uinsaizu.ac.id/index.php/celti/article/view/544 (Accessed August 24, 2024.)

Cortazzi, M. & Jin, L. (2020). Elicited metaphor analysis: Researching teaching and learning. In M. T. M. Ward & S. Delamont (Eds.), *Handbook of qualitative research in education* (pp. 488–505). Edward Elgar.

Wan, W., Low, G. D., & Miao L. (2011). From students' and teachers' perspectives: Metaphor analysis of beliefs about EFL teachers' roles. *System*, *39*(3), 403–415.

M12: Multimodal and Visual Methods

Ibrahim, N. C. (2022). Visual and artefactual approaches in engaging teachers with multilingualism: Creating DLCs in pre-service teacher education. *Languages*, *7*(2), 152.

Mason, S. & Chik, A. (2020). Age, gender and language teacher identity: Narratives from higher education. *Sexuality and Culture*, *24*, 1028–1045.

Melo-Pfeifer, S. (2021). Exploiting foreign language student-teachers' visual language biographies to challenge the monolingual mind-set in foreign language education. *International Journal of Multilingualism*, *18*(4), 601–618.

M13: Object and Material Analysis

Canagarajah, S. (2021). Materializing narratives: The story behind the story. *System*, *102*, 102610.

Frimberger, K., White, R., & Ma, L. (2018). "If I didn't know you what would you want me to see?": Poetic mappings in neo-materialist research with young asylum seekers and refugees. *Applied Linguistics Review*, *9*(2–3), 391–419.

Toohey, K. (2018). *Learning English at school: Identity, socio-material relations and classroom practice*. Multilingual Matters.

M14: Reflective Writing and Journals

Ahmed, A. M. (2019). Students' reflective journaling: An impactful strategy that informs instructional practices in an EFL writing university context in Qatar. *Reflective Practice*, *20*(4), 483–500.

Farrell, T. S. C. & Macapinlac, M. (2021). Professional development through reflective practice: A framework for TESOL teachers. *Canadian Journal of Applied Linguistics*, *24*(1), 1–25.

Peercy, M. M., Sharkey, J., Baecher, L., Motha, S., & Varghese, M. (2019). Exploring TESOL teacher educators as learners and reflective scholars: A shared narrative inquiry. *TESOL Journal*, *10*(4), e482.

M15: Stimulated Recall

Gass, S. M. & Mackey, A. (2017). *Stimulated recall methodology in applied linguistics and L2 research* (2nd ed.). Routledge.

Morris, S., Yamamoto, K., & King, J. (2023). Practitioner researcher intuition in stimulated recall studies. *Journal for the Psychology of Language Learning*, *5*(2), 34–44.

Sanchez, H. S. & Grimshaw, T. (2020). Stimulated recall. In J. McKinley & H. Rose (Eds.), *The Routledge handbook of research methods in applied linguistics* (pp. 312–323). Routledge.

M16: Stories and Narrative Frames

Barkhuizen, G. (2014). Revisiting narrative frames: An instrument for investigating language teaching and learning. *System, 47,* 12–27.

Barkhuizen, G. & Consoli, S. (2021). Pushing the edge in narrative inquiry. *System, 102,* 102656.

Benson, P. (2018). Narrative analysis. In A. Phakiti, P. De Costa, L. Plonsky, & S. Starfield (Eds.), *The Palgrave handbook of applied linguistics research methodology* (pp. 595–613). Palgrave Macmillan.

M17: Questionnaires and Surveys

Dörnyei, Z. & Dewaele, J.-M. (2023). *Questionnaires in second language research: Construction, administration, and processing* (3rd ed.). Routledge.

Pitura, J. (2023). Using the e-questionnaire in qualitative applied linguistics research. *Research Methods in Applied Linguistics, 2*(1), 100034.

Wagner, E. (2015). Survey research. In B. Paltridge & A. Phakiti (Eds.), *Research methods in applied linguistics: A practical resource* (pp. 83–99). Bloomsbury.

References

Bailey, K. M. (2006). *Language teacher supervision: A case-based approach.* Cambridge University Press.

Bakhtin, M. (1981). *The dialogic imagination: Four essays* (M. Holquist , Trans.). University of Texas Press.

Banks, C. P. (2017). *The American legal profession: The myths and realities of practicing law.* SAGE Publications.

Capron, A. M., Cash, R., Saxena, A., & Wikler, D. (Eds.) (2009). *Casebook on ethical issues in international health research.* World Health Organization.

Curtin, J. H. & Uştuk, O. (Eds.) (2024). *Building a culture of research in TESOL: Collaborations and communities.* Springer.

Darling-Hammond, L., & Hammerness, K. (2002). Toward a pedagogy of cases in teacher education. *Teaching Education, 13*(2), 125–135.

Doecke, B. (2004). Professional identity and educational reform: Confronting my habitual practices as a teacher educator. *Teaching and Teacher Education, 20*(2), 203–215.

Freeman, D. (1989). Teacher training, development, and decision making: A model of teaching and related strategies for language teacher education. *TESOL Quarterly, 23* (1), 27–45.

Freeman, D. (2016). *Educating second language teachers.* Oxford University Press.

Gooden, A. B. (2021). *A casebook of inclusive pedagogical practices for second language teacher education.* University of Michigan Press.

Gooden, A. B. (2024). *A casebook of decolonizing pedagogical practices for second language teacher education.* University of Michigan Press.

Haley, M. H. (2004). Implications of using case study instruction in a foreign/second language methods course. *Foreign Language Annals*, *37*(2), 290–300.

Harrington, H. L. (1995). Fostering reasoned decisions: Case-based pedagogy and the professional development of teachers. *Teaching and Teacher Education*, *11*(3), 203–214.

Harrington, H. L., Quinn-Leering, K., & Hodson, L. (1996). Written case analysis and critical reflection. *Teaching and Teacher Education*, *12*(1), 25–37.

Heitzmann, R. (2008). Case study instruction in teacher education: Opportunity to develop students' critical thinking, school smarts and decision making. *Education*, *128*(4), 523–542.

Jackson, J. (1997). Cases in TESOL teacher education: Creating a forum for reflection. *TESL Canada Journal*, *14*(2), 1–16.

Johnson, B. (2010). *The hedge fund fraud casebook*. Wiley.

Johnson, K. E. & Golombek, P. (2020). Informing and transforming language teacher education pedagogy. *Language Teaching Research*, *24*(1), 116–127.

Kelch, K. & Malupa-Kim, M. (2014). Implementing case studies in language teacher education and professional development. *ORTESOL Journal*, *31*, 10–18.

Kubanyiova, M. (2020). Language teacher education in the age of ambiguity: Educating responsive meaning makers in the world. *Language Teaching Research*, *24*(1), 49–59.

Kumar, R. (2016). *Strategic financial management casebook*. Elsevier Science.

Kunselman, J. C. & Johnson, K. A. (2004). Using the case method to facilitate learning. *College Teaching*, *52*(3), 87–92.

Lundeberg, M. A. (1999). Discovering teaching and learning through cases. In M. A. Lundeberg, B. B. Levin, & H. L. Harrington (Eds.), *Who learns what from cases and how: The research base for teaching and learning with cases* (pp. 3–27). Erlbaum.

Mercer, S., Farrell, C., & Freeman, D. (2022). *Self-directed professional development in ELT*. Oxford University Press.

Merseth, K. K. (1991). The early history of case-based instruction: Insights for teacher education today. *Journal of Teacher Education*, *42*(4), 243–249.

Merseth, K. K. (1996). Cases and case methods in teacher education. In J. Sikula (Ed.), *Handbook of research on teacher education* (pp. 722–744). Macmillan.

Mostert, M. P. (2007). Challenges of case-based teaching. *The Behaviour Analyst Today*, *8*(4), 434–442.

Ochs, E. & Capps, L. 2001. *Living narrative*. Harvard University Press.

Orsini, D. L. (1988). *The neuropsychology casebook*. Springer-Verlag.

Owen, C. (2020). *Becoming an English teacher: The shaping of everyday professional experiences in early career teaching*. Unpublished doctoral thesis, Monash University, Australia.

Prince, M. & Felder, R. (2007). The many faces of inductive teaching and learning. *Journal of College Science Teaching*, *36*(5), 14–20.

Reichelt, M. (2000). Case studies in L2 teacher education. *ELT Journal*, *54*(4), 346–353.

Richards, J. C. (Ed.) (1998). *Teaching in action: Case studies from second language classrooms*. Teachers of English to Speakers of Other Languages.

Richards, J. C. & Farrell, T. (2005). *Professional development for language teachers: Strategies for teacher learning.* Cambridge University Press.

Schröter, E. & Röber, M. (2022). Understanding the case method: Teaching public administration case by case. *Teaching Public Administration, 40*(2), 258–275.

Shulman, L. S. (1992). Toward a pedagogy of cases. In J. H. Shulman (Ed.), *Case methods in teacher education* (pp. 1–30). Teachers College Press.

Tinker Sachs, G. M. & Ho, B. (2011). Using cases in EFL/ESL teacher education. *Innovation in Language Learning and Teaching, 5*(3), 273–289.

Wasserman, S. (1994). *Introduction to case method teaching: A guide to the galaxy.* Teachers College Press.

Wright, T. (2010). Second language teacher education: Review of recent research on practice. *Language Teaching, 43*(3), 259–296.

Zlateva, M. N. & Gooden, A. B. (2018). *A casebook for second language teacher education: Reflecting on the language classroom.* University of Michigan Press.

Index

ADHD, 19, 63, 70, 72–73
Afrikaans, 166, 166–167
AI, 6, 19, 29, 38, 41–44, 112, 129–131, 133, 256, 290
assignments, 35
assistant language teacher (ALT), 77
Australia, 88, 91, 109, 111, 124–125, 187, 213, 216–217, 220, 267, 275, 281, 298
Austria, 162, 169, 292

Bangladesh, 102, 112, 126–127, 129
benefits of the case method, 13
Botswana, 20, 240, 255–256
Brazil, 95, 95, 102
bullying, 81

Cambodia, 267, 274–275
Canada, 19, 23–24, 88, 98, 125, 137, 158, 240, 248, 251, 259–261, 298
Canvas, 32, 130, 137, 147–150
case method, 3, 16
casebook, 1, 4–7, 9–11, 16–18, 21, 24, 28, 30, 32, 35, 297–299
ChatGPT, 129
Chile, 137, 154–156, 267–268, 270
China, 38, 48, 88, 94–95, 97, 102, 144, 148, 158, 187, 191–193, 198–199, 224, 248
collaborative research, 207
College English teacher, 48, 198–199
Colombia, 20, 162, 172–173, 240
colonialism, 240
conference, 25, 42, 53–54, 73, 83, 132, 152–153, 162–167, 180, 183, 196–199, 203–204, 208–211, 227, 230, 241, 249, 252–257, 265, 289
continuing professional development (PD), 1
cooperating teacher, 232–234
Covid-19, 113, 147–149, 210, 221, 223, 268, 270
critical reflection, 4
critical thinking, 14

decolonization, 240
dilemma-based cases, 10
dissertation, 20, 25, 37, 148, 187–188, 191–194, 256
doctoral colloquium, 169

Egypt, 38, 55–57
England, 91, 119, 130, 187, 191, 213, 235–236, 239, 251
English for Academic Purposes, 130
English medium instruction (EMI), 95
ethics, 36, 195–198

Farsi, 85
field trip, 158
first-year teacher, 224

Gender, 63, 81
German, 44–46, 259–260, 294
Germany, 45, 240, 259–261
Global Englishes, 38, 51–55
Gujarati, 101

heritage language school, 219
Hong Kong, 3, 95

ideological discourses, 8
IELTS, 120–121, 123–125, 141–142, 282
India, 63, 74–77, 88, 101–102, 282
Indigenous language, 216
Indonesia, 88, 91–93
Iran, 63, 84–85, 194, 240, 244, 248
Ireland, 137, 147–148
isiXhosa, 52, 166

Jamaica, 88
Japan, 19, 63, 77–78, 88, 97, 108, 110, 267, 271, 289

Kazakhstan, 267, 278, 281

Index

large classes, 19, 38, 48, 58, 60–61

Malaysia, 42, 88, 105–106, 172, 213, 253
maternity leave, 271
mediational spaces, 9
mentoring, 244
Mexico, 63, 67, 187, 202–204
multigrade classroom, 74–77
Myanmar, 278

narrative frame, 61, 76, 100, 136, 153–154, 280
narrative inquiry, 6
native-speakerism, 280
Nepal, 162, 183
Nepali, 183
New Zealand, 63, 84–88, 101–102, 112, 119, 122–124, 213, 228–229, 267, 288–289
non-native English-speaking teacher (NNEST), 101

older language learners, 63, 67, 69

Pakistan, 112
Poland, 19, 137, 151
practicum, 194
publishing, 202

Qualtrics, 44, 90–91, 122, 150, 175, 190, 223, 231, 243, 284

racial prejudice, 111
refugee student settlement, 262
retirement, 288

Scotland, 88, 105
self-inquiry, 9
Sesotho, 115
sexual harassment, 107
sexual orientation, 81–82
Shona, 133

Singapore, 38, 41, 162, 176–177, 213, 220–221
sociocultural theory, 4
South Africa, 38, 51–52, 112, 115–116, 162, 165–166
Spanish, 67–68, 71, 92, 172–173, 188, 195–196, 202–204, 232, 240–242, 268
Sri Lanka, 63, 217
stereotypes, 6
study abroad, 20–21, 68, 172, 174–175, 188, 217, 240, 259, 261, 267, 274–277, 281–282

teacher emotions, 60, 226
teacher research, 16
Thailand, 19–20, 137–138, 140, 240, 252–252, 255
third-age learners. *See* older language learners
time management, 141
transgender identity, 83, 248
translanguaging, 19, 38, 44, 46–48, 97, 162, 167, 183–186
Tunisia, 162, 179–180
Türkiye, 38, 44–45, 67–68, 187, 209

United Kingdom, 20, 38, 58, 59, 95, 104, 108, 111, 112, 125, 129, 172, 180, 191–192, 213, 235, 252–253, 292
United States, 4, 19, 20, 38–40, 53, 55–56, 63, 70, 71, 91–92, 109, 111, 137, 141, 144, 162, 187, 194–195, 202–203, 213, 232, 240, 241, 244, 262–263, 268
Uruguay, 63, 81
Uzbekistan, 213, 224

Venezuela, 162–163
Vietnam, 20, 176, 187, 205–206

Wales, 267, 285–286

Zimbabwe, 112, 133

For EU product safety concerns, contact us at Calle de José Abascal, 56–1°, 28003 Madrid, Spain or eugpsr@cambridge.org.

www.ingramcontent.com/pod-product-compliance
Ingram Content Group UK Ltd.
Pitfield, Milton Keynes, MK11 3LW, UK
UKHW022139240226
468380UK00018B/372